HISTORY
OF RUSSIA

Sergei Mikhailovich Soloviev

The *Academic* *International* *Press* *Edition* *of* *Sergei* M. *Soloviev's* History
of Russia From Earliest Times. *Peter* *von* *Wahlde,* *General* *Editor.*

Contributing *Editors*:

HUGH F. GRAHAM
JOHN D. WINDHAUSEN
ALEXANDER V. MULLER
K. A. PAPMEHL
RICHARD HANTULA
WALTER J. GLEASON, JR.
WILLIAM H. HILL

SERGEI M. SOLOVIEV

History of Russia

Volume 45

The Rule of Catherine the Great

The Legislative Commission (1767-1768)
And Foreign Affairs (1766-1768)

Edited and Translated

by

William H. Hill

Academic International Press

1986

The Academic International Press Edition of S.M. Soloviev's *History of Russia from Earliest Times* in fifty volumes.

Volume 45. *The Rule of Catherine the Great: The Legislative Commission (1767-1768) And Foreign Affairs (1766-1768).* Unabridged translation of the text of Volume 27, Chapters 2 and 3, of S.M. Soloviev's *Istoriia Rossii s drevneishikh vremen* as found in Volume XIV of this work published in Moscow in 1963, with added annotation by William H. Hill.

Library of Congress Catalog Card Number: 75–11085
ISBN 0-87569-091-2

Composition by Jayne Berndsen and Mary Virginia McDaris
Title Page by King & Queen Press

Printed in the United States of America

A list of volumes published by Academic International Press is found at the end of this volume.

ACADEMIC INTERNATIONAL PRESS
Box 1111 Gulf Breeze FL 32561

CONTENTS

Confrontation: The Confederation of Bar—The Turkish
Reaction—Religious and National Ferment in the Ukraine
—War with Turkey—European Reaction to Turkey's Dec-
laration of War

WEIGHTS AND MEASURES

Linear Measure

Verst: 500 sazhen, 1166 yards and 2 feet, .663 miles, 1.0668 km
Sazhen: 3 arshins, 7 feet, 2.133 m
Arshin: 16 vershoks, 28 in. (diuims), 72.12 cm
Chetvert: 1/4 arshin
Fut: 12 diuims, 1 foot, 30.48 cm
Vershok: 1.75 in., 4.445 cm, 1/16 arshin
Diuim: 1 inch, 2.54 cm
Desiatina: 2400 square sazhens, 2.7 acres, 1.0925 hectare
Chetvert (quarter): 1/2 desiatina, 1.35 acre (sometimes 1.5 desiatinas or ca. 4.1 acres)

Liquid Measure

Stof: Kruzhka (cup), 1/10 vedro, ca. 1.3 quarts, 1.23 liters
Kufa: 30 stofy
Vedro (pail): 3.25 gallons, 12.3 liters, 10 stofy
Bochka (barrel): 40 vedros, 121 gallons, 492 liters
Chetvert (quarter): 1/4 bochka, 32.5 gallons

Weights

Berkovets: 361 lbs., 10 puds
Pud: 40 funts, 36.113 lbs. (US), 40 lbs. (Russian), 16.38 kg
Funt: 96 zolotniks, .903 lb., 14.4 ozs., 408.24 grams
Grivenka: 205 grams
Korob (basket): 7 puds, 252 lbs.
Rad: 14 puds, 505.58 lbs.
Chetvert (grain measure): 1/4 rad, 3.5 puds, 126.39 lbs., ca. 8 bushels
Chetverik (grain measure dating from 16th century): 1/8 chetvert, 15.8 lbs.
Zolotnik: 1/96 lb., 4.26 grams

Money

Chervonets (chervonny): A gold coin minted in the first half of the 18th century worth about 3 rubles
Muscovite Denga: 200 equals 1 ruble
Novgorod Denga: 100 equals 1 ruble
Ruble: 100 copeks, 200 dengas
Altyn: 6 Muscovite dengas, 3 copecks
Grivna: 20 Muscovite dengas, 100 grivnas equals 1 ruble, 10 copeks
Poltina (Poltinnik): 50 copecks, 100 dengas
Polupoltina (-nik): 25 copecks, 50 dengas
Poltora: 1 1/2 rubles
Peniaz: 10 equals one grosh (Lithuania)
Kopa grosh: 60 groshas, one Muscovite poltina
Chetvertak: silver coin equal to 25 copeks or 1/4 ruble (18-19th centuries)
Copeck: two Muscovite dengas
Foreign Denominations: 1 efimok or 1 thaler (Joachimsthaler)—about 1 ruble
1 chervonets or chervonnyi—a ducat, about 3 rubles
Levok—Dutch silver lion dollar

Note: Weights and measures often changed values over time and sometimes held more than one value at the same time. For details consult Sergei G. Pushkarev, *Dictionary of Russian Historical Terms from the Eleventh Century to 1917* (Yale, 1970).

PREFACE

This book is an unabridged translation of Volume 27, Chapters 2 and 3, which are, respectively, pp. 71-133 and 134-262 in Volume XIV of the multi-volume edition of Soloviev's *Istoriia Rossi s drevneishikh vremen* (History of Russia From Earliest Times, 29 vols., St. Petersburg, 1851-1879) published from 1959 through 1966 in Moscow.

The present translation endeavors to render the text and Soloviev's thought as accurately as possible. No attempt has been made to reproduce his style and text word for word for this would have yielded a bizarre Russianized text. The main consideration has been to make his history as readable as possible consistent with accuracy, while retaining at least something of the flavor of the language of the era. An effort has been made to find English-language equivalents for all technical terms Soloviev employs (ranks, offices, titles, legal, administrative and so forth) in the belief that English is no less rich in such terms than other languages. This is intended to smooth the flow of the narrative for the reader and to avoid marring the pages with annoying untranslated words. The exception involves Russian words which have become common in English —boyar, tsar, cossack. In all of this the translator remains painfully aware of the inevitable shortcomings that may remain.

Soloviev's pages are featureless and interminable, one long and complex sentence marching after the last. To make the text easier to follow for today's readers, long paragraphs and sentences have been broken into shorter ones. Most of the subtitles are based on the descriptive topic headings clustered at the beginnings of the chapters in the Russian edition. These headings have been moved into the body of the text as subtitles to mark and ease for the reader the transition from one subject to another. In some cases, to even the frequency of breaks in the text or to show topics not listed by Soloviev at the beginning of chapters, new subtitles have been added. Soloviev's arrangement of the material has been followed strictly.

Brief explanatory or interpretive materials have been inserted into the text enclosed in brackets, or added as footnotes to each chapter at the end of the book. All material enclosed in brackets has been added by the present editor and all material in parenthesis is the author's. Emphasized words or phrases in italics are the author's.

The general policy followed in annotating has been to identify prominent personalities at first mention and to give explanation and elucidations of less common or obscure terms and passages, assuming the typical reader to have relatively little familiarity with Russian history. If brief, these have been included in the text in brackets; otherwise they appear as numbered footnotes found at the back of the book by chapters. Most of the author's own notes are not included because their highly specialized archival, documentary and bibliographic nature is of value solely to specialists who, in any case, will prefer to consult the original Russian text. In addition, most of the notes added by the editors of the edition published in the Soviet Union also are technical in nature—fuller bibliographic citations than those in Soloviev's notes—have not been included. When the author's notes and those of the Soviet editors are included, they are so designated. All other notes are those of the present editor.

Russian personal names are preserved in their Russian form except for Alexander, Alexis, Michael, Nicholas, Catherine and Peter, which English usage has made familiar with respect to Russian historical figures, and important ecclesiastics whose names largely have been recast into Latin or Greek equivalents, especially for the earlier period of Russian history. This applies to prominent individuals; Russian forms usually are used for the less prominent. Certain other names and terms have been anglicized for the sake of clarity and because they are used widely—Casimir, Sophia, Dantzig, boyar, rubles, versts, Dnieper river, and others.

The editors of the edition published in the USSR frequently have added patronymics and other names, and these have been retained without brackets; patronymics appearing in the original edition also have been included. Plural forms for names and terms which might be confusing have been anglicized—Vologdians rather than Vologzhane, Voguls not Vogulichi, the Dolgorukys not Dolgorukie, and so forth. Even so, in a few cases the Russian plural form is used when this form is common. Most Slavic surnames show gender, and this has been preserved. Since an "a" at the word end usually indicates a female, Golovkin would have a wife or daughter, Golovkina. The final "iia" in feminine personal names has been shortened to "ia"—"Maria" and "Evdokia" instead of "Mariia" and "Evdokiia."

Non-Russian names, locations, terms, ranks and so on are spelled according to the language native to the person or particular to the city, region or culture when this can be determined. Confusion arises at times because the text is not clear about nationalities. An excruciating example is Lithuania where at least three languages intermingle. In such cases the context is the guide used and as a last resort the Russian spelling in the text is accepted. Individuals whose families were once non-Russian but had been in Russian service for generations are named by the original spelling of the family name. Turkish, Tatar, Persian and other names and terms are spelled in the original according to accepted froms in scholarly books. In some instances, if not otherwise ascertainable they are transliterated from the Russian as given by Soloviev. The names of geographical locations conform to commonly accepted English usage—Podolia, Moscow, Copenhagen, Saxony, and so forth.

Finally, with respect to transliteration, this translation follows a modified Library of Congress system omitting diacritical marks and ligatures, and rendering the initial "ia" and "iu" as "ya" ("Dmitry Poliansky" instead of "Dmitrii Polianskii"), and the form "oi" has been replaced by "oy" ("Donskoy" not "Donskoi"). In some cases "i" has been inserted in place of hard and soft signs, or apostrophes indicating these signs. Hence Soloviev and not Solov'ev. The soft sign is not indicated by an apostrophe, as in some transliteration systems, but is dropped completely.

All dates, as in the original, are according to the Julian calendar ("Old Style"); that is, for the eighteenth century, eleven days behind the Gregorian used in the West.

A table of weights and measures is included at the front of this volume for the convenience of the reader.

William H. Hill

History of Russia

Volume 45

The Rule of Catherine the Great

The Legislative Commission (1767-1768)
And Foreign Affairs (1766-1768)

I

THE LEGISLATIVE COMMISSION
1767-1768

OPENING OF THE COMMISSION

The thirtieth day of July, 1767, was designated as the opening of the Legislative Commission. Deputies numbering some 450 had arrived in Moscow and had assembled in the Miracles (Chudov) monastery by seven o'clock in the morning. Prince Viazemsky, confirmed not long before as the procurator general and chief supervisor of the Commission, preceded the delegates.

Three hours later at ten o'clock Empress Catherine, in her imperial robes and with a small crown on her head, left Golovin Palace with great solemnity. Her carriage was drawn by eight horses. Before her, courtiers rode in sixteen parade carriages. The cavalier guards, commanded by their chief, Grigory Grigorievich Orlov, followed the empress' carriage. Grand Prince Paul Petrovich rode in a carriage following the cavalier guards.

When the empress reached the cathedral of the Assumption, the deputies approached in ranks of two, led by the procurator-general (attorney general), carrying a marshal's baton. Deputies from government offices came first, followed by deputies from the gentry, the cities, the poorer nobility, other old service people, and finally the general population. Within the classes, seniority among the deputies was observed according to provinces, ranked as follows: Moscow, Kiev, Petersburg, Novgorod, Kazan, Astrakhan, Siberia, Irkutsk, Smolensk, Estland, Livland, Vyborg, Nizhny Novgorod, Little Russia, Slobodsko Ukraine, Voronezh, Belgorod, Archangel, Orenburg and Novorossiisk. Personal seniority among the deputies was determined according to their time of arrival in Moscow and registration in the list of deputies.

Christian deputies entered the cathedral, while those of other faiths remained outside. After the end of the service, the empress set out for the Kremlin Palace. The deputies signed an oath in which they vowed "to invest pure-hearted effort in the great affair of the composition of a project for a new Code of Laws, corresponding to the trust of their electors, so that this effort might be begun and finished according to just rules, inspiring brotherly love and an impulse to preserve happiness and serenity, from which all justice flows." After taking the oath they asked God that "He grant them the power to keep their hearts and thoughts free from blindness stemming from prejudice, personal interest, friendships, enmities and hateful envy, from all of which might result severity in their thoughts and cruelty in their counsel."

After signing the oath the deputies went to the palace and then to the audience hall, where Catherine stood on the steps to the throne. On her right was a table, covered with red velvet, on which lay her Instruction to the Commission, the procedures for administering the Commission, and the Instruction for the procurator-general. The grand prince, government officials, courtiers and foreign ministers stood to the left of the throne, while prominent ladies stood to the right. Vice-Chancellor Alexander Mikhailovich Golitsyn stood on the second step of the throne.

After the procurator-general had presented the deputies to the empress, the deputy from the Synod, metropolitan of Novgorod, Dmitry (Sechenov), gave a speech in which he artfully derived Catherine's legislative powers from Justinian: "Rome and sometimes ancient Greece found glory in their legislation. But they could not attain full glory, not being enlightened by the teachings of the Gospels, which are the prerequisite basis of all morality. But you, through the light of this guidance, are Christians receiving strength from these sources of truth. There have been Greek Christian states which have received the glory of lawgivers, but which have changed in the course of things stemming from God's unfathomable will (as a result of the Turkish attacks) and where the force of the laws has ceased. Yet in these sad cases we see a fortunate fate for us, for with the passage of the faith from the East to us, the right of lawgiving also has been assigned to you, whom the present drives sternly and the future orders beneficially."

When the metropolitan finished, the vice-chancellor gave a speech to the deputies, in the name of the empress, in which he invited them to begin their great task. "Embark upon this great affair and remember with each line that you have the opportunity to demonstrate to yourselves, your contemporaries and your heirs how great was your care for the general good, for the happiness of mankind, and for instilling love and morality in each human heart; for the quiet, peacefulness, security and happiness of each and every one of your fellow citizens. You have the opportunity to glorify yourselves and your era and to acquire the esteem and thanks of future ages. All men under the sun await an example from you—their eyes are upon you. Your fame is in your hands, and the path to it is open. The perfection of all these things, useful to the fatherland, will depend upon your agreement."

ORGANIZATION OF THE COMMISSION

Early in the morning of the next day, July 31, the delegates began assembling in the Palace of Facets. At ten o'clock, upon the invitation of the procurator general, 428 delegates took their places. They proceeded to choose a marshal. The deputy of the Viazma gentry, Count Ivan Grigorievich Orlov, received the most votes (278 electoral and 150 advisory); after him came his brother, the Koporsk deputy, Count Grigory Grigorievich Orlov (228 and 200); then the Volokolamsk deputy, Count Zakhar Grigorievich Chernyshev (179 and 249); the Kostroma deputy, Alexander Ilich Bibikov (165 and 262); the Orel deputy, Count Fedor Grigorievich Orlov (159 and 269); the deputy from the Senate, Prince Michael Nikitich Volkonsky (147 and 254); and the Moscow deputy, Peter Ivanovich Panin (137 and 296). The three top candidates were to be presented to the empress for confirmation. But when the procurator general announced to the assemblage that the two Orlovs—Ivan and Grigory—had received the most votes, Grigory rose and asked the assembly to excuse him from the post of marshal because of the many other tasks given to him by the empress. The assembly agreed, but then the candidate just behind him, Count Chernyshev, made a similar request. However the assembly did not agree this time and as a result the three candidates presented were Ivan Orlov, Count Chernyshev and Bibikov.

On August 3 at the second meeting of the Commission, Catherine's decision, written in her own hand, was read. "Since Count Orlov asked to be excused from the post, and Count Chernyshev has many responsibilities, the marshal shall be the delegate from Kostroma, Alexander Bibikov." Upon reading this decision, the procurator general gave Bibikov his baton. Then the reading of the Instruction was begun.[1] According to the daily minutes, this reading was greeted enthusiastically; many wept, especially when the words were read: "God grant that after the conclusion of this legislative session there shall be a more just and consequently more prosperous Russian people. Otherwise the intention of our laws would not be fulfilled, an unhappy event which I do not wish to live to see." At the fifth meeting on August 9 the deputies began to ask: "What can we do for our empress, treating her subjects so well and serving as an example to all monarchs? How can we show how much all the happy peoples ruled by her owe her?" They settled on the idea of bestowing on Catherine the title of "all-wise and great mother of the fatherland."

Following dinner on Sunday, August 12, the empress received the deputies in the palace, and Marshal Bibikov made a speech to her. His speech concluded: "Having become by your deeds the wonder of the earth, through your Instruction you will be the benefactress and teacher of all mankind. All of humanity ought to step forward with us here and give to your Imperial Majesty the name of mother of nations, as a debt owed to you. But as in universal fortune because we are the first to take on this debt then Russia is first, in the persons of her chosen deputies, standing before your throne, bearing hearts filled with love, devotion and gratitude. Look upon their sincerity as a sacrifice which only you deserve! Be gracious, great Sovereign, for we ourselves are glorified before the world by this great title which Catherine the Great, all-wise mother of the fatherland, receives from us. Deign, most merciful Sovereign, to accept this title as a presentation from all your loyal subjects and, having received it, glorify this calling. The world will follow us and call you mother of peoples. This is the voice of blessed mighty Russia! God grant this voice to be the voice of the universe!"

The vice-chancellor responded that the empress "accepts with pleasure the expression of the deputies' feelings all the more since this thankfulness clearly presages the zeal which they are prepared to demonstrate to the world in implementing the rules formulated in the 'Instruction.'" Regarding the proposed title, the empress answered: "As to the titles which you wish me to accept from you, I respond: (1) *the Great*—I will let time and our heirs judge my deeds dispassionately; (2) *all-wise*—I can in no way call myself such, for only God is all-wise; (3) *mother of the fatherland*—I consider it a duty of my position to love the subjects entrusted to me by God, and it is my wish that I be loved by them."

The following two meetings of the Commission were devoted to the choice of members for three special commissions: an executive committee, an expediting committee and a committee for compilation of the deputies' instructions. The executive committee was responsible for constituting the other special committees for various branches of legislation (justice—criminal law, property rights, trade, etc.) and for choosing the members of these committees from the whole assembly by ballot. The executive committee supervised the work of the other committees through weekly memoranda received from each committee. Were deviations from the rules observed in these memoranda, the executive committee would correct the wayward committee. When each committee completed its work it presented the results to the executive committee, which then confirmed that the work accorded with the empress' 'Instruction,' and certified that its parts were consistent and that all portions of the work advanced the preservation of the unity of the empire through high moral standards, well-being of the people and humanitarian laws.

The expediting committee made certain that the labors of all other committees were written in correct grammar and style. It was charged with assuring that there should be no passages or words that were ambiguous, murky, vague or unintelligible. This committee was essential because the thinking of Russians, on account of their recent exposure to modern secular knowledge, grappled clumsily with the new world of political and juridical concepts and relationships, all of which was reflected in obscure, heavy and incorrect speech. The committee for the compilation of deputies' instructions was to arrange the instructions and projects according to their content and to present excerpts to the entire assembly, which then would send them with its comments to the executive committee.

At the eighth meeting of the Commission the reading of the projects of the delegates began. Twelve were read and discussed in fifteen sessions. Then the reading and discussion of the laws on the rights of the nobility commenced. Before the conclusion of discussion on this subject the deputies moved on to the laws of the merchantry and then to the privileges of the nobles of Livland and Estland. Following these discussions the 1767 meetings of the Commission in Moscow concluded on December 14.

The Commission's next meeting was in St. Petersburg where it went back into session on February 18, 1768. This time the deputies read and discussed laws concerning the judiciary before recessing once again. When Marshal Bibikov announced that the executive committee had forwarded a project of rules for the well-born, composed by the committee on state categories, the Commission returned to session on July 10 for consideration of gentry rights. The discussion of this project consumed much time. In December the Commission finished its deliberations with a discussion of laws concerning service landed estates (pomestie) and patrimonial estates (votchina).[2]

Catherine wished to hear the frank opinions of the various segments of the Russian people, wished to get to know, as it was said then, the popular "frame of mind." Into these outlooks she hoped to introduce principles reflecting contemporary thought and secular knowledge. She wished to learn the popular frame of mind in order to test the soil before sowing, to find out what was possible, what would evoke response, and what could not be done. Her interest was practical. For us, her heirs, our interest is no less, if historical in character.

COMPOSITION OF THE COMMISSION

The representatives of the various estates gathered for joint discussions of matters of highest interest. This was an assembly of different ranks, and therefore we can expect to find in each rank an effort to define relations with other estates to its own advantage, all the more so since each deputy received instructions to that effect from his electors and considered it his duty to justify their trust. Here the noble estate presented a duality of two factions, men of old families and those from new clans or families. Old Russia had not known a higher noble class. There had been no class connection, solidarity or equality of rights among people standing highest on the service ladder and those on the lower rungs—between the boyars, lords-in-waiting (okolnichii), and "the leanest petty boyars."

These groups had two traits in common—the obligation to military service, which links them to the retinues (druzhina) of the early princes, and the right to receive compensation for this service in the form of landholdings, sometimes converted from temporary into permanent holdings. Despite the absence of an upper noble class and despite the gulf which separated a boyar from a "boyar's son (syn boiarskii),"[3] all of these people, as military men, placed themselves higher than those engaged in peaceful occupations and thought of themselves solely as warriors and true men. They considered the others to be lesser men and called them in the familiar diminutive, "little peasants." At the end of the sixteenth century an important complication in the relations between these groups arose. All of the landowners, those with service and hereditary tenure alike, received for their lands a serf population and took on a new significance in relation to the bulk of the population. This was the status of master which they had held before only in relation to slaves.[4] It was then that the principle was established of separating landowners and serfowners as masters from the rest of the population not having the right to possess peasants. The principle of a *landlord* class, an upper or noble class, was instituted. Bonded peasants were the peasants of lords; privilege appeared and with it a privileged estate.

In this situation the transformation under Peter the Great took place. The essence of the new era demanded the most precise names and definitions for everything. The upper privileged class had to receive one general name, all the more since it was that way in Western Europe where Peter found his model. But from where should that name come? The Russians turned to the nearest national ethnic group, the Poles, and took from them for a time the term gentry (szliachta). Little by little this title began to be displaced by the old Russian one—the nobility (dvorianstvo).[5] At first this name could not be assimilated. The time was still fresh in the popular memory when the word "nobles" (dvoriane) signified only one clear branch of military servitors and when boyars and lords-in-waiting would have made anyone who offended their honor by referring to them as a "nobles," pay dearly. But when the boyars and the lords-in-waiting disappeared, the title of noble was the most esteemed for the mass of landholders and became a class title for all masters, landowners having the right to own peasants.

However in the new Russia there soon appeared a distinction among the nobility leading to trouble. In ancient Russia the right to hold land along with the right to own peasants had belonged to military men. This right was subjected less to contradictions between the various ranks than to those arising from otherwise unthinkable but imperative relations of state. The penurious state could give no other reward for service but land and had to supplement this land with bondaged workers. Conflicts arising out of service or family seniority and honor were vented in the system of ranks.[6] But in the new Russia, as a result of new demands, there appeared phenomena giving rise to a special kind of conflict. First, a standing army was created in which a soldier could rise by merit from the ranks to officer. Being an officer gave him entry into the estate of the well-born, the nobles or the lords. A lord might witness how his peasant, or *his own man,* could enroll in the army and become equal to or even greater than he. It could happen that the peasant would surpass the master in the service; while the noble remained a soldier, the peasant might rise through the officers' ranks and become the superior of his former master. Second, in the natural course of development the civil service appeared alongside the military. People of low origin earned a rank in the civil service giving them entrance into the nobility. Such men bought populated lands with money earned by any means in the service, lived alongside of the old masters and often eclipsed them with their wealth. A military man, obligated to difficult and dangerous service, was offended deeply to see a man of poor family somehow prosper in easy, peaceful service and become equal to or higher than he.

Finally, the epoch of Petrine reforms brought forth new demands, and the agricultural state came to be based partly on manufacturing. Necessary factories and workshops began to be established, but one could not run them with freely hired labor from the underpopulated country. Those same factors which had forced the binding of the peasant to the land for the maintenance of the military now forced the binding of the peasant to the factory and the workshop. Along with the lords who were military people owning peasants, now there appeared factory and workshop owners who also were lords owning peasants. Some of the new lords were themselves peasants who had become rich through trade. This was a new affront to the old lords, the military men.

DEBATES ON THE RIGHT TO NOBILITY

Therefore one heard in the Palace of Facets voices raised against the law of Peter the Great which allowed one reaching a certain rank in the service to become a noble. Prince Michael Shcherbatov, the deputy from the Yaroslavl nobility, addressed the assembly and soon attracted attention by his erudition, the literary craftsmanship of his speeches, and the fervor with which he delivered them. One of his opponents made the following comment about him: "I have noticed that in the opinions offered by the distinguished deputy Prince Michael Shcherbatov that he very rarely stands on previous laws, and that he reinforces his opinions with extremely prudent considerations with which he has been endowed excellently by God."

Shcherbatov replied, "The circumstances of the times and various occasions forced Peter the Great to create for our benefit certain practices, which now due to changing customs, not only are not useful but, more likely than not are harmful. The laws as now written contain the rule by which every man attaining the rank of officer is considered a noble and his children entered in the registers of the nobility. Such a premium on earning an officer's rank was necessary then to attract the gentry into government service. But now when we can see that the Russian gentry is inclined to service and education out of love for the fatherland, glory and devotion to their monarch, it seems that the right of including in that class anyone who somehow attains an officer's rank should be abolished. The Sovereign alone in her discretion can award this right not only to him who has been shown worthy by important services but also to his heirs.

"It is well known that the first difference among statuses arose from the individual brilliance of selected individuals compared to the general populace. Their heirs duly distinguished themselves by rendering services to the societies in which they lived. Thus the prime foundation of the title of noble is that he is the type of citizen to whom, at the moment of birth, the fatherland, as if embracing him, states: 'You have been born of virtuous ancestors; not yet having done anything useful for me, you still have the esteemed title of noble; therefore, more than others you should show me your virtue and your devotion. The rights given by my laws, predating your services, oblige you to this. The deeds of your ancestors move you to this. Imitate their virtue and you will satisfy me.' Born in such a position, raised with such thoughts, will a man not exert special effort to be worthy of such a title and calling? The title alone and the reminder of the glorious deeds of his ancestors are strong enough to move superior persons to all sorts of great deeds.

"This policy was so widespread among the Romans that they attributed the source of their noble families to their heroes. According to St. Augustine, the noted Roman writer Terence stated that it was very useful for the state that the leading people thought themselves the descendants of heroes, even if untrue, since the thought alone of such an origin could motivate them to undertake and complete the greatest deeds.

"Natural reason assures us, just as all the best writers recognize, that honor and glory are found more in the nobility—since these qualities have a greater effect on those who hear almost from birth of the illustrious deeds of their ancestors, see their images, and recall those feats which glorify them—than in those who look at fathers who reached the lower officers' ranks either by seniority or intrigue and not through outstanding service and do not see anything which might incline them toward glorious deeds. The names of their ancestors already have vanished into obscurity. I must cite here the opinions of Baron Pufendorf, renowned for his scholarship and legal knowledge. Pufendorf states that ranks themselves usually do not confer nobility, but that the sovereign awards the title of noble to those whom he deems fit.

"I am so bold as to add that the right by which every man without rank (raznochinets),[7] having achieved an officer's rank, may enter the ranks of the gentry without any examination of his conduct or opinions can be the source of many abuses. Such people know that to attain officers' ranks and thus to become nobles depends on the power of their commander. They will not refuse to play up to his passions and to use other base devices to win his good will. This of course harms the morals of both the servants and the commanders. Once they have reached officer levels and see that they are nobles, these people lose all motivation to achieve higher rank and want only to get themselves an estate. They seek out all possible paths and refuse not one; this results in bribery, embezzlement and all sorts of similar evils.

"I do not propose at all to deprive people, no matter what class they come from, who possess those qualities which lend dignity to such an award. I suppose it quite just to reward such a man, no matter what. However, I wish to reward only real merit and to have the reward come from that person who alone has the undoubted right to give such rewards to a man and his heirs. That person is the monarch."

Other deputies repeated the same thoughts, filling in some details. Ignatiev, the deputy of the nobility of Rzhev-Volodomir, added: "Many of the clerical and townspeople and others like them—having reached staff or senior officer ranks in various state posts—buy large villages, multiply the numbers of factories and workshops, and thus undercut the native gentry in the purchase of villages. When a noble who farms the land and makes his living with his own labor wishes to buy a village from a neighbor at a modest price, several non-nobles with large sums raise the price three times or more. Such villages are left to themselves. In this way a noble is deprived of increasing his estate. He becomes poor and the villages which he held previously fall into decay.

"It is my opinion that the right to nobility and to buy villages should be forbidden to those who are not of the gentry but who have achieved staff or senior officer rank in the service. Some of the latter might ask if they are not given the rights of the nobility and permitted to purchase estates, how will they get their support when they have retired from the service and receive no salary. One should answer that they should invest those funds which they might have used to buy villages and, receiving a percentage from their capital, they should be as content with this as with income from villages."

The deputy of the Oboyansk gentry, Glazov, then stated: "Many people in the military, the guards, the navy, the artillery or the field regiments have stated that they come from the gentry and claim to have estates when they have none for they know that in the military service accurate lists of such things are not kept. By some sort of false information they rise in the ranks. They also have acted in the same way in the civil service. Beyond this, many have coupled themselves with noble families. They use bribes in the military administration to get patents which allow them to add another last name to their own. Having sought out the last member in a certain noble family—a prodigal who does not preserve the honor of his calling—those seeking noble status convince the prodigal noble to sign such patents, duly witnessed, that they are from the nobility and are closely related to him although they really have no true family and can hardly honor the other family name with their own. Through this device many have received promotions and have bought estates. At present in the regiments there are very few nobles. Most of the people serving in the regiments are like those whom I have described."

These opinions did not go unopposed. The deputy of the Izium gentry, Zarudnyi, replied: "I will not begin to explain how varied and heavy are the duties of service in the navy or army for this is too broad a subject. Those who have served and those who now are serving can tell those who do not know about the incredible hardships they suffered in the past Turkish and Prussian battles and campaigns. It can be certified from these stories that the ranks and titles of nobility which those servitors won were not achieved easily.

"As for the civil service, both in managing domestic affairs and in conducting relations with other nations, the work is undoubtedly necessary, useful and not without difficulties. Consequently, to think of rescinding the title of nobility earned in military service—onerous but useful to the fatherland—earned by so many hardships, wounds or even loss of life or, in the same vein, to think of such deprivation of a title acquired by constant labor and honor in the civil service—to think, I say, of taking the title from those on whom it has been conferred seems to me to be consistent neither with the general good of the gentry, nor with that prosperity which our most merciful Sovereign deigned to offer, nor with that precept which Her Majesty propounded in her Instruction—that is, mutually to do good to one another as much as possible.

"Such a thought—depriving state servants of their nobility—can be ascribed to self-interest. Those giving opinions on limiting the means of achieving nobility bespeak a wish that they and those like them alone should enjoy nobility, but others—no matter what their worth, honor and devotion to their monarch and fatherland and no matter what services they have rendered—should be deprived of nobility forever."

The deputy of the Dnieper lancer regiment, Kozelsky, added: "If the ancestors of the present Russian nobles received their titles as rewards for their services, faithfulness and virtue and not through the fame of their family, their descendants should not belittle or scorn the present officers' ranks. If those persons, although not of illustrious birth but only well and morally educated, who by the law of the sovereign, Peter the Great, earned senior officer ranks and have shown themselves to be proficient in military affairs and in managing the soldiers under their command—if such people are indisputably worthy of being considered noble—then they should enjoy all the perquisites of the gentry.

"There is no question that this title is valuable. But to whom has it been dearer—to the ancestors who themselves earned it or to their heirs? If, as some wish, only the ranks of the old nobility are multiplied and newly commissioned servants once again are neglected, then in my opinion this will lead to an upheaval in the state service. The other non-noble classes, seeing themselves not compensated equally with the nobility for service, will serve out of necessity without any initiative and love for the fatherland. Not having the prospect of earning any distinction in the service of their fatherland, they will not be true sons of the fatherland. There will be no reason to take any care about their education, knowledge or virtue. And what kind of order will there be in state affairs, what kind of peace in society, when—instead of mutual brotherly love—hate and enmity are multiplied from such neglect? The nobility, having increased the distinction of their own title, will scorn both military and civil servants. Instead of an improvement of morals, pride and scorn for what is dear will be established."

According to the deputy of the Tersk Cossack army, Mironov, "The calling of noble does not originate in nature but is acquired through virtue and service to one's fatherland. Can the esteemed Russian nobility say of their ancestors that all of the latter were born into the nobility?

I suppose, to the contrary, that in Russia will be found more who received that title through military activities or other virtues."

The old nobles had to defend themselves. Especially telling were the assertions that the ancestors of the people now parading their ancient lineage were people of rather common background who had earned their honors. The most ardent defender of the rights of the old families, Prince Michael Shcherbatov, began to speak "from the depths of his soul," in trembling voice: "The deputy from the Dnieper lancer regiment has offered the opinion that all the ancient Russian noble families were of low birth and that now these ancient nobles do not wish to allow deserving people to join their ranks out of their own haughtiness. I am thoroughly astonished that this esteemed deputy should attribute a base origin to the ancient Russian families since not only Russia but also the entire universe can testify to the contrary. I need refer only to historical events to refute his statements. Some Russian nobles stem directly from Grand Prince Riurik or from the subordinate line of Grand Prince Vladimir. Others who have become prominent people are descended directly from crowned heads. Many families do not come from landholding origins but are descended from quite illustrious people who entered the service of the grand princes of Russia, who count their ancestry in centuries and who have graced themselves with outstanding service to the fatherland.

"How can Russia, assembled here in the person of its deputies, hear accusations of baseness against such families, who in an uninterrupted stream of centuries have rendered her such services? How can she not remember the blood which these worthy men spilled? Be my witness, beloved fatherland, to the service rendered you by your true sons—the nobles of ancient family! You will be my witnesses also, these hallowed halls, where we have assembled for our common good! Were you not in the power of a predator's hands? You, divine cathedrals, were you not defiled by non-believers? And Russia, in your hour of downfall, who came to your aid? Your true spirits, the ancient Russian nobles! They forsook all and sacrificed their lives; they freed you from the yoke of the foreigner and regained for you your former liberty! I imagine that I can see the blood of these worthy men still flowing, reminding their heirs to act as such and sacrifice their lives, as they have been taught, to the fatherland. There is the prime right and demand of the nobles of old family that no one shall be made equal to them without sanction of the highest authority. They do not create barriers to excellence out of superciliousness, but they desire that those who wish to join them as brothers should achieve this status through true virtue, which the monarch herself would reward with a title to nobility."

The deputy of the Mikhailov gentry, Semen Naryshkin, tried to explain what, in his opinion, should constitute the difference between an officer and a noble. "Promotion into the officer corps serves as a reward for good conduct in the lower ranks, while inclusion into the gentry is a reward for designated services to the fatherland." Naryshkin also spoke on the relationship of the gentry toward the owning of peasants. "The title of noble is considered something sacred by us, which distinguishes any one man from others. It gives him and his heirs the right to own other humans and to care for their welfare."

However, the defenders of the law of Peter the Great, "such a great lawgiver," would not yield and one of them, the deputy from the city of Ruza, one Smirnov, proposed to limit the rights of inheritance of the gentry: "Ranks and stations are received not through inheritance but for services to the fatherland and are tied to the persons receiving these honors, who then die. Heirs should not enjoy rewards which they have not earned with their own services. They should not develop an aversion to earning their ranks themselves. Nor should they deny others who have earned their own rewards the approbation and same hope for rewards which their predecessors enjoyed. We should strengthen in the heirs a proclivity to service and ward off apathy, lack of enthusiasm, and despair. We should encourage people of the lowest class toward the achievement of the highest level of honor. For all these reasons I consider it useful to propose a decree that nobility and its immovable property should not be inheritable but that every man should try to attain them through his own services.

"Conferral or removal of noble status can be accomplished in the following manner: (1) Every man, regardless of his family, can be rewarded for his services with the title of noble and all the perquisite advantages of this status, beginning with the first honorable level earned by him, for example, senior officer rank. (2) Each such noble, just as all other nobles, should be subject to the same law to which others are subject. If some noble commits a misdemeanor, then, depending on its severity, he should be deprived not only of his nobility but also of the advantages belonging to an honorable citizen. (3) As for the heirs of nobles, I suppose that to be deprived of nobility without considering the services of their ancestors would be unjust and unacceptable, but to leave them their estate in perpetuity would be even more unjust for the reasons I have given before. (4) Consequently, it is fitting that the nobility of each man be extended to several generations, according to his services and rank—for example, for staff and senior officers, if they are nobles, one should grant nobility to their children and grandchildren; for generals, nobility should be extended to their great-grandchildren, and so on. (5) If any individual in the following generations does not demonstrate the required devotion and does not renew his nobility, his children should be deprived of that title. (6) When an heir falls several ranks below his ancestor who had earned nobility, the inherited nobility of his heirs shall be reduced the according number of steps. (7) Through such carelessness about himself a man's heirs shall be deprived. With this the inevitable discouragement with themselves and the despair and laziness of non-nobles will be rooted out, and in each person will arise an eagerness to make himself useful for society and his heirs.

"Finally, our gentry should form one body, not torn into different factions fighting one another, but including and uniting all citizens striving for the same goal, foreseen by our wise monarch, whose wish is not to raise up some and to turn others into nothing but to make all, without exception, as much as is humanly possible, the most fortunate on the globe."

PRIVILEGES OF THE GENTRY

The ownership of estates and peasants, that is, *lordship* in its true sense, was that dear right which the old nobles especially did not want to share with the new men who recently had earned their nobility with sabre or pen. And both the old and new nobles looked askance at people who had not earned nobility at all, did not belong to the noble class but, despite this, enjoyed the valuable right of owning estates and serfs. These latter were the factory owners. In the instruction from the Yaroslavl nobility to its deputy, Prince Michael Shcherbatov, it was written: "In the decree of Peter the Great to urge the Russian merchant class to build factories,[8] the merchants were allowed to buy villages around their factories. The merchants not only have made use of this right but also have exceeded it by more than is proper, having bought villages in places far from their factories. This not only does not correspond with the intentions of Peter the Great but violates them. Factory owners, envisioning themselves as the holders of many estates, have begun to neglect their factories and to receive the revenues of landowners. Those who really have bought villages for their factories have taken all the peasants out of the villages to work in their factories for such meager wages that it is hard for the workers to obtain their daily sustenance. This places an obstacle on the growth of the people, undercuts tillage and oppresses the peasants themselves with such labors that they often rise in revolt. Therefore, would it not be desirable to take from the merchants the villages which they have bought and distribute them so that they are not left at a loss? For factories constructed in the future the following appropriate disposition should be made: the factories shall have artisans and workers according to the amount of work and the size of the plant, and other workers shall be hired on a temporary basis. This could force factory owners to attend more zealously to the improvement of Russian factories and the production of Russian goods for trade. The gentry also will gain through greater circulation of money when their peasants with slack times in the fields go to the merchants to work in the factories."

In their effort to restrict landowning privileges to themselves, the old nobles could not help but remember the right of primogeniture. In the instruction of the Moscow nobility to its deputy, Peter Ivanovich Panin, the following article was inserted: "In correspondence with other well-ordered Christian states in Europe, one should petition for the right of each landowner to designate a part of his movable and immovable property as an indivisible inheritance to go to whomever he wishes with directions for the manner in which it should pass from generation to generation. Our previous law borrowed some examples from several European lands, but it could not last because, of course, it restricted the will of property owners within extremely narrow limits through the directive to give all one's immovable estate, the most important property of a noble in Russia, to one heir only, even if that heir were of his own choosing."

The instruction of the gentry from the Mikhailov district to their deputy, Senator Melgunov, attempted to avoid the break-up of villages and the resultant open field system of landholding. The instruction demanded whenever the peasant lands of any landowner were surveyed that those lands—entire villages or hamlets, in fact—should be deemed indivisible. Consequently, in sales, rentals, gifts or inheritances those villages would be transferred according to the survey.

The instructions of the gentry from Pereiaslavl-Zalessky to General Stupishin said: "It would seem to be useful for the preservation of families and homes if it were permitted that any landowner, while alive or upon his death, could keep one or several villages, as he wished, from being split up among his family."

The deputies spoke much more vociferously about the necessity of creating regional assemblies of the gentry and of their right to participate in the local courts and administration. The nobles of the Borov district wrote in the instruction to their deputy, Golokhvastov, that nobles should be allowed to have a meeting every two years in their district. This meeting should investigate and judge whether all activities in the district were being conducted according to the laws—whether anyone was being oppressed by the courts, by regiments quartered in or passing through the district, or by anyone whatsoever and whether any illegal activities or oppression of the gentry or the serfs could be seen. If any such abuses were found, the chosen deputy of the nobles should report them to the Senate. At the same assembly the nobles should choose from among themselves a district councillor [landrat][9] and a district commissioner [distriktnyi komissar] for every locality or district. The district commissioners should obey the district councillor and preside over all nobles and peasants, including those from court holdings and lands under the administration of the College of Church Landed Property.[10] The district councillor should hear and decide small cases involving not more than twenty-five rubles. The commissioners should make a record and inform the district councillor whenever a violation of the law occurs. The district councillor will then investigate and pass judgment, based upon his review of the case. If robbery occurs in the district, the local commissioner immediately should assemble the nobles with their servants and peasants and try to catch the robbers. He also should inform the district councillor and the other commissioners, who also should take all measures to apprehend the robbers and send them to the chancery of the military governor. The district councillors and commissioners should act likewise in the case of illegal sale of liquor. The commissioners also shall accompany troops in transit, see that they are kept provisioned, and see that the inhabitants are not subjected to any insult.

Upon the passage of two years, the district councillor should assemble the nobility and inform them what has happened in the district during those two years as a way of giving an account of his administration. The assembly should choose a new district councillor and new commissioners; the incumbents may be reelected. If the district councillor or commissioners have managed their posts unfittingly, after removal the assembly should pass judgment on the offenders and, by majority vote, levy fines. Proceeds of such fines should be sent to foundling homes. Fines also should be levied upon those nobles who disobey the authority of the district councillor or commissioners. The district councillor, in sum, should serve as guardian and protector of his district in all matters.

The Kostroma gentry requested the establishment of local courts, elected by the gentry and composed of retired nobles. These judges should mete out swift justice and punishment in disputes occurring among the gentry over land ownership, cutting wood, harvesting grain, cutting hay, peasant fights, and theft of horses and cattle. Furthermore, the judges should keep the roads in order, arrange for the quartering of military units, and appoint and supervise guardians for insane or underage nobles.

In the instruction to their deputy, Count Bruce, the Kozelsk gentry requested: "Military governors are sent to the cities by the Senate.

However, because of the great number of persons involved, the Senate is unable to ascertain the qualifications of each person for that position. Therefore, could it not be considered to give the choice of military governors to the nobles so they might choose the most fit of their comrades?"

The Mikhailov gentry requested that courts dealing with affairs between the gentry or their servants and peasants in minor disputes, not exceeding ten rubles, be composed of the marshal of the nobility and four assistants. The Sudislov gentry requested the founding of an oral hearings court with judges and four assistants chosen by the gentry so that nobles would not have to suffer losses or bureaucratic delays for many nobles did not know the bureaucratic procedures. Others were totally illiterate or too poor to hire counsel, especially widows and orphans. The Sudislov gentry also asked for the election of military governors by the gentry from their own number. The Yaroslavl gentry requested that nobles be allowed to elect assistants to the military governors from their own ranks. Every petitioner, before the beginning of his case, should appear before one of these assistants, who would be obliged to try to reconcile the rivals in the case. Should he be unsuccessful, he would be obligated to assure that neither plaintiff nor defendant suffered in court because of excessive formalities and procedures.

The instruction of the Vladimir gentry stated: "Crown agents obscure legal matters with their own fantasies. Those in the wrong prolong matters by various intrigues, inquiries, inapplicable citations of statutes and other improprieties. Having taken money from one side in a dispute, they do not look at all for the cause of cases; those who trust them often are indicted. Thus, should not people so harmful to society be eliminated entirely from legal proceedings and civil matters and be replaced by nobles, whose worth and knowledge is attested by the Senate?"

The gentry of Klin requested the right to choose a noble supervisor for each district every three years. Nobles would turn to this supervisor with their complaints. Having received a complaint, the supervisor would call in the plaintiff and his opponent and demand that, to aid them in reviewing their case, each should provide a representative from the gentry of the district with certification that they trusted him. When these representatives had been presented from both sides, the supervisor would be sworn in and decide the case with them as a court of three. The supervisor should attend to the affairs of the nobles of his district which arise in the military governor's chancery. Finally, he should guard the local estate boundaries. The gentry of each district should have in Moscow its own deputy, chosen for a year, to look after all the affairs of the district in the College of Hereditary Estates and other judicial offices so that these affairs might be settled expeditiously. These persons would enjoy the protection of a state deputy who should be a man of the first or second class.

The gentry of Peremysl and Vorotynsk districts proposed that a magistrate be chosen by election by the gentry. The Aleksin gentry requested that courts be founded in every district to be elected by the gentry rather than chosen by the military governors and their assistants. In the event of doubt about any matter, the judge would inform the marshal of the gentry who would have the affair settled in a general assembly of the gentry. The Dmitrov nobles requested the right to choose local judges who would settle orally in the shortest possible time all arguments and disputes between nobles or peasants without written opinions.

The old nobles, opposing the easy achievement of nobility by persons of low birth, prided themselves upon their superior upbringing and higher education. But the means to give their children such an education were far from accessible to all, and therefore they requested the establishment of schools. The deputy of the Kashin gentry, Kozhin, stated: "Although there is the noble Corps of Cadets in St. Petersburg, one such institution is not enough for the multitude of the gentry in Russia. Furthermore, many young people have passed the age established for admission to this newly-founded corps, and the shortage of proper teachers prevents giving them a moral education befitting a noble at home. But since gentry are required to serve her imperial majesty and the fatherland, we therefore request an order to found a Corps of Cadets for nobles in Moscow on the basis of the decree of 1731.[11] To support this academy, the tax on marriages should be renewed. Non-nobles getting married should pay fifty copecks per marriage. All nobles who hold hereditary estates should procure from the Treasury College[12] a document indicating how many souls [adult males] they own and pay two rubles for each one hundred souls[13] when they marry. Nobles who own fewer than one hundred but more than ten souls should pay one ruble. Those who do not own immovable property but who earn a salary should pay one ruble for each one hundred rubles of salary."

The deputy of the Serpeisk gentry, Count Alexander Stroganov, noted that it was necessary to found a school in Moscow for poor nobles, but that the proposed tax for this was unjust since it contradicted the articles of the Instruction which proposed advantages and incentives for those entering marriage. A tax burdening those getting married would prevent growth of the population. Besides, every levy on society should benefit all of that society, and not just one part. Therefore, the school should be maintained at the expense of the gentry alone. Every landowner having more than two hundred souls should pay a fixed yearly sum. The corps, however, should admit only the children of nobles owning fewer than two hundred souls. Nobles with more than two hundred souls also could place their children in the school but at their personal expense.

In their instruction to their deputy, the Kostroma gentry wrote: "Many poor nobles not only are unable to raise their children decently and teach them the subjects necessary for a noble but also are unable, because of extreme want, to send their children to the distant state schools. Because of this, their children grow up in ignorance and lethargy and not only become unfit for the service but also do not have the slightest trace of nobility in their lives and conduct. To preserve these children for the use of the state and to raise and teach them reading, writing, and the rudiments of mathematics and foreign languages, especially for a dignified upbringing, schools or seminaries should be founded in the cities of gubernias and provinces."

The Tula gentry requested that small gymnasia [high schools] be founded in provincial cities with one professor and two assistants. The Moscow gentry requested the establishment in Moscow of a Corps of Cadets for young nobles and two schools to educate noblewomen, one for children and one for adults. The gentry would undertake to pay for these schools themselves. The Serpukhov, Tarus, and Obolensk nobles asked for the establishment of guardians for young nobles and of schools for poor nobles as well as for children of civil servants and merchants. These schools would teach Russian grammar, arithmetic, geometry, German and French. The education of the nobles was supposed to give them service rights. The gentry of the city of Opochka requested that nobles be exempt forever from serving as soldiers or non-commissioned officers and that every noble who had been taught to read and write well and had learned arithmetic, geometry and a bit of Russian geography be allowed to enter the service directly as a commissioned officer. These same nobles who at their own expense had learned various sciences, foreign languages, arts and skills should be rewarded with the rank of first or second lieutenant.

NOBLES, MERCHANTS, AND PEASANTS—THE DEBATE ABOUT CLASSES

The gentry demanded for itself the exclusive right to own serfs. The merchants demanded for themselves the exclusive right to conduct trade. The deputy from the merchants of the Rybnaia settlement (Rybinsk), Alexis Popov, said: "Instead of the remedies we expected, we see with great sorrow from the opinions offered to the commission by many of the lord deputies that great exactions are being prepared for the Russian merchantry, as if it were completely unneeded by the state. Instead of affirming the edicts of Peter the Great on the rights and freedoms of the merchants and forbidding people of any other class from carrying on trade, whereby the merchantry naturally might achieve greater prosperity, the aforementioned deputies propose to harm the merchants by advocating that the gentry and the peasantry should enjoy the merchants' rights on par with the merchants. The lord deputies urge that merchants be forbidden to own any factories or mines. In support of such an arrangement they claim that the operation of factories and workshops by merchants brings society no good and that it would be much more useful if ownership of factories was permitted to retired nobles living in the villages. They also propose that peasants bringing their products to the towns be allowed to sell them at retail. If all this is approved, the merchantry inevitably will be ruined and trade will fall into total decay.

"For although peasants and people of various ranks are forbidden now by law from engaging in trade, the merchants are suffering a great deal of injury and interference from them. What would it be like if the law allowed everyone to engage in trade?" Popov made a demand: "Give the merchants the right to construct factories and workshops and to buy peasants for the necessary work, but not in excess, only corresponding to the number of looms or furnaces. Let the merchants buy as much land and people on it as are needed for the factories. Do not allow the gentry to engage in trade and do not let anyone in any manner purchase merchants' rights; the gentry has its own rights, which include great privileges and the bearing of the precious title of nobility. Therefore, it is not fitting for the gentry, by their very calling, to enter into such commercial activities as running factories, workshops or other aspects of trade. They should offer for sale only that which is produced on their estates by their own industry without buying anything from others. The well-born Russian nobleman should attempt to improve the agriculture of his peasants and assure that the latter work the land with diligence and zeal.

"In Russia at present many agriculturalists neglect agriculture altogether and engage in commerce instead of keeping to their calling and expanding cultivation. Because they do not know the fine points of commercial exchange, many of the agriculturalists who enter commerce end up bankrupt. They do not pay the merchants for the goods they have received from them, hide out in the countryside and do not go back to agriculture. This leads to the great evil whereby the agriculturalists left in the villages pay the head taxes and rent[14] for those who have fled and thus become poorer. To eliminate such an unfavorable situation, one should recognize the necessity of requiring agriculturalists, for the good of the entire state, to engage solely in cultivation of the land and not to engage in any kind of trade. If it is necessary that the

Russian merchantry render the state useful services, other people of any class should be forbidden absolutely from engaging in trade."

Prince Michael Shcherbatov came forward to defend the right of the nobility to own factories and workshops. He began with the proposition that "the state becomes strong when it rests on illustrious and well-endowed families who are like the firm and unshakeable supports which bear the weight of a heavy building. If the supports are weak, it does not matter how many their number. In actuality we see that the greatness of the French and Spanish states is based on illustrious families. Let us look at the essence of workshops and factories. Merchants alone, unless by exception from the rights of nobles, should not own metallurgical factories which take ores from the ground and transform them by fire for ownership of land should be allowed only to nobles. Is it really the desire of the esteemed deputy from the Rybnaia settlement that the merchants, having deprived the gentry of the opportunity to obtain some sort of profit, should become monopolists of all manufactures in Russia and set the prices for both goods and workers? As for purchase of lands around factories, it seems indisputable to me that the merchants should be permitted this; but they should be allowed no more land than each of their workshops requires. Although workers are necessary for a factory, if one takes into account the number of agricultural laborers in Russia, it surely does not follow that workers for factories should come from the land. On the contrary the nobles should strive in every way to increase the number of agriculturalists. At present, if you examine the use and lives of these workers, you will see that aside from a small number of master craftsmen who are kept almost as captives so that they do not impart their expertise to strangers—aside from these, I say, the rest are in a very bad state, both materially and morally. This very capital city [Moscow] can attest to the dissolute state of these people."

The peasant Vonifatiev, deputy from the Olonets crown peasants, spoke for the right of peasants to engage in trade: "Several deputies write in their opinions that in order to trade peasants will travel far from their homes and will not attend to agriculture. To this I can reply that peasants absent themselves from home not just for trade but for the most part to get money for state taxes through various trades and jobs. Moreover, it is usually those peasants whose families consist of five or six people that go off. While one or two are away, the others remain home and tend to agriculture. All honorable people attend to the field in which they find themselves. Yet people who do not take care of themselves can, I think, be found in all families."

The merchants continued to insist that the peasants engage only in agriculture, or else higher prices would result. The deputy from the city of Serpeisk, Glinkov, stated: "There are about seven million peasants in the country. If one excludes minors, the aged, the dead, military recruits and personal servants of landowners—barely half are left who are fit to till the soil. Without doubt, almost half of these are engaged in trade or off on other activities, and therefore the number actually engaged in agriculture is very small. Because of this, a significant amount of arable land remains idle and the cost of living in Russia rises. It must be decreed that peasants traveling about the country be prohibited from purchasing goods and selling them in cities, at fairs or trading posts as items of their own manufacture. A peasant can get every sort of food for himself and feed for his horse from his own household but a merchant has to buy his."

Speaking on the exclusive right of the merchants to own factories, Glinkov added an observation on the difference between the establishment of factories by merchants and by landlords. "When a merchant builds a factory all the peasants of the region derive benefit from it. They sell wood, boards, shingles and so on and are hired to build the works. They get good money for this and they also can sell the produce of their land there. This makes them better able to pay their state taxes and quitrent to the landlords. When a factory is built the peasants receive another great advantage. They are hired to haul all kinds of materials from distant places to the factory and to haul the products of the factory off to the markets. Other factories are constructed by landlords who use their own peasants for this. They begin by demanding that a certain amount of timber, boards, pitch, and shingles be brought from each household. Each peasant is called unwillingly from cultivation of his fields to bring whatever is demanded. Then the peasants have to work on the construction without pay and feed themselves. After such a factory is built the peasants are forced to work in it, again without pay. This happens especially when the owner of such a factory goes into debt for its construction and does not know the secret of running it properly."

In light of these arguments, the deputy from the College of Commerce, Mezheninov, offered a curious opinion. "Several lord deputies have considered whether it is better for merchants or nobles to own factories and workshops and whether trading activity might not be shameful for an honorable noble. It is absolutely useless, it would seem to debate this question. Let everyone find what is good for him. There is no shame in that for anyone. Only no one should interfere in the affairs of another. It would be all for the better if nobles established those types of factories which do not yet exist in Russia. But in this case the Russian people are like birds which find a bit of bread, take it from one another until they crumble it into tiny crumbs, mix them up with dirt and sand, and lose them entirely. Only some twenty years ago the nobles learned that sailcloth brought big profits. Not imagining that quite a sufficient number of such factories had been built, they also began to build these factories and did not see their mistake until they practically were ruined, when the owners hardly knew where to turn with their sailcloth. (How do you get your big profits out of that, you tempted nobles?) People now have started doing the same thing with soldiers' broadcloth. The poor broadcloth manufacturers hardly had begun to reap the fruits of their work—after many years of effort and great expense for construction of their factories—when the nobles, envying them, began to build similar factories and took from the previous manufacturers all hope of profit. It seems unnecessary that nobles should be allowed to construct factories and workshops. Hence their competition against one another and excessive production will ruin neither themselves nor the old factory owners, and then agriculture, necessary for every factory, will not be neglected. There are already so many iron works that from year to year a significant quantity of iron for domestic consumption and for export is not used. Why should poor factories be added when there are already a great many good ones? Just to destroy the forests, so that our heirs will burn straw instead of wood?"

This same Mezheninov suggested several things that harmed trade and caused the merchants losses: "(1) The draymen take most of the money agreed upon from their masters but do not take the goods entrusted to them to their proper destination, and offer various excuses. They store the goods someplace along the road with peasant conspirators who live in the area and receive from the peasants the money not paid by their masters, usually as much as they think to demand. Having received the goods and pilfered a part of them, the peasants do not return the merchandise to the owners until the latter pay them all that they demand for storage of the goods and compensation for what the peasants have paid the drivers. The poor merchants, above their ordinary loss, also are responsible for non-delivery of goods to the destination and for breach of contract. The merchants have no way of avoiding such losses for they find it quite hard, in fact, impossible to get as many wagons as they need on consignment or on their written assurances. (2) When barges carrying goods on the rivers are damaged or have to be lightened to make a shallow passage, the owners of the lands along the rivers will not allow portage without toll. Nor do they allow outsiders to do the work but insist on using their own peasants at a great price. (3) These same landowners will not allow barges to be pulled by the merchants' own horses and insist that the merchant hire their horses at exorbitant cost."

The deputy of the town of Yaransk, Antonov, portrayed the general position of the merchant in somber hues. "For insult or injury merchants are supposed to receive seven, six or five rubles per man for the first, second or third guild, respectively.[15] Therefore the merchantry is extremely neglected and is in danger; merchants often suffer not only insult but also cruel beatings and mutilation by various kinds of people who are not held in check by any restrictions or danger of punishment. Although some merchants can seek satisfaction for an injury in court, this does not do them any good. It only wastes time and profits because the judicial process and proclamation of a decision never take less than half a year. When such a case is finished, even if a merchant of the first guild is involved, he receives only seven rubles for the injury. Meanwhile, during the time that he is attending to the litigation, he loses incalculably more in his business affairs. Besides this, he runs an extreme risk of retaliation in the form of abuse or beatings, sometimes even at the hearing of his case."

Antonov demanded an increase in the amount paid for insult to merchants. The deputy from the town of Kronstadt, Rybnikov, claimed that the merchants of Russia found themselves in a position far different from that of merchants of other European states; the Russian merchantry enjoys neither appropriate freedom nor sufficient privileges and renders service in the form of state taxes. The deputy of the city of Serpeisk, Glinkov, thought it necessary to give the right to wear swords to factory owners and merchants of the first guild because, above their usual duties, they made payments for the poor, supporting from ten to fifteen souls each; they also carried on trade with foreign merchants in the seaports. "The Germans scorn a Russian merchant if they see that he is without a sword, especially at the commodity exchange. When a foreign merchant stands next to a Russian it appears he is with his servant and deals with him like a superior to an underling."

Prince Michael Shcherbatov answered the complaints of the Russian merchants with an attack on their own remissiveness: "Did the Russian merchants respond to the instructions of Peter the Great? Did they establish offices in other countries? Do they have correspondents to inform them what goods and how many are needed where? Did they send their children off to learn their business? No! They did not do any of these. Therefore it is vain to complain that the peasants and men without rank are taking all the means for trade from the merchants. All foreign trade remains in their hands.

"We Russians assembled here should be ashamed that Hamburg and Dutch merchants, farther from the Arctic Ocean then we are from Kola by fifteen to eighteen degrees on a straight line, without counting the

distance around Norway, come and kill whales and make a profit practically right on our shores. All this despite the fact that arming their
ships and hiring sailors costs them quite a lot. Just look at how profitable
it would be for Russian merchants to undertake such trade—given the
proximity, the low cost of labor and the cheap firewood for melting
blubber. These are the true keys to the wealth of merchants! Let them
turn to such ways and see that real usefulness to the fatherland is connected with their own enrichment."

The deputy from Simbirsk, Larionov, offered the following information about the conduct of the rich merchants who demanded swords.
"Some crown contractors have other merchants in their service and
count on them illegally for great sums of money. As if in very important
court cases, they hold the latter for eight months and more in underground prisons, inflict corporal punishment on them, and do not allow
anyone in to see them. All this is known at the Treasury College. The
merchantry of European countries, and even Asiatic countries, treat
their assistants like their own children. Therefore I propose a law that a
rich merchant, who has in his pay assistants from the merchantry, should
not behave barbarously nor do anything wicked. If they should have
some dispute about accounts, it should be ordered that it be settled by
the town council."

The one general demand in the requests of the state or crown peasants
was improvement of the courts. The peasants of Kazan district wrote:
"We are like a voiceless people, not conversant with the laws. We sell all
we have to hire agents to represent us, but these agents deceive and ruin
both petitioners and defendants. In these affairs many witnesses also are
assembled and many depositions are taken, and thus the case is drawn
out. The plaintiff and defendant are ruined, and things get to the state
where we not only cannot pay our crown taxes but cannot even feed
ourselves."

They requested that in cases of less than thirty rubles, except where
robbery was involved, they be allowed to hold court themselves and to
pick a suitable judge from their number. Others demanded that resolution of domestic quarrels, insignificant disputes over debts and division
of haymowing be left to their village elders.[16] The deputy of the newly
baptised Votiaks,[17] Ivanov, proposed giving peasants the right to hold
oral hearings court in cases of not over thirty rubles. For this, the
peasants could pick one judge from each hundred. This judge would
have the right to punish the guilty according to law and to mediate civil
suits. Ivanov considered it inappropriate to appoint nobles or salaried
officials as judges of crown peasants because these nobles or commissioners acted high handedly; they demanded transport, victuals and so

forth. Furthermore the peasant did not dare argue and if he did start to say something such judges would beat him for speaking disrespectfully. When the deputy from the College of Audits,[18] Kartashov, expressed the opinion that it was necessary to limit the cutting of timber and game and bird hunting by explicit rules, the deputy of the crown peasants of Archangel province, Chuprov, noted: "If game and bird hunting is allowed at all times, they will not grow scarcer; and if it is forbidden, they will not increase since their increase or loss lies in the power of Almighty God!"

THE QUESTION OF SERFDOM

The private serfs were not heard from for there were no deputies representing them. We have seen how the initial draft of the empress' Instruction was altered in those articles dealing with the serfs. Among the articles in the instructions to the deputies from government offices we see one article dealing with improvement of the condition of the serfs and an article on the application of the law on how to proceed in cases where serfs are killed by beatings by their masters.

Concerning the question of runaway serfs, the deputy of the Kozlov nobility, Korobin, pointed to the cruel treatment of serfs by landlords as one cause of their flight. He also cited overly high quit rent payments, cases in which indebted landlords hired out their peasants for labor, paying only interest, and thus removed the serfs from farming, and cases in which landlords took from the serfs property earned by their own labor. Referring to the articles of the empress' Instruction, Korobin proposed limitation of the power of the landlords over the property of the serfs. Eighteen persons rose to speak against Korobin; only three agreed with him. His opponents pointed out the impossibility of separating two rights: leaving landlords their power over the person of the serf while removing their power over the serf's property.

We have seen that the gentry demanded for themselves as their chief right the exclusive privilege of owning people, the right to be masters. But the merchants also demanded this right, claiming that it was necessary for them. The deputy of the city of Yaransk, Antonov, stated: "According to existing law, merchants do not have the right to buy or own servants although they need them very much. Merchants hire peasants at great cost, but there are very few such free laborers, and they are for the most part people who are in extreme need of money and hire out on the condition that they receive in advance a certain amount of money which they will work off. Many of these people flee their employers before they have fully earned this money. And when they live with their masters, knowing that they are not serfs, and therefore having no fear, they act up and cause their employers much grief for it is necessary to lodge any complaints against them in the courts, which is ruinous and leads to loss of time. The merchants cannot rely on such employees under any circumstances. When it is necesssry to ship goods or send money, one cannot use such employees; employers are forced to neglect their own crying needs and go themselves or else to put off delivery of the goods or money with the fear of losing their reputation."

The deputy from the city of Serpeisk, Glinkov, stated: "A certain number of serfs definitely should be assigned to factories because the shop masters should be serfs. In the case of the death of one of them, it is necessary to put another in his place expeditiously for when I teach a stranger and show him secrets, he can go off to another factory owner or demand higher pay than the factory can afford. It would be useful to decree that the merchants of the first guild could buy serfs, from three to five souls. Merchants trading in the ports hire crews for loading and unloading, but the crews often take their pay and never show up to work. The merchants cannot abandon their business. They lack the means of pursuing and prosecuting the crews and therefore suffer losses unnecessarily. They hire private peasants as household servants. These are rarely proper servants for they often turn out to be idlers, and many even bring robbers into the homes of their employers."

The demands of the merchants naturally met strong opposition from the nobles, who stood by the principle that the right to own people, to be masters, belonged solely to them. Prince Michael Shcherbatov stated: "The nobility is a title of honor, an honor which separates them from all others whom it might adorn (the words of the Instruction), and all rights and advantages of the noble estate should stem from this fundamental principle. This title obligates the nobles to serve the fatherland and sovereign with special zeal and to prepare themselves through their upbringing to be capable of this service and command of other subjects of their monarch. They thereby acquire the right, incidentally, to own villages and slaves so that, having learned from childhood to manage their villages, they will be more capable of administration of parts of the empire and from their own experience will know all the needs of the various kinds of people in the state. In the Instruction it is declared that the burghers (meshchanstvo)[19] live in the towns and engage in various crafts, commerce, arts and letters. Therefore it is clearly indicated that the burghers, of which the merchantry is a part, shall have and engage in the above activities personally, but not with the aid of unfree persons. The right demanded for the merchants makes the lack of freedom of the lower class even more sensitive since, upon their sale, they would be forced to serve people whom not long ago they had looked upon as equals.

"We turn our gaze upon humanity and are ashamed at the very idea that things could become so severe that a man equal to us by nature should be compared with cattle and sold without his family. We are people, and the serfs under our power are essentially people like us. The vagaries of fate have put us in a position of owning them, but we must not forget that they are created essentially equal to us. Would it correspond to this indisputable truth when a master, solely for his own profit, takes some boy or girl from their parents and sells them like livestock to someone else? Just imagining this makes my blood boil, and of course I do not doubt that the esteemed Commission will forbid the sale of people, separately, without land.

"It surprises me that hired people supposedly are not as faithful to their masters as personal serfs. This is the same as if someone said that man works more willingly unfree than in following his own inclinations. If a free man serves me, especially for a long time, he works independently of salary out of zeal, but I cannot penetrate the mind of a serf and tell whether he is eager to serve me. And how can you say that the merchants cannot get along without such bonded servants, when we see all of Europe, where no one has slaves and yet no one complains of the impossibility of getting along without them or of the lack of enthusiasm of free laborers?"

In conclusion Prince Shcherbatov stated: "The number of peasants subject to the poll tax is now calculated to be 7.5 million.[20] The nobility, clergy, merchants, military, other types of people and foreigners supposedly number about one million. If we presuppose the largest number, one still cannot presume that there are more than four million workers among the peasantry. From this number you must subtract people in the personal service of their masters, those assigned to factories, and the landless peasants who wander about in search of work—carpenters, stonemasons, bricklayers and so on. All of these might number up to 700,000. If you exclude this number from the four million, there are only 3.3 million actual agriculturalists. Consequently every one who tills the soil must provide bread for some five persons. If merchants are allowed to buy people for themselves and if one postulates that of 20,000 merchants each purchases two families this will result in a loss of 40,000 cultivators."

But the merchants were not swayed by these arguments and did not give up their demands. The cossacks also demanded the right to have serfs. Finally, even the clergy demanded that right!

Such a solution of the question of serfdom by Russia's chosen deputies in the latter half of the last century stemmed from moral, political and economic backwardness. To own people, to have slaves, was considered

the supreme right, a ruling assumption that made up for all other political and social disadvantages. It was a right which its holders therefore
did not wish to share with others and thereby lessen its value. This right
was so valuable, this position so esteemed and advantageous, that even
the best people shut their eyes to the terrible abuses which naturally
and necessarily flowed from this right and position. Those notions which
little by little undermined the value of this right and position in the eyes
of leading people had only just appeared and were beginning very weakly
to penetrate society. There was the scientific concept of the state—of a
higher authority and its relations to its subjects—relations unlike those
of landowner and serf, lessening the latter's tsarist hue. Then there was
the notion of slavery as the stamp of a barbaric society, a notion insulting for people with pretentions to refinement. There was the concept of
nationality and that the honor and glory of a people consisted not in
the fact that they were all beaten and oppressed but in an effort to
assure that as few as possible should be beaten and oppressed. It was
necessary for a century to pass before all these ideas, strengthened more
and more by the ways of European life and disseminated more widely
by the spread of education, gradually undermined the idea of the lofti-
ness of the right to own slaves.

Beyond the aforementioned lack of development, economic backwardness also militated mightily against a favorable solution of the serf
question. From the beginnings of our history we note in Russia a phenomenon which has led to many unfortunate consequences. This is the
discrepancy in the size of the country as compared to the size of the
population. A small population is scattered about a vast land which
constantly is adding more and more wastelands. There are not enough
hands for the work, and no work goes well in the absence of cooperative
activity. Land is cheap and the worker dear. There are hardly enough
workers to satisfy the basic requirements of society, not even thinking
about industrial development. Because of a shortage of labor Russia was
doomed to remain agricultural, rural and poor. The worker was valuable
and he was lured and enticed. Finally, so that a less wealthy man in the
service would have constant labor on his land and so that his rich neighbors would not lure away his workers, the worker was tied to the land.
The serf laborer ran away and others continued to entice him, hide him
or send him further away where he could not be found. The owners of
runaways wailed, demanding the help of government in locating those
who had fled, and Russia presented the curious spectacle of the pursuit
of men to provide labor power—to acquire, catch, settle and bind the
worker. Russian society lived in the period when slavery was a common
phenomenon. Society had developed beyond the era of elementary

existence when each family or clan satisfied all of its own unpretentious needs, but had not yet attained civilization and the division of labor allowed by a significant population. It was most important in that society for a man to have at his disposal a living, thinking force that would deliver him from manual labor which, with the appearance of classes, began to be considered vulgar. Given the economic backwardness, each separate family had to satisfy almost all its needs itself, and this was made all the easier by using slaves. The more such living, thinking beings a man had, in full dependence upon him, the more self-sufficient, independent, strong and illustrious he became. The right to own such beings became the most valuable right.

Russia was in such a position when the acknowledged necessity of raising the country from the poverty and helplessness of an agricultural state led to a transformation that aimed to eliminate its unbalanced agricultural character through commercial and industrial development. But the feature which was so prominent in old Russia lived on into the new for the country remained poor in population. When factories, workshops and seagoing trade appeared, permanent serf workers were needed for there were no free workers to be found. The peasants were bound to the factories and workshops just as in the sixteenth century they had been bound to the land. We have cited the curious request of a shipowner that he be allowed to keep his serfs as sailors. From their youth he had taught them a difficult trade. Were they to be taken away from him, he would not find any free workers for no free man would agree to take up and learn such a difficult trade. The owner would have to give up his ship and sea trade, so profitable for the state. The merchants demanded serf workers and stewards, claiming they could not rely on free laborers. The nobles, wishing to retain for themselves the exclusive right to own people, in theory victoriously refuted the arguments advanced by the merchants, but in practice the latter were correct. One could not make do with free labor. The free population presented no choice; there were few of them, and it was necessary to take whoever came along. In addition, when considering one factor at a particular time in a particular society, all other related factors require attention, such as jurisprudence and administration. With one's own man no courts were necessary; but a free man could go to court, and a Russian of the eighteenth century winced at the word "court." It was not accidental that the *Russian Justice* [legal codes of the Kievan period] decreed that a free man who became keeper of the keys for another also became his slave and did not allow a free man to be keeper of the keys.[21] The declarations of the merchants in the Commission on the Law Code that one could not rely on free assistants demonstrate that the conditions in which the Russian

Law appeared had not wholly disappeared at this time when nobles, merchants and clergy alike voiced that unanimous and terribly sad cry: "Slaves!"

This cry naturally had to disturb above all the author of the Instruction.[22] Catherine was prepared for it, however, as the alteration of the original draft of the Instruction demonstrates. The propositions in the Instruction were good seeds, but before sowing them Catherine wished to test the soil. Hence, she assembled deputies from all quarters. But the soil turned out to be completely unsuitable for the liberation of the serfs, and Catherine proposed the patient improvement of the soil by means of the moral and political development of the people.

Prince Grigory Orlov, according to Catherine, was enraptured by the theses of the Instruction. He was chosen as a deputy of the Koporsk gentry, but he did not wish or was not able to include in his instruction a demand for liberation of the serfs. With respect to the peasants, the Koporsk instruction was limited to one demand: "We find it necessary to found schools for both Russian and Baltic children in order that knowledge of the law at least somewhat might improve their morals. To this end, one might found schools in the churches which peasant children from seven to twelve might attend in the winter for a moderate fee to learn reading, writing and the rudiments of the law." The Yamburg gentry demanded the same thing.

The instruction of the Pskov gentry expounded especially on the sorry state of the peasants. "We do not begin to intend to address ourselves to all the ruin and hardship we find among agriculturalists and chronically poor workers. Whether necessary or not, people of every calling always ride in wagons and take horses from the peasants without any accounting. When poor people do not have an old nag or, if they do, they are worn out from hauling, as almost always happens, the poor are punished mercilessly and told they should not stand on the road. What hardships doesn't the poor cultivator suffer? They beat him because he hasn't anything to haul peoples' baggage! Not having ploughed the soil or sown a crop, he scarcely knows how he can feed himself and his family. A soldier quartered in a peasant's home is a lord; in fear the poor agriculturalist does all he orders. Although he has nothing for himself and his family to eat, he dares not refuse the soldier the last morsel he possesses. When a soldier goes on patrol, to headquarters or to requisition provisions, the host serves as drayman without pay. Often the soldiers berate him, beat him and leave him in utter ruin."

We have seen how Prince Michael Shcherbatov insisted that merchants not own serfs and with what pathos he spoke against the sale of serfs singly. Other deputies also opposed the sale of serfs singly, repeating the words of Peter the Great, that such sales take place nowhere else. But a deputy appeared who defended the sale of serfs singly. The deputy of the gentry of the Kurmysh district, Alfimov, claimed: "There are many nobles who own no more than two or three peasant families and some even fewer. In some circumstances one of these nobles becomes indebted for an amount which he cannot pay except by selling one of his peasants. Only in this way can he retain the rest of his estate and is deprived of only one person and not ten souls or more, comprising one family. Even among the peasants of well-to-do nobles there are in some families negligent people and those inclined to crime. Separation from their families serves to punish such persons and restrains them from bad conduct."

The fate of this same issue in the Free Economic Society[23] explains the negative decision on the questions of peasant freedom and property. At the end of 1765 an unknown person (the empress herself) put to the Society the question of whether it is more useful for agriculture when land is owned individually, or collectively by a family. The questioner was inclined to the former. There was no answer. The following year the empress, again acting incognito, sent a new question: "What constitutes the property of an agriculturalist? The land which he works or his movable property? And for the common good, what right does he have to the one or the other?" A reward of one thousand gold rubles was offered for the most satisfactory solution of the question, expenses for publication would be paid and so forth. The Society publicized the problem and offered for its solution a prize of one hundred gold rubles and a medal worth twenty-five gold rubles.

But before any answers were sent in, the impatient Sumarokov[24] sent the Society a refutation of the whole problem. "The problem," he wrote, "cannot be resolved clearly. For example, if you ask whether it is necessary for a noble to write Russian, then you must say a Russian nobleman, since an English noble can get along without knowing Russian. It is the same with peasants—free peasants or serfs? Before anything else it must be asked whether it is necessary for the general welfare for the serfs to be free. To this I say: Does the canary which amuses me need freedom or a cage, and does the dog guarding my house need a chain? The canary is better without a cage, the dog better without a chain. However, one will fly away and the other will bite people. Thus one thing is needed for the peasants, but another for the sake of the nobles. Now it is left to decide which is more needed for the general welfare. If peasant freedom is better than bondage, one must settle the announced problem. To this, all true sons of the Society and even the slaves of society will say that, of two evils, it is better that the peasants not own land. In fact, it is forbidden for land is all property of the gentry. Here is another question. Must the nobles yield to the peasants their purchased, earned, inherited and other lands when they do not wish to, and can peasants own lands in Russia since that is the right of the nobles? What will the gentry be if the peasant and the land are not his? What will be left to him? Indeed, peasant freedom is not only harmful but disastrous for society, and it is not proper to argue over why it is disastrous." Sumarokov's declaration was placed in the archives.

By the deadline set as November 1, 1767, one hundred twenty answers had been sent and forty were received after the deadline. The works received were in Russian, French, German and Latin, but most were in German. The work of Beardé de l'Abaye, a member of the Dijon Academy,[25] was unanimously recognized as the best. Now the question arose whether to publish the work and in what language. They decided to translate the composition into Russian and present it to the empress for approval. Catherine approved the translation, announced that she found nothing in the work which should not be published but all the same left it to the Society to make the decision about publication.

The Society voted thirteen to three against publication. But then several members sent written opinions. The two Orlovs, Grigory and Vladimir, sent a suggestion that the work should be published in French and Russian. Baron Cherkasov announced he was against publication. The procurator general, Prince Viazemsky, claimed to be unable to decide the matter since he did not know French even though the work already had been translated into Russian. Count Roman Vorontsov sent a statement that the work was worthy of publication and the public might enjoy the fruits of its use. Counts Chernyshev, Zakhar and Ivan, were also for publication as were the governors of Novgorod, Sievers, and Teplov. Thus eleven votes were collected for publication and sixteen against.

The majority was opposed but high court officials, especially the Orlovs, and the empress herself were for publication. The matter was decided in favor of the minority on the grounds that "it is more fitting and proper for those Russian lords holding very important state positions, and who submitted their opinions in writing that the piece should be published, than for the others to pass judgment on such a matter, which concerns more a political than an economic problem." In his work, Beardé resolved the question by stating that the peasant should be free and should own land—that the peasant should be freed gradually. Besides Beardé's work which was awarded the first prize, five other works were judged worthy of second prizes. One of them was by a Russian, Polenov.

THE CLERGY

There were no deputies from the local clergy. The clergy was represented by deputies from the Synod.[26] A particular [credentials] commission assigned the clergy to the middle classes. The Synod protested, arguing that the entire clergy, both black and white, constituted a special class and that the two were united so closely they could not exist separately. According to the Synod clergymen should have the same rights as nobles. The particular commission responded that it was not concerned with church rights since secular principles guided it, requiring placement of the clergy in the same rank as scholars, as teachers of the people.

Regarding the inclusion of scholars in the middle classes, the Academy of Sciences announced that such persons should not be subject to personal taxation and conscription for if scholars did not enjoy great advantages over merchants and artisans there was no hope that the sciences would grow in Russia.

In general there were confused notions about the middle class although there was much debate on the subject. The empress attempted to clear away the presuppositions on this subject by citing history and the position of the French third estate [tiers état].[27] The members of the commission for classifying the population were Prince Alexander Golitsyn, Count Fedor Orlov, Count Yakov Bruce, Baron Ungern-Sternberg, and Nicholas Sveshnikov. In the meeting of September 19 Orlov suggested dividing the commission into three parts. The first would consider the gentry, which it divided into four levels: prince, count, baron and noble. The second would deal with the middle class or burghers. Here there were eight levels: poor clergy, scholars, artists, artisans, merchants, civil officials, men without rank, and free men. The third part would deal with the peasants, among whom there were two types—free peasants and serfs. Orlov's suggestion was adopted.

There are several curious propositions concerning the clergy in the materials of the Commission. For example, there were the following proposals: Men from all ranks of society should be able to enter the clergy and the clergy to enter all secular ranks. The clergy should be liberated from unseemly labors. There should be no obstacles to tonsuring for those who wish it. The parish clergy should be maintained on a suitable basis and their salaries fixed. Priests should not demand more than a specified amount of money for church needs. And finally, priests, church workers, merchants and other various classes should be permitted to buy peasant and household serfs. Along with a proposal that the clergy should be forbidden to buy land, there was a suggestion that the agricultural lands which had been taken from the bishoprics and monasteries should be returned. This proposition came from the city dwellers.

In the instruction from the nobles of Krapivna district it was stated: "We ask that all churches have educated clerics on a sufficient salary for preaching of the holy law, confession of the true faith, prevention of evil things, and teaching of the laws of her imperial majesty. Where the church owns lands, they should be sold. Church readers and sacristans should teach male peasant children from the age of seven to read and write at their parents' expense. In this way it is hoped that in the future the common people will gain some enlightenment." It was proposed that bishops demand from the priests attestations of good conduct, signed by their parishioners. Those lacking attestations should be deprived of the cloth. There was also a curious proposal to reduce the number of holidays and to allow free religious services by persons of other faiths.

COURTS AND JUSTICE

As might be expected, strong complaints were heard in the Commission concerning the state of justice. The nobles protested that they must complain to the episcopal hierarchy about the clergy, to the College of Mines and Manufactures about the millowners, to the College of Mines about the factory owners, to the town councils about the merchants, and to the Chancellery of Posts about postal coach drivers. Should it not be decreed that all should be judged equally in all types of courts? Addressing the unholy extortion common in court cases and the accursed system of bribes, they asked if all presiding lords, secretaries and civil servants in all posts could not be obliged to take an oath not to turn to bribes. Anyone guilty of accepting a bribe, no matter how small the amount, should be subject to capital punishment.

The deputy of the Galich gentry, Lermontov, spoke out against the College of Justice. "Because of the number of cases in this college and its offices, it is a rare petitioner who receives satisfaction within the legal time without incurring great losses. The entire assembly knows that a slanderer does best in the College of Justice because of the frequent transfer and postponement of cases. They waste away time and drive the petitioner to exhaustion and utter ruin. It also often happens that the college holds a case for a considerable time and then sends it off for resolution to some other judicial office." Lermontov proposed abolishing the College of Justice and sending all cases straight from the provincial chancelleries to the Senate. The *guberniia*, provincial and military governors' chancelleries should resolve cases within half a year without fail.

The deputy of the Rostov nobles, Yazykov, declaimed: "I consider it excessive to explain in detail all of the complications which arise in court cases from the brainstorms of slanderers and court assistants. One should cite here the proverb: Don't fear the court, fear the judge. Would it not be prudent to order that the decision of the court be reached solely on the basis of the petition of the plaintiff and the written response of the defendant, who should be given a copy of the sworn complaint and a definite period for compiling and composing a reply?"

The deputy from the Ukrainian College, Natalin, proposed that in all courts both plaintiff and defendant have lawyers under oath, of honorable station, who know the law and are of commissioned officer rank. The deputy of the nobles of the Bakhmut hussar regiment, Rashkovich, added to this that the courts should accept as judicial aides only persons who had been educated in jurisprudence at the Academy of Sciences, had passed examinations and had been placed under oath. The deputy of the nobles of Gorokhovets district, Protasov, proposed the establishment of justices of the peace according to the examples of England and Holland.

But if there were vigorous complaints against the judges such as dragging out cases over ten years with red tape, not attending court every day, having reported themselves sick, meanwhile going off on a visit someplace, there were also defenders of the judges who laid the blame for slowness on the petitioners themselves. The plaintiff and defendant themselves drag out the course of their affair under various pretexts. During the deliberations they focus suspicion on several of those present, and sometimes on all, with stealthy and deceitful ruses. They do not pay proper attention to their cases and do not present them for resolution on heraldric paper.

We have seen how strongly the author of the Instruction opposed torture and how previous decrees had placed limitations on it. Yet the instructions from private persons contained demands to eliminate these innovations and limitations. For example, the instruction of the Vereia district stated: "Can it not be allowed to inflict torture without admonitions according to the previous laws on bandits and robbers brought in to *guberniia*, provincial, and subordinate chancelleries in order to produce great fear and suppress evildoing once and for all? Without this no form of evildoing can be rooted out and criminals cannot be made afraid. Many criminals, caught red-handed and brought in for a burglary, admit their guilt to that one crime and conceal their previous crimes." The instruction of the Kineshema gentry cited the increase of burglary and robbery as a result of the fact that it was forbidden to inflict torture in local centers. The Suzdal gentry complained in their instruction about the abolition of capital punishment and the limitation of torture since "some people, seeing that murderers are not suitably tortured or executed, not only murder innocent bystanders, but serfs and peasants kill their masters and mistresses. Tormenting abuse, robbery, beatings and such crime increase time and again." The Suzdal gentry thus instructed their deputy to request protection and to increase torture and justified retribution for such evildoers in their trials.

The instruction of the Krapivna gentry stated: "Could it not be ordered that as before in district towns there be searches and executions in order to reach the quickest solution and root out criminals by instilling fear into others? The admonition against this should be abolished because the common people are uneducated and do not know the law. One does not learn the truth from a man by hanging him, and because of this various criminals have become more numerous. It should be decreed that investigations of the old style be permissible."

Several instructions demanded limitation of corporal punishment, torture and execution in a class sense, exempting only nobles. To this, the deputies from the towns replied: "Those laws are proper which are founded on truth and in agreement with holy and natural laws. Holy and natural laws do not countenance partiality and look not at the individual but solely at the truth. A criminal is always a criminal, whether commoner or noble. The only difference is that the former does not understand the sin and crime of ignoring the laws of God and the sovereign as does the noble doing the same. In fact, nobility is natural only when one performs deeds consistent with one's honor. Consequently, when a nobleman performs some base act, the thought naturally occurs that he deserves a crueler punishment than the common man, who is driven to crime by extreme need as well as by ignorance. By God's power, Russia has had through the centuries a monarchical and not an aristocratic regime. Both noble and commoner—in other words, people of all families and stations—are all equally the devoted slaves of the all-merciful sovereign."

The deputies demanded torture and cruel punishments for thieves and robbers. They complained of an increase in the number of criminals and at the same time pointed directly at the chief source of the evil which, however, they tried with all their powers to preserve. "We request," said the nobles, "discovery of reliable methods and promulgation of new laws to root out thieves and robbers and thus achieve deliverance from the harm these villains do to all of society. Runaways of various classes are for the most part responsible for this harm, but at the very root of this evil are the people who take in and hide these runaways. We request elimination of bandits, thieves, robbers, and all kinds of miscreants, for the danger from them prevents quite a few nobles from going to or living in their villages. Because of this the village economy is

declining and decaying more and more. People living in the country, out
of necessity or for want of any other haven, must have more than the
needed number of personal servants, living off their grain reserve, for
protection of themselves and their home. Thus it is that the masters are
ruined and the number of peasants and cultivators decreases. Although
there are laws for the extermination of brigands and thieves, these are
little help since orders for the deployment of the needed detachments
for pursuit and capture of criminals are given so slowly that the villains
succeed in robbing many and carrying on the same trade in other places
or districts. It is dangerous, difficult and almost impossible for nobles
and peasants to catch these scoundrels. When these miscreants, captured
somehow or other, are brought into town, they are freed on their own
signature or, due to the lack of a real guard, they escape from jail and
cruelly revenge themselves on the nobles and peasants who reported or
captured them."

Independent of the complaints about brigandage and robbery, the
instructions of the nobles contained strong denunciations of the flight
and hiding of peasants. "For many years the strictest edicts forbade the
harboring of runaway serfs and peasants, but even now nothing restrains
the reception and harboring of runaways. Many serfwomen—widows,
wives and daughters without husbands—steal many valuable things and
money from their masters, flee their masters and marry a soldier, for
they have heard that there is no specific law which mandates their return. Hence the poor nobles suffer great losses and even more annoyance
and abuse from their serfs. Others see this and are tempted to flee. Some
flee to Poland where the border is close, for all Russian peasants know
the Polish customs allowing everyone to sell spirits and salt and that
there is no conscription or collections for payment of state taxes. Lured
by this, without any oppression from their owners, local peasants flee
there, not only singly or in families, but as entire villages with their
property. As they flee, they openly rob and ruin their owners. Others
steal secretly. Some gather in Poland in small bands of robbers, come
back openly into Russia to attack and rob peasants and landowners and
return again to their refuge, where their Polish owners willingly receive
them and take what they have acquired. Jews have some Russian runaways in their service. The runaway serfs who returned from Poland
according to the terms of the edict of 1763 and settled in the empty
lands on the Polish border, have proved to be in cahoots with peasants
living both on the border and up to 200 versts[28] from the border, inciting whole families to flee into Poland. They have also helped supply
robbers and bandits and the movement of criminal bands to ruin the
local inhabitants. Others run away within the country. Many flee to the

Finnish areas and Livland, which are close and free for runaways, since there are no forts or outposts there. Runaways are practically never returned from there. To find and catch them is completely impossible, especially for those who are not important or rich. Although someone might know where a runaway is living, if the owner sends someone or comes himself to find and catch the runaway, the local resident will lose himself without a trace before turning in the runaway. At conscription time, as soon as the peasants find out, all men fit for conscription flee to Poland and hide out there until the conscription is over. It is estimated that more than 50,000 runaway peasants of both sexes have fled and are now across the Polish border from Smolensk *guberniia*."

Besides runaways, the nobles pointed out others who were guilty of theft. "Theft stems to a large part from the large number of people from the clergy without posts. These people are registered with the church administration with their fathers, but many of their fathers have little church land and two, three, or more children. They have no income of any kind; it is well known that these people are lazy. Therefore, should it not be ordered that people related to churchmen without positions be sent off as soldiers, and those unfit for the military be subjected to the poll tax?" Finally, the nobles lashed out against the gypsies, "who wander around the entire country, deceive people by various tricks without any punishment and burden society by living off the fruits of the cultivator's work."

ECONOMIC COMPLAINTS

Concerning financial affairs, the Klin nobles proposed relieving the peasants of the poll tax "since they render the state its foremost benefit by their farming," and instead taxing or raising the prices of spirits, beer, tea, coffee, sugar, wine, tobacco, playing cards, horse collars and carriages, hounds, clothing using gold or silver, other luxury items, as well as the passports of free workers, and hemp. If this sum does not equal the poll tax, salt should be taxed for "although salt is needed for food, it is better voluntarily to buy it more dearly than to pay the poll tax improperly and to see peasants languishing in prison for this."

The nobles of several districts requested the establishment of reserve grain storage facilities. They also pointed out that the state banks founded in Petersburg and Moscow were not sufficient. Those living at a distance from both capitals had the same need to borrow money, and they therefore requested the establishment of banks in the *guberniia* and provinces according to the number of nobles living in each.

The Kaluga, Medynsk and Tula nobles wrote in their instruction that in their areas and in other provinces almost all forests had been hauled away and what was left was diminishing hourly. The residents suffered a lack of lumber for construction and firewood. They therefore requested that in these areas the construction of metallurgical factories and distilleries, which consumed a great amount of wood, be forbidden, especially in the vicinity of Moscow and for some 200 or more versts around. The nobles of Pskov also complained of a lack of wood and asked that the export of wood overseas be forbidden.

The Romanov nobles spoke out against hunting because hunters assembled in great numbers on horses with many dogs, ran through other peoples' estates without permission, trampled the gardens, trampled the grain fields and pastures, and stampeded the cattle. If a peasant dared to complain of the damage done him, the hunters would beat him for supposed lack of respect. The nobles requested that all hunts be limited according to the example of the German states where a hunter could not enter an estate without a ticket from the owner.

THE EASTERN FRONTIER

Special conditions and special demands appeared concerning the outlying areas of Russia. The Siberian nobles came from beyond the Ural mountains and announced that they were descended from people who had gone or been sent to Siberia to pacify the local peoples and had rendered onerous service. The heirs of the conquerors of Siberia now asked that they be given hereditary nobility and allotments of land with people to work it. They asked to be allowed to purchase these people. As one might easily guess, the zealous defender of the rights of the old noble families, Prince Michael Shcherbatov, rose against this demand. In his words, a Siberian noble was not a member of a class but a holder of a rank which could not be transferred from father to son. Mere similarity of names could not be a sufficient basis for linking the Siberian nobles with the rights and advantages of the illustrious noble class. Therefore the Siberian nobles, granted that calling by the local governors, should be deprived of the title of noble so that they would not intermingle with the true nobility.

The governor of Orenburg province, Prince Putiatin, sent the Commission a presentation on the province. It long had been uncultivated and the property of the crown. The fields and forests had been assigned to various native peoples who paid quitrent or other tribute. These peoples were the Chuvash, Cheremis, Tatars, but chiefly Bashkirs. Together with the vice-governor of Ufa, Aksakov, Senator Nepliuev proposed to the Senate that a new direct road be built from Orenburg through the town of Sakmara to Kazan and that people leaving the interior of Russia be settled along the road. This road was settled and now is called the Moscow highway. A census was taken of the settlers along it, and they were placed on the poll tax rolls. Also at the suggestion of Nepliuev, the empty lands were ordered to be distributed in return for service to officers and crown officials serving in the Orenburg Commission. Finally Nepliuev resettled in his province some resin makers serving beyond the Kama, peasants sent from various provinces, and retired dragoons and soldiers.

But after Nepliuev the expanse, abundance and safety of the lands offered for settlement to Great Russians aroused great longing among nobles, the non-Orthodox and new converts to own some of this land, and they began to acquire it through various swindles. First, the landowners who had received land under Nepliuev for service and built their first houses began to buy land from the Bashkirs without asking whether the latter had the right to sell. If a Bashkir sold some land, it was recorded in the deeds as a very large tract, 200 versts or more. Having bought a large tract and not having the means to settle it, they started to sell to others. Such spurious sales reached the point that identical land was sold by different Bashkirs to different people. The Ufa Provincial Chancellery did not exercise proper supervision and wrote deeds without checking whether the sellers had proper titles. Many of these falsely acquired lands still lie empty. Some landowners, unsated by this land grab, got involved in bitter quarrels or lawsuits. The outcome of all this was much disruption and useless destruction of forests, fields and meadows.

There was no visible success in planned or direct settlement in terms of homes, agriculture, livestock raising, preservation of the forests or in any of the good and peaceful purposes. It was hopeless for there was no one to teach or from whom to learn proper ways. The majority of the non-Orthodox and new converts settled not because of crowding in their previous home areas, and some came out of criminal motives or laziness. This applied especially to the newly baptized Tatars, none of whom voluntarily accepted Orthodoxy. They were baptized after being sentenced to torture or death for their crimes. The Chuvash avoided living in Christian righteousness and remained free to pursue their paganism and idolatry. The unbaptized Tatars grew closer to their fellow Tatar-infidels.

THE UKRAINE

We have seen the results of the decree on the selection of deputies in the Ukraine and the Baltic regions. We also have observed that Catherine was not disturbed by the stubbornness displayed in some places in the Ukraine in preserving and restoring the old ways and customs with which the government had dealt already. Catherine anticipated that, together with instructions demanding restoration of the office of hetman[29] there would be local instructions which would clarify the situation in the country for the government. This in fact is what happened.

The instructions of the Ukrainian gentry requested equality of Ukrainian military and civil ranks with those of Great Russia. They also asked for the establishment of a heraldry for the Ukrainian gentry because patents attesting nobility had been destroyed in wartime and many Ukrainian families had appropriated noble status for themselves improperly. As with the Great Russian nobility, the Ukrainian gentry also requested a permanent marshal of the nobility to protect their interests, asked permission to select judges from their own ranks and for an oral hearings court, and petitioned for the founding of a university in Pereiaslavl or some other place, a Corps of Cadets and a finishing school for noble girls, the chartering of a bank, and elimination of the burdens of military billeting.

The presentation of the cossacks must be linked to the presentation from the old Ukraine. We have seen that under Khmelnitsky in the Ukraine, during the time of its liberation from Polish rule, there was a turnabout in land ownership. The previous landowners were eliminated or driven out, and the military replaced them—the cossacks with their elective seniority from captains [sotnik] to hetman. As usually happens during times of military activity, the Ukraine acquired a military organization and administration. A simple cossack warrior became a free landowner. The military or cossack elders became the rulers of the country and began to use their position to amass the greatest profit and landed property. They began to think that exalted position which they called noble to restrict the free landowners and cossacks, and to take their land from them. We know from Teplov's writings how this was done.[30] There remained in the Ukraine the memory of those times when many cossacks would sell their lands for a jug of vodka because obligation to military service went with the land.

Thus in the Ukraine in the seventeenth and eighteenth centuries there occurred the same process of disappearance of small free landholders that had occurred in the West in the Merovingian and Carolingian epochs. As in the West the government in the Ukraine used all its powers to prevent this disappearance of free people, who depended directly on it, to keep them from falling under the sway of rich landowners and government personages. The cossacks did not know how to protect their interests constantly and collectively. They did not know how to cure their ills and complained strongly to the elders about the aristocratic aspirations of the latter. These captains and colonels had enriched themselves by every means, had attempted to separate themselves and their names from the cossack community and had raised themselves by becoming nobles. These were the same men who had been elected by the cossacks to their positions; yet every cossack considered himself a free landowner and warrior, a noble.

At the beginning of the seventeenth century, as we have seen, the discontent of the cossacks with the new relationships introduced by the elders led to serious disturbances. Zaporozhe,[31] representing the democratic principle and original equality, supported the cossacks. But in the eighteenth century, despite the support of the Imperial government, which incidentally received no aid from among the cossacks, the elders won out. The cossacks sold them their lands and vanished into the peasantry and were able only to complain and talk about the good old times when they elected their hetmen. They forgot that these hetmen had thought only of themselves and not at all of the cossacks.

Yet now several cossacks demand a hetman as in old times. In general, they demanded restoration of the old right of choosing elders by free vote; yet no one ever had taken that right away from them. They demanded equality with the nobility and requested that no one might buy their lands. The instruction of the Chernigov Cossacks stated: "It is clear from the privileges granted by the Polish kings that the cossacks managed their military service well and easily for they had sufficient arable land, hayfields, forests, mills and every variety of landed property. But now, because of the coercion of landowners, the cossack elders of all families and church monastery landowners have been deprived of their lands. The rootless captains and cossack army elders seek out cossack lands as soon as they enter their posts. First they build huts to live in, then a big residence, and then to go with their mansions they buy from the cossacks—by threats or cajoling—land, forests, hayfields and all the best places. They restrict the cossack in numerous ways and use the cossack for their own private work. Other cossacks leave their families and households because of great burdens, beatings and threats by the elders, and go off to unknown places. Still other cossacks are enslaved and bear the same burdens as serfs."

Thus the confused question of cossack lands owned by the so-called nobility possessed great significance in the Ukraine, just as the confused question of Bashkir lands had in the eastern Ukraine. The Ukrainian nobles, guided by ideas circulating in higher circles, were not loath to introduce some humanitarian changes in their old law code, the Lithuanian Statute. For example, they were willing to abolish the law by which a noble who had killed a common man was punished only by the loss of his hand and a small fine. After all, "This law," it reads in the

Chernigov instruction, "can be tolerated in Poland where all poor people, especially those who have not acquired the distinction of nobility, groan under the yoke of slavery and torture." However, as far as the Cossack lands which they had bought were concerned, the gentry requested that the empress confirm them in their possession forever out of her special maternal generosity toward them. The nobles promised to obey whatever decree on this subject might be issued in the future.

After the transformation brought about by Khmelnitsky's revolt and the union of the Ukraine to Great Russia, the Ukrainian cities remained strongly discontented with the military administration. The city dwellers offered incessant complaints that the Cossack elders restricted and robbed them, and they demanded that they be sent Great Russian military governors, even though, as has been shown, these were far from being distinguished by their gentle or unselfish relationships with the populations they governed. The instructions brought by the deputies to the Commission on the Law Code reveal the sad state of Ukrainian towns and their extreme poverty, which resulted as much from the military government of the country as from their locations, quite unsuited for commerce. Their poverty arose also from the military-agricultural way of life prevalent from the beginning in the Ukraine with the usual consequences of this type of existence—backwardness in commerce and industry. Finally, the cities suffered from the character of the Ukrainian people, disinclined to trade, so that to the present day the majority of businessmen there are Great Russians. The instructions portray the Ukrainian cities as having fallen behind the development of those in Great Russia and reveal the same conditions that existed in Great Russian cities in the seventeenth century.

Just as the residents of the Great Russian cities requested in their instructions the retention and development of the city self-government granted by Peter the Great, the inhabitants of the cities of the Ukraine asked to preserve their old forms of urban self-government, the Magdeburg Law, which indisputably had served as an example for Peter the Great in introducing the self-administration of cities into Great Russia. But forms alone signify nothing. Forms are beneficial and solid when they are the result of independent internal development. They benefit those to whom they have been given if they find the proper conditions. The poor, scanty city population in the Ukraine could not satisfy the necessary demands of the state in money form; city inhabitants had to pay in kind with their own labor. This brought them terrible hardship and finally ruined them. To escape their burdens, they fled or sold themselves into bondage to rich or influential people. This made it even more burdensome for the rest. These are conditions well known in Great

Russian towns in the seventeenth century, circumstances inescapable when the demands of the state develop out of time and step with the economic development of the people. It happens whether the society is still young and undeveloped like Russia of the seventeenth and eighteenth centuries, or already decaying like the Roman empire at the time of its fall.

On February 28, 1768, Rumiantsev wrote to the empress: "I had occasion to meet with some deputies who have been given leave and who were departing again. I found them unfailingly constant in their demented ideas. Skoropadsky is the leader of all the others for he dreams of being chosen hetman. There are quite a few people here who blindly follow such ignoramuses. However, I dare think that when he and people like him, who are very prominent, end up without any activity or business while well-intentioned people, who are not infected by this diseased idea of autonomous rule and independence, are distinguished and given rank and power by your imperial majesty, and when the government and the service acquire clear rules—the constant desire for rank and especially for salary will change rapidly their ideas and conduct." Catherine answered: "What you write about Skoropadsky is quite just. He acts here like a wolf and doesn't want to have anything to do with our people."

Many instructions expressed the desire to erect a monument to Catherine, but she wrote to Rumiantsev concerning the collection of money for such a memorial: "If the money for the monument has not been collected, prevent the collection for such expenses for the people are unnecessary. Thank them appropriately for their good intentions."

THE BALTIC PROVINCES

Rumiantsev also wrote about the Ukrainian deputies who had gone home for a recess: "Many of them were quite proud here that, like them, the Baltic deputies were intent on retention of their old rights and freedoms." In the Commission session of October 2, 1767, the Estland deputy from the nobility of Virsk kreis [district], Rennenkampf, presented a proposal that the Estland nobility should be mentioned in the draft of the new law code and that they should retain unchanged their perquisites by virtue of the privileges confirmed by the monarch. The deputy of the Livland gentry of Estnitsk district, Vilboa, offered the same resolution. He was joined by other Livland and Estland deputies. But in the session on November 22 Tolmachov, the deputy of the Liubim nobility, argued that it was necessary to keep in view the general good. Since the Senate was aware of shortcomings in the rights enjoyed by

Livland and Estland and since ignorance of these particular rights produced crimes among those living along the borders, it was necessary to compose general laws for all of her majesty's subjects. An extraordinary number of the noble deputies shared Tolmachov's opinion.

In the session on November 27 the deputy of the Novosilsk gentry, Shishkov, gave the following speech: "The laws being enacted must be the same in the newly conquered provinces as they will be for us. In this I presuppose equality of state taxes and revenues. Therefore the task of the esteemed deputies sent from these new provinces should consist in trying to deliberate with us jointly for the general benefit of all. The laws for the Teutonic Knights, written in the sixteenth and seventeenth centuries by the grace of God and Pope Nicholas, no longer can be the laws there for now there is no bishopric where the immovable property of the nobility can be registered and there is now no enemy with which the Teutonic Knights can wage war or conclude peace. A capitulation forced by arms is not a distinctive service on the part of a captive but the victor's magnanimity.[32] Therefore, would we not do more honor to the provinces in question if we called their inhabitants not conquests but citizens equal to us in one society? This cannot be until they live under the same laws as we."

Vilboa opposed both Tolmachov and Shishkov. He said of the opinion of the former that the privileges and rights of Livland corresponded fully to the disposition of the people living under them. Their suitability to the faith, climate and customs of this people, proven over a long time, and the unforced observance of these laws by the inhabitants of Livland prompted him, Vilboa, more than ever to request that the rights and privileges of the Livland nobility be preserved in perpetuity in the new law code. Then Vilboa mentioned that the people of Livland faithfully fulfilled their oath of loyalty, which was proved by their willingness to serve, to pay taxes regularly and to bear the general burdens. There was no need that all laws should be the same for all of her majesty's subjects. As for Shishkov's opinion, Vilboa said that it was more like one calling for autonomy and intolerant of contradiction than the moderate and modest view adopted by the assembly. Shishkov had noted especially the privilege of Bishop Silvester of 1449 which began with the words: "By the grace of God and Pope Nicholas" and made fun of these words. This may well have given him pleasure, but he would not have said this publicly had he read attentively article thirty-two of the Instruction of the empress: "A man receives great benefit in those circumstances when passion pushes his thoughts toward evil, but he considers it useful for himself not to be evil." Preservation of the terms of capitulation granted by the victor, which was in the treaty signed by both sides, proved the justice of the sovereign.

Even so, opposition from the Russian deputies did not cease. Demidov, deputy from the town of Romanov, noted that the ancient privileges of Livland could not be found in the original agreement. The deputy of the Kromsk gentry, Pokhvisnev, declared that all peoples under Russian rule should be governed by the same laws for such unity contributed to the might and glory of the empire. The Kazan deputy from the nobility, Yasinov, said: "If on the occasion of this most useful drafting of new laws someone unexpectedly wishes to retain his old rights, he is seeking merely his own good and not society's. He is violating the duty of an honorable citizen in relations to his fellows. Above and beyond this, it is singularly strange to hear that Livland and Estland, which long have been subject to Russian rule, are governed even now by foreign laws issued by sovereigns who have no business in these regions."

The deputy of the Livland Assembly of the Land, von Blumen, argued against this. "Many of the esteemed deputies have claimed that in the future identical laws should be composed for all parts of this broad empire and that for this the Livland privileges should not be taken into consideration, as if the well-being of Russia cannot be assured by the promised new law code without annihilation of the privileges of all the German lands. These esteemed deputies are infringing upon the power of our most wise sovereign who has confirmed these privileges, but who now should destroy them because of the desire expressed by these deputies. These men, so to speak, move against those great emperors who previously confirmed these privileges."

But the "most wise empress" was not pleased with the Baltic deputies. "The lords of Livland," Catherine wrote Rumiantsev, "from whom we expected exemplary conduct, enlightenment and courtesy, have not lived up to our expectations. They have requested and demanded from the start that their laws be considered substantively on a par with our Russian laws. But when the deputies began to examine these laws and speak about them as they did of other laws, the Baltic deputies reproached not only the deputies who had spoken but the entire Commission for usurping power not given to it. In short, I expected that they would loudly accuse the whole commission of 'high treason.' When they saw that many had been tempted by their conduct, the men of Livland as a group signed and presented to the Commission a statement that they neither needed nor wanted additions to or changes in their laws.

"In response to this, one of our Russian deputies presented to the Commission excerpts from some twenty or more petitions from Livland nobles and townsmen in which they had asked as a body in various years, from the time of the conquest in 1710 on, that their laws be supplemented for they were quite insufficient and burdensome in some instances. This man added that he wanted to find out whether to believe the petitions or the statement of the Livland deputies. This ended the sessions of the Commission in Moscow, and here (in Petersburg) the laws about the judiciary are being deliberated. Thus, we still do not know how the gentlemen from Livland are going to extricate themselves from their contradictory actions."

They desired to extricate themselves by submitting a draft of a law code for themselves. Catherine looked over the draft and with obvious displeasure made some curious notes on it. For example, she wrote, "When the commission for drafting a new law code considers previous drafts in this matter, the project drawn up in Livland will be considered if it was commissioned by the crown. If it was written without imperial authorization, it should be sent to the sub-commission where such drafts are to be sent. It is an old habit of these gentlemen, when they see that their desires will be difficult to fulfill, to bring some sort of suit or proceeding before all conceivable institutions. There were daily examples of this in the Riga Commerce Commission although they did not succeed in a single case by these means. Most often when their words prove insufficient, they pour money in. The city of Riga alone has designated 60,000 rubles a year for such things. When they sent a deputy here to seek changes in the commercial code of 1765 he was provided with 13,000 gold rubles, which went back with him intact when he found that no one had the power to change the law. This new draft that they have written is quite harmful for the city. I will not confirm anything that is not brought to me through proper channels. They are subjects of the Russian empire, and I am not empress of only Livland but of all Russia."

To the request for restoration of an academy in the Baltic region, the empress noted: "We can readily agree to the reestablishment of their academy. However there is the catch that they will demand the parcels of land (haaki) which had been given to the academy; but these parcels either have been assigned (granted) to someone or rented out in the name of the crown. If the cities or nobles agree to support this academy, it can be restored swiftly. Without it, they may send their children abroad, or on the other hand they can send them to Russian schools where there are places everywhere for them."

INCIDENTS IN THE DEBATE

We have seen that there were heated quarrels in the Commission as a result of the clash of differing interests, but these quarrels were conducted within the bounds of moderation. The following incident was an exception. At the fifteenth session, the Oboiansk deputy of the gentry, Glazov, took upon himself to speak rudely about the opinions of a deputy of the free homesteaders and a deputy of the crown peasants. He was stopped by the marshal, and as a result of his conduct a rule was made which would make anyone else hesitant to make similar outbursts. The following comment was entered in the minutes about Glazov's statement: "Although his objection takes up twenty-three large pages, it is difficult nevertheless to find in it a single decent point or issue. The ideas are all mixed-up and obscure. Almost every expression is indecent. But its insufficiencies seem inconsequential compared to the other improprieties with which this document abounds. The deputy from Oboiansk abuses the deputy from Yelets without the slightest restraint, attributes a perverted opinion to him and reviles all crown peasants. Finally, he denounces the instruction from the Kargopol crown peasants and says that it should be burned. He wishes to deprive their deputy, who prefers only truth and has proved that there is nobility even in the lowest rank, of his deputy's badge and privileges. Of course such a strange argument intrinsically produces amusement, derision and disapproval— which indeed happened. The marshal stopped the reading on the ninth page so that the solemnity fitting the assembly should not be totally violated."

When this paper had been read, the marshal announced that such libelous words and statements were contrary to article fifteen of the rules, which prescribed that a deputy who insulted another deputy in the assembly be punished by a fine or temporary or permanent exclusion. On this basis the marshal called for an opinion from the Commission on what should be done with the deputy from the Oboiansk nobility. The decision was expressed as follows: "The Commission on the Composition of a Draft of a New Law Code has heard most of what was said by the deputy from the Oboiansk nobility, Michael Glazov, about the proposal of the Yelets deputy from the free homesteaders, Michael Davydov. The Commission has judged that these expressions, poisonous words and abuse violate all of the principles of decorum and justice accepted by society. Glazov does not just state that deputy Davydov is arrogant and thinks in a perverted fashion. Glazov also notes without the slightest cause that all crown deputies should take their *Speculum*[33] out of their pockets more often, whereby we are to suppose that their conduct has heretofore been disorderly. Finally, the Oboiansk deputy dares to call for the strictest punishments when he has no right to judge. He wants to cast the Kargopol instruction into the fire and deprive the deputy of that district (whose sober conduct merits greater praise) of his deputy's badge and privileges. Considering all of these circumstances and adhering to article fifteen of the rules, the Commission has determined to return the paper in question to the Oboiansk deputy with a reprimand, to levy a five-ruble fine, and to have him apologize before the entire assembly to those whom he insulted."[34]

Aside from this incident several deputies acting outside of the assembly took a strange action, stemming from a lack of understanding of their responsibilities. They permitted themselves to sign in their own names, instead of for others, petitions and reports to the Senate and then to lobby for them in the Senate. The Senate passed an order through the Commission forbidding this. The deputy chosen from the peasants assigned to the Goroblagodatsk factories, Ermakov, took three copecks each from his electors for his expenses. For this and other transgressions he was deprived of his post as deputy, his gold deputy's badge and instruction, and was returned to his previous station. For the future he was barred from being chosen to deal with any important matters of state. This was the sentence of the Senate. The empress added: "As for the money he collected, it should be taken from him only when the peasants themselves demand it since they should not have obeyed his orders any more than he should have issued them."

THE FATE OF THE INSTRUCTION

Catherine had the right to be dissatisfied by several developments, but she could not but recognize that the general goal for which she had convened the Commission had been attained. "The Legislative Commission," she wrote in one of her notes, "assembled and gave me insight and information about the entire empire—with whom we are dealing and for whom we must show concern. It collected and organized all parts of the law by category and would have done more if the Turkish war had not begun. The deputies were dismissed and those from the military returned to the army. The Instruction to the Commission achieved a hitherto unseen unity to public debate and administrative practice. Many began to consider colors as colors and not as a blind man judges colors. At least they came to know the will of their lawgiver and started to act upon it."

Catherine was right to ascribe such an enlightening and educational significance to her Instruction. The deputies, gathered from all places and all classes, heard the Instruction, used it and relied on its words in their opinions and disputes. However its further use was limited. Heeding the proposal of the procurator general, the Senate ordered in September 1767 that copies of the Instruction be sent to the higher institutions, the departments of the Senate, the colleges and their offices, the Chancellery of Justice and the Chancellery of Confiscations. The order excluded the provincial, regional and military governors' chancelleries. In fact, the decree stated in respect to higher institutions "that copies of the Instruction should be held solely for the information of the offices mentioned and that they should not be given to the civil servants in the lower chancelleries or to others for copying or even for reading. Hence, all copies must be held under official seal [zertsalo] [35] in judicial offices."

Those serving in higher offices were to read the Instruction in their free time, when not occupied by current business, that is on Saturdays. While reading, only their secretaries and recording secretaries might be present. The Instruction thus was accessible only to senior officials and was a forbidden book for their juniors. A decree similar to that of the Latin church respecting the Scriptures was issued regarding the Instruction. It was found that the work of the autocratic sovereign, subjected to the strict censorship of her subjects, still contained axioms which could "tear down the walls," as Nikita Ivanovich Panin had put it. [36] The explanation for this order is found in the edict of the Senate concerning the personal serfs and peasants of General Leontiev, the wife of General Tolstoi, Brigadier Olsufiev, and Lieutenant-Colonel Lopukhin and his brothers. These personal serfs and peasants had sent the empress a complaint against their masters. "From the circumstances of this case one can see," says the edict, "that such crimes originate for the most part from things divulged by persons of evil intent. They sow rumors which they have dreamed up about *changes in the laws* and collect fees from the peasants under this pretext. They hold out the chimera that they will lobby for various gains or advantages for the peasants. Instead they use these collections to satisfy their own greed. The poor peasants do not know the laws, divert this money from the dues owed their masters and end up in ruin and extreme misery."

DEALING WITH DOMESTIC UNREST

At the very beginning of the meeting of the Legislative Commission in August 1767 the Senate was informed of discontent among the factory peasants. An investigation of the general uprising of the factory peasants in the northeast, assigned first to Prince Viazemsky and then to Bibikov, was completed; the insurgents were quieted and the prime offenders punished. The factory managers guilty of inflicting hardships on the peasants were punished also, and the wages due the peasants but withheld by the factory managers were confiscated. An improved division of labor was introduced, differing depending upon location. But the discontent was not eradicated for the relationships remained essentially the same. Similar investigations presented exceptional difficulties despite the good intentions behind the investigation.

One should be very careful, separated by a century from the events, in judging the results of these inquiries. An example is the depositions of the peasants who filed complaints against the Demidov factory managers.

The *first* states: "Back in 1759, I don't remember just when, the fore-
man hit me once on the head with a club for nothing at all. I dropped
and barely recovered, but there weren't any more beatings." A *second*
claimed: "The factory steward and his son beat me mercilessly with a
sapling for nothing at all." A *third*: "They whipped me with a stock because I didn't get to work on time." A *fourth*: "I have never worked in
a factory and no one has beaten me." The *fifth*: "I was late to roll call
and they put me down as absent, and for this the factory steward whipped
me with a knout, not hard enough to injure but moderately." A *sixth*:
"The son of the steward gave out special work for the day, so much that
I couldn't finish, and for this they whipped me with a stick one time
without pity. Besides this, nobody beat me and there weren't any witnesses." A *seventh*: "The factory steward nearly whipped me to death
with sticks and he broke two sticks on me, but aside from this nobody
beat me." An *eighth*: "The factory steward said that I came late, and he
whipped me with a stick really hard so that for some days I couldn't
bend over." A *ninth*: "The factory steward didn't believe that I was sick
and he beat me pitilessly with a stick. This whipping made me worse
and I had to stay in bed for a week." A *tenth*: "They beat me really
cruelly with many lashes and said that this was a threat for everyone
working at Demidov."

Several peasants claimed that they had lain ill for four to eight weeks
from beatings. They added that some beatings resulted in death. But
what means were used to verify the depositions? The accused were
locked up and even tortured. These same factory peasants were pushed
aside as prejudiced witnesses. The exhumation of corpses and medical
testimony were impossible then, and the magistrates decided according
to their own judgments whether the alleged beatings could have led to
death. If they concluded that they could not, what evidence is there
now to accuse these magistrates of an incorrect decision or indulging
oppressors? It must be recognized that Russians living a hundred years
ago had more experience in these things than we do, fortunately for us.
If one wishes to be just and impartial, it must be recognized that complaints about serious beatings could not produce as strong an impression
on Russians then as on us now. It must be remembered that corporal
punishment in its most severe forms was in general usage and was considered necessary. Even our generation remembers abuse of schoolchild-
ren, quite injurious abuse at that. What must it have been like a hundred
years ago? One must recall that at that time the voices of a few worthy
pastors only had begun to speak out against the horrible tortures to
which the clergy were subjected in the monasteries. These moral outrages were encountered all over Russia where it was only the strong man

with power who engaged in conflict with someone weak—the father-superior with the simple monk, teacher with pupil, master with servant, employer with worker and, yes, father with son. The egregious example of criminal prosecution of factory managers for cruel punishment of factory peasants would have made many people look about and raise a howl since they too could have been subjected to similar prosecution. These things were not oddities or departures from normal practice.

As proof of the difficulties encountered by Prince Viazemsky and Bibikov—difficulties to which the latest investigator of these sad events has been subject—the following incident can be cited. There were many complaints about the Demidov factory steward, Ensign Kulaleev. Viazemsky found him a man with an unclean conscience, a bribetaker, and discharged him from supervision of the peasants there. But Viazemsky did not subject him to criminal proceedings although there was a complaint that in 1760, for unknown reasons, he had fatally slashed with a sabre the peasant Alekseev in Dubrov. Kulaleev answered the accusation as follows: "The peasant Letkov from the village of Kotlovki came to me and said that some bandits traveling along the Kama river had crossed over to the mountainous side. I assembled the peasants of Kotlovki and sent them to hunt for the bandits. I myself took some other peasants and at night in the woods we met up with some strangers. We began to round them up. One of them fell upon me with an axe and struck my horse. I hit him on the shoulder with my sword, but he ran away. The peasant Talanov caught up to him, but he knocked Talanov off his feet. I chased him on foot and overtook him. He attacked me again with his axe. I defended myself and cut him in the leg. He fell and died on the spot. We captured the comrades of the dead man; they were runaway factory peasants. They said that the one who was killed was also a runaway factory peasant, Michael Alekseev Bolonkin." Kulaleev was exonerated. Finally, the difficult position of the investigators was exacerbated by the fact that some peasants revolted while others remained calm and went on with their work. The rebels attacked the latter and forced them to take the side of the rebels.

Viazemsky's and Bibikov's situations were extremely difficult. If we have no right to demand that they should have acted according to concepts and conditions not of their time but of ours and therefore do not recognize their services, we must admit on the other hand that their directives could not completely eradicate the evil. As a means of effecting a basic cure for the illness, the question was put by Catherine. Was there a possibility of replacing the bonded peasants with freely hired laborers? Understandably, the answer was negative. If this possibility had existed, serfdom would have vanished throughout Russia. As long as

the bonded status of the workers to their master was preserved, no defi-
nition of their relationship could achieve the desired success—even with
constant, vigilant supervision and always just, impartial resolution of
disputes.

But was it possible to demand such conditions in outlying regions,
given the admittedly sad state of the judicial process? The factory peasants certainly did not want what was imposed on them. They did not
want a more bearable determination of the relations binding them. They
wanted full freedom from factory work for their lot was the most onerous
one in the system of serfdom. No matter how cruel or greedy the master
or overseer that fate sent them, the peasant agriculturalist remained at
his usual place engaged in his usual activities; but factory work was in
essence "unfree slave" work as the peasants put it. Peasants who lived
very far away, sometimes several hundred versts, were assigned to the
factories. They had to appear on time, they had to spend all they had
and sometimes ruin themselves to make the journey. If they did not
arrive on time, they had to be prepared for beatings from the factory
steward which were more or less injurious depending upon the character
and inclinations of the latter. In addition the owners or stewards attempted to drain as much profit as possible out of the worker, who was
entirely in their hands. They drove him, paid him too little, forced him
to work overtime and sold him necessities at high prices. All this hardly
could reconcile the peasant to factory work and his constant wish was
to get away from it. The first serious peasant uprisings during the reign
of Elizabeth were among the factory peasants. It should not be expected
that they would stop even after the pacification of the first years of
Catherine's reign.

In the summer of 1767 the peasants bound to the Yugov mining
factories of Count Ivan Chernyshev, the factory owner Pokhodiashin,
and the late Chancellor Vorontsov went on strike. The Solikamsk military governor's chancellery determined that Major Dervetsky was at
fault for ordering the peasants to work in the salt mines only. The Senate
sent a military detachment headed by Major General Irman, the commander-in-chief of the Goroblagodatsk and Kemsk factories, to subdue
the peasants. In October a report came from the chancellery of the Main
Administration of Factories concerning resistance and walk-outs of the
peasants bound to the Anninsk factory of Count Chernyshev in the
Solikamsk and Cherdyn districts. The chancellery wrote that there was
no hope of suppressing the revolt and turned for help to the governor
of Kazan.

In the same month Riumin, owner of the Riazan needle factory, and
his partner and manager, Brigadier Prince Kildishev, lodged a complaint

with the Senate after the College of Manufactures had freed their serfs, which were being held and accused of disobedience, that the serfs had loosed even greater disobedience and mischief at their factory. The petitioners asked that a military detachment be ordered to pacify the peasants. The Senate ordered deployment of a detachment and let the College of Manufactures know that it had acted quite unwisely and carelessly in liberating the serfs in question without satisfying their owner and ordering that the serfs be used only at the needle factory and not be sent to an iron factory to make wire. The college answered that it had released the peasants in compliance with a decree not to hold arrested persons too long. It had just assigned the chancellery of Riazan gubernia to investigate their case and determine their guilt. As for the order that the peasants should work only in the needle factory, the college claimed that to have done otherwise would have produced confusion since it supervised the needle factory whereas the College of Mines supervised the iron factory.

At the end of the year Irman reported that the rebellious peasants had been forced back into line and obliged to return to factory work except for thirty-seven persons from the village of Burdakova, assigned to the Pyskorsk factory. The Senate resolved to recommend that Irman act secretly and in a moderate way so that the peasants would not become inflamed. The chancellery of Riazan gubernia reported that the peasants of Riumin's needle factory had been punished, some with the knout and some with the lash, for their resistance to authority and had been brought back to proper obedience.

As a result of a report from the governor of Voronezh about resistance among the Lipetsk workers, the Senate noted that it was apparent from the affair that the disobedience of the factory workers had originated and continued chiefly because of the oppressions by Prince Repnin's managers. Repnin, the Senate suggested, should be told secretly that without violating his own interests he should take timely measures to prevent the workers from having direct cause for complaints. For greater stability he should discharge his present managers and assign new ones as long as his factories suffered no harm from this.

At the time that the Legislative Commission gathered from the ends of the Russian empire to render "light and information" to the empress about the entire empire and about topics appropriate for discussion and her solicitude, and at the same time that various classes in this Commission continually demanded the right to own serfs, the sovereign signed a sentence in an incident which demonstrated to what lengths serfdom could go, placing as it did one human being in the power of another. This incident occurred within the ranks of the people who proclaimed in the Commission that they held the sole right to own serfs. They portrayed the management of serfs as a preparatory school for senior government posts and pointed out their own great moral qualities and education. Yet it happened that a terrible deed could be committed among just these people because among them there was found the necessary freedom from punishment. The wife of Gleb Saltykov, a captain of the horse guards, Daria Nikolaevna, had been a widow for twenty-five years and enjoyed control of inhabited estates and a host of personal serfs. She ruled them with monstrous cruelty. She beat her servants mercilessly, men and women without distinction, with her own hands. She burned their ears with red-hot tongs and poured boiling water over them. On her orders male and female servants were beaten and whipped, sometimes to death—all for the slightest misstep. Saltykova's fury increased in proportion to the agony of her unfortunate victims and eventually reached madness. "Beat him to death," she would shout at someone being punished. "I am responsible and not afraid of anyone, even if I have to give up my patrimony. No one can do anything to me!"

Aware that punishment was improbable and that it was possible through family ties and wealth to frighten and bribe judges, Saltykova felt unbridled. More than six years of peasant complaints against her accumulated without consequence. Those who complained were punished and sent back to their mistress, who told them: "You won't do anything to me. No matter how much you complain, they won't do anything to me and they won't exchange me for you."

Finally in 1762 a complaint that Saltykova had killed some one hundred persons since 1756 found its way to Catherine. The complaint was referred to the College of Justice and an investigation began. At the end of 1763 the college reported that Saltykova "was clearly under suspicion of murder and should be tortured to discover the truth." The battle which Catherine waged against torture has been described. She did not want to allow it now for she felt that it was not a sound means for penetrating to the truth of a matter. Instead, she ordered: "Inform Saltykova that all circumstances of this case and the testimony of many people mandate that she be tortured, which indeed will be done unless she makes a clean breast of everything. Meanwhile, send to her for a month a clever, honorable priest who knows the Scriptures to convince her to confess. If she feels no remorse, he should prepare her for inevitable torture and show her the cruelty of the punishment meted to a criminal sentenced to torture. Should she still not confess, present her to her majesty but do not tell her of this last provision. Await a final decree."

These measures did not help. Saltykova would not admit guilt in anything. Catherine still did not want to use torture. A full investigation was made which indicated commission of murder. Prosecution began on the basis of these findings in the Gendarme-General Chancellery, the Chancellery of Investigations and the Secret Office, but all cases were decided in Saltykova's favor because she bribed the presiding officials. Saltykova's serfs accused her of murdering seventy-five people of both sexes. The College of Justice, after examining the evidence, found grounds for positive indictment for the murder of thirty-eight people and suspicion of murder of twenty-six more.

In October 1768 the Senate received an imperial decree: "Having considered the report presented to us by the Senate concerning the criminal proceedings against the notorious, inhuman widow Daria Nikolaevna, we have found that this monstrosity of humankind—making so many assaults on her own servants of either sex at so many different times—cannot be attributed only to outbursts of fury peculiar to a depraved nature. One must suppose, although it is a bitter insult to humanity, that compared to many other murderers in the world she has a completely apostate and extremely torturous soul. Because of this, we order our Senate: (1) to deprive her of her nobility and forbid that in the future she ever be allowed to use her father's or husband's family name with anyone, in any court or in any matters of any kind; (2) to order in Moscow, where she is now under guard, on a day specially designated for it and announced to the population, that she be taken out to the first (that is chief, or Red) square and placed on a scaffold; to have the sentence passed upon her by the College of Justice read to all the people along with this edict from us; then tie her, standing on the same scaffold, to a column and chain around her neck a sign with the words in big lettering: "torturer and murderer;" (3) when she has endured an entire hour of this disgraceful exposure, then, in order to deprive her evil soul of any further human contact in this world and to give her body, smeared with the blood of other humans, to the providence of the Creator of all things—order that she be taken from there in irons to one of the nunneries on the outskirts of the city and put in a specially made underground cell, not next to a church, and keep her there until death so that she never sees the light of day again. Feed her the usual elders' (monk's) food. Light a candle while she eats and put it out as soon as she is done. Take her from her cell whenever there is a church service to a place where she can hear the service without entering the church." Saltykova was incarcerated in the Ivanov convent. In 1779 her punishment was eased and she was transferred from her underground cell to a stone annex of a church, with a window. Saltykova died in 1801, and to this day the memory of the terrible "Saltychikhe" lives on.

A special commission handled the case of the Liven landowner, Lieutenant Mishkov, also without torture. Among other things Mishkov was accused of four times sending his peasants, free homesteaders and Ukrainians, disguised as brigands, into the house of the free homesteader Pisarev. Mishkov himself went on two expeditions, stole Pisarev's possessions and completely ruined Pisarev's house. Mishkov then took the house for himself and had Pisarev beaten with sticks. Then Mishkov ordered the free homesteader Pikhtin, the runaway peasant Nikiforov who was hiding with him, and the soldier Medvedev—after getting them drunk—to break Pisarev's legs with the flat of an axe. They did this, and then Mishkov himself put out Pisarev's eyes with a shoemaker's awl. Pisarev died from this after nine days. Mishkov also ordered the free homesteaders Zhiliaev and Pykhten, living in his house, to kill the homesteader Enin, which they did, and so on.

The widow of the privy councillor, Maria Efremova, was ordered to church confession for the murder of one of her serf girls. It is not known what kind of relationship with his peasants the Serpeisk landowner and retired lieutenant of the guards Shenshin had. One knows only that at night unknown persons attacked his home with muskets and spears, wrecked his house and killed him, his wife and his peasant elder. It turned out that Shenshin's own peasants were involved in the killing.

In 1768 the governor of Kazan reported an increasing number of assaults and murders. He cited the lack of manpower in the garrisons there and the need to send further military detachments. The Senate decreed that although the detachments could be formed they would not get there in time. In any case in the winter bandits could be chased down without these detachments, and the Senate sent an edict to the governor that he catch the robbers in their winter hideouts with posses of ordinary citizens and the detachments on hand. Since it was obvious that the peasants and servants did not offer any resistance to the robbers when they fell upon the houses of their masters—despite the fact that the peasants and servants at times outnumbered the bandits a hundred times or more—and that the peasants ran off, hid or surrendered the lives of their masters to the ferocity and cupidity of the bandits, it was announced in a printed edict that henceforth the peasants and servants who did not offer resistance, despite their numbers, would receive suitable monetary and corporal punishment. To demonstrate the initial application of the edict, the Senate wrote to the governor of Kazan that he should order investigations in all parts of his domain where robberies or murder occurred. If he found an incident where the peasants had not defended their lords because of indifference or malice he should deal with the guilty according to the laws. The commander-in-chief of Moscow,

Count Soltykov, also wrote to the empress that in Moscow and its environs robberies and brigandage had increased greatly.

DESCRIPTIONS OF RUSSIAN LIFE

The deputies to the Legislative Commission attributed such assaults to runaway peasants. The landowners in the border regions also complained of the flight of their peasants into the Baltic provinces. But the complaints had two sides. Sievers, the governor of Novgorod, sent a report to the Senate that the Baltic nobility were complaining that he would not return their runaways from Novgorod gubernia, primarily the Pskov region, although it was known precisely where the runaways were hiding. The great difficulty arose from the fact that the runaways could not be returned without court action. If runaways from Livland and Estland converted to Russian Orthodoxy, they could not be returned to their old masters and had to be bound to whatever Russian lord they wished. In Sievers' opinion it was necessary that both sides be able to recover their runaways without court action or without consideration of the fact that some had converted to Orthodoxy. In Livland there were enough Greek churches so that anyone who had converted did not have to go far to reach a city or regimental church.

Sievers also gave the Senate a curious report on the condition of the cities of his gubernia: "Because of its scenic location and its suitability for trade, the city of Pskov could be much better off and not arouse such pity. I cannot find the words to express my feelings at the ruin of this city. I will say only that it is very unfortunate, like Great Novgorod it suffers from the same consumptive disease. The causes of ruin are almost the same in the one as in the other, not only political but moral. The habits of the people are so depraved that human reproduction has almost ceased. In all of the cities of my gubernia the number of inhabitants has increased by one-seventh from the second to the third census. Where habits and order are good, this increase has been from one-fifth to one-fourth. Only Novgorod and Pskov have lost a full third. Over the course of 150 years, practically no townsmen remain in Pskov. Here are some means to halt this decline: (1) increase the number of merchants by moving them in from outlying towns; (2) include in the merchantry or artisan guilds all crown and former monastery peasants who live in the town and nearby settlements; (3) transfer one regiment to another town for it is almost unbelievable that two infantry regiments are quartered in the same place as 450 merchants; (4) found a bank to eliminate the ruinous loans from the Narva offices. The stone building of the provincial chancellery in Pskov has become rundown. This is the third year that I have now recommended that the chancellery be removed to a private dwelling. There is no house for the military governor; he lives in such a common decrepit house that I am ashamed and afraid to go there. I did find a fairly good garrison school, built by the commander.

"The town of Ostrov is just a glorified village with about 120 merchants. Only swallows and crows live in the governor's house, and I found no squares or shops there. In Kholm I came unexpectedly into a salt warehouse and ordered the sacks of salt to be counted. According to the records there were 7,000 puds[37] on hand, but actually there were only 1,000; the rest had been loaned out to almost the entire town, right down to the priests. In Kholm there are more than 700 males and only one knows how to write. Toropets is the best town in all of Novgorod gubernia. Although the people of Toropets have the bad reputation of importing many goods without paying tariffs, the receipts of the nearby customs points show that several, the best of them, conduct themselves decently. They trade mainly in silks which they buy at fairs in Königsberg, Dantzig, Breslau and Leipzig. Several send flax and hemp to Petersburg. One of the merchants scarcely succeeded in building himself a stone house when the lieutenant of a regiment entering the city took it as the best in town. The owner was left to live in his old wooden house. No one has built any more stone houses. I found great disagreement between the commandant and the town council. The offices of both had more petitioners than in any other town. The commandant's residence was so dilapidated that one could not live in it, and the chancellery was no better. There was no jail or prison of any kind; they put prisoners temporarily in the homes of men without rank instead of billeting soldiers there, something that I have never seen or heard of.

"Rzhev Volodimerov may contest with Toropets for being worse in one respect: there are few people with large sums of capital and their trade is hurt by borrowing great sums from Englishmen and others at very high rates of interest. They have considerable quarrels with the men without rank, especially with retired cannoneers and coachmen over land. This fundamental split is the town's great vice.

"Belozersk is the worst of all the towns. I did not find the town council there exercising the same kind of supervision over the town as in Torzhok. I was satisfied with the Tver chancellery, except for the large number of prisoners. I noticed from the office reports that two-thirds of the prisoners were always from Rzhev. I found the same thing in the town council. The merchants themselves had no education, and their children were not receiving any education. Their commerce was conducted in total disorder, rarely with written records, ledgers and receipts. They held no trust in one another which is the very soul of commerce.

"The chief damage to the merchants comes, it seems, from the poll tax. Each town pays a special levy in a flat sum instead of the personal levy. This special tax is collected from the estate and trade of each resident of the town. This group of people [merchants and townsmen] also would improve their thinking were they not subject to investigations with torture in criminal cases.

"I should note about the peasantry in general that it deserves even more pity for its illiteracy; this ignorance subjects it to a multitude of indignities."

Sievers demanded that the gentry serve by lot in outlying areas in police surveillance and as district commissioners. Sievers also spoke about the decline of noble families as a result of the division of estates. "I was in one village where I found seventeen landowners in fifteen peasant huts, and all of the people whom I found harvesting grain were nobles."

There was a curious happening concerning the clergy in Tambov. The Tambov merchants presented the Synod with a petition signed by 106 persons, both lay and clergy. They requested the return to Tambov of Bishop Pakhomy, who had been transferred to Ustiug, and the replacement of the present Bishop Feodosy, who had been transferred from Ustiug. The Synod found that there were no lawful reasons set forth in the petition and gave the Senate the list of lay persons who had signed the petition with the statement that it had dealt already with the clergy who had signed. The Synod further stated that Pakhomy had been transferred again, from Ustiug to Moscow, because of age and infirmity. The Senate removed from their posts the Tambov, Nizhelomov, and Verkhnelomov commandants and their deputies who had signed the petition. Bishop Feodosy reported that the clergy had been motivated to sign the petition by the Tambov merchant Rastorguev, who invited the clerics and got them drunk.

During this period another curious incident took place in the church. A well-known owner of bronze-casting and iron factories who had been awarded the rank of director of these factories, Peter Osokin, joined the schismatics with his wife, two small foster children and several personal servants. The Senate sentenced him to deprivation of his director's rank and double payment of the regular poll tax. The empress wrote on the Senate's report: "In my journey along the Volga I happened myself to see this man, who is eighty years old and blind. Although he is reputed to be a virtuous man, in view of his old age and infirmity, he hardly has his full memory. A response should be obtained from him whether he really knows about joining the schismatics or whether someone has taken advantage of his age and blindness. His fate may be decided far better because of his answer."

The governor of Siberia, Denis Chicherin, reported how non-believers were converted to Christianity in his gubernia. "Preachers initially were sent out with expenses and transportation supplied by the non-believers. Since this is now forbidden, they have found means to travel to distant settlements of non-believers at the expense of the lower clergy living along the highway instead of visiting non-believers living near the city in large villages. During my entire tenure not one of the latter has been converted. They try to reach remote and wild areas where they preach in Russian to people who have never heard Russian speech, and they always seduce those who hope for a better living to be baptized. They entice them with the lure of rewards, get them drunk or frighten the inhabitants. It isn't known how they act at baptism. After baptizing the natives, they ride their horses off to other places with the offerings of the new converts. They leave the new believer a symbol of faith written out on some paper which that Christian mindlessly considers divinity. He doesn't know what is really written there. After a year or more the preachers return to inspect the new Christians and commit great frauds. At fast times they bring dishes smeared with milk or butter and horses' bones, accuse the converts of not observing the Christian faith, threaten them with cruel punishments and thus rob them inhumanely. If someone doesn't give a contribution—they take him with them, making him pay for his own food, put him in stocks and settle him somewhere else. If someone is richer and has wood stored in some secret places, they search it out.

"The priests cannot judge these cases themselves and so send them to a higher court where consideration takes years. There are other means of robbery. Preachers go to some new convert. If they learn that a dead person was buried without a priest or a youth is not baptized, they ask why the youth has gone so long unbaptized or why the burial without a priest. Obviously, because of the remoteness, priests can visit only once every few years. Since the natives cannot marry in a church, they get married at home, and this too serves as a chief source of bribery. The preachers tax them for performing these services, shout about violation of the faith and threaten the natives with having to go 300 or 400 versts if they don't pay. Whenever the priest, a spiritual father from another people, arrives for confessions—his charges don't know a word of Russian, only that the priest must be paid. This disorder can be eradicated only by the appointment in Siberia of a new metropolitan, a man who would be able to dig into these cases intelligently. Although conversion of non-believers should continue, it should occur only in places close to a church. Schools should be founded to educate priests to serve the natives, but proselytizing and conversion in remote areas should be halted for the time being."

As a result of this communication a commission was formed, consisting of the Novgorod Metropolitan Dmitry, the bishop of Pskov, Innokenty, and Teplov. They recommended that Paul, the metropolitan of Tobolsk, be replaced for lack of diligence as well as other causes. A new, more talented metropolitan should be chosen and given the following instructions about missionary activity from the Synod: (1) God's word should be spread by citation of the Gospels, and the acts and letters of the apostles only, without teaching the legends of the Holy Fathers, except when absolutely necessary, as a symbol of faith; (2) the missionary should have three responsibilities: to teach, to exhort, and to remind; orders, threats and stern punishment with imprisonment are violations of conscience and therefore evil; (3) missionaries should not be allowed to go where they wish. Church officials will draft a map of the country showing where the various pagans live, will choose honorable missionaries—especially men who are not self-seeking, but who are sober, rational and gentle—and will designate the time and place of missionary assignments. It is desirable to begin near the towns and spread the faith little by little. New converts should not be forced into church observances which might be difficult to bear for those unaccustomed to them. The missionaries should make reports to the church administration; (4) the missionary should give the impression of being a volunteer rather than ordered to the locality. The missionaries absolutely should not propagate the true faith through superstition or tales of false miracles and revelations. The missionaries should accept nothing more than their daily bread and they should pay for that; (5) when a missionary does not know a native tongue, he should use an interpreter. Hereafter new converts should be chosen for the seminary with the proviso that they never forget their native language. Better yet, instruction in other languages should be introduced.

News came from the eastern steppe frontier that the Kirghiz were preparing to attack some Turkmen roaming around Khiva. The Russian border officials grew nervous, fearing that the Kirghiz would change their minds and attack the Kalmyks. They sent warning to the regent of the Kalmyk khanate and also to the Saratov Bureau of Guardianship of Foreigners, since they feared for the German colonies on the meadow side of the Volga. Catherine commented: "These people who have written this don't know the map at all. The Yaik Cossacks shield the Kalmyks and the Kalmyks shield the German settlements, so people are trembling over nothing. Look at the map. All this is like the news from Little Russia, reporting repeatedly that the king of Prussia is advancing to take the unconquerable city of Kiev."

The appearance of pretenders to the throne also did not cease. In 1769 a deserter, Mamykin, revealed on the road to Astrakhan that Peter

III was still alive, would take his crown again and reward the peasants. Peter III was talked about on the Astrakhan highway and around Petersburg. In discussing the Baturin affair, it was seen that his sentence was not carried out during Elizabeth's reign. Under Peter III the Senate wanted to exile him to hard labor in Nerchinsk, but the emperor ordered him left in Schlüsselburg[38] and given better treatment. In 1768 the soldier Sorokin came up to another soldier, Ushakov, took two pieces of paper from his pocket and said: "I was in Shliushin (Schlüsselburg) in the cell of one prisoner who said he was a colonel, Ioasaph Andreevich Baturin. He gave me these two bits of paper and asked me to give the small one to the empress and the other to Peter Fedorovich. Baturin told me that if I gave them these papers I'd get a big reward." Ushakov first unfolded the big piece of paper and saw that it was addressed to the former sovereign. He said to Sorokin: "This is no good for he's long since dead. Why, you remember, we were out on a campaign and everybody already knew then that he really had died." But Sorokin answered: "No, brother, Baturin knows the planets. He looked out of a window in the prison, picked out the sovereign's planet and said that he was alive and free and that he'll come back in a year or two."

Ushakov took both notes and sought a chance to give the small one to the empress but never found an opportunity. Once, when he got into a drunken fight with the owner of his lodgings, he dropped both notes on the floor. They were picked up and given to the proper authorities. Ushakov told about his conversation with Sorokin, and the latter added: "Baturin told the guards that he wanted to place Peter Fedorovich on the throne. The guards said to him: 'If you did such a service for Peter Fedorovich, then why didn't he free you from here when he was alive?' Baturin answered: 'You're lying, the sovereign didn't die, he's alive and just went off to wander, and he left me here as a ruse. I know from the planets that he's alive. I see the planet, and you'll see that in two years he'll return to Russia.'" Sorokin admitted that he took the papers from Baturin solely to give one to the empress and one to Peter Fedorovich when he returned to Russia. After these discoveries it was deemed best to exile Baturin to Kamchatka. But we will have cause to say more of him later.

Also in 1768 a doctor, Lebedev, reported that an eighteen-year-old adjutant, Opochinin, the son of a major general, passed himself off as the son of the king of England and Empress Catherine, and put together a conspiracy to depose Catherine and put Grand Prince Paul Petrovich on the throne, after destroying the Orlovs, among whom Catherine supposedly wanted to divide up Russia. Opochinin declared that he got the idea of his lineage from the cornet, Batiushkov, who had said: "My late grandmother, Anna Prebyshevskaia, told me that when the ambassador from England was here, the king of England himself was in his suite disguised as a cavalier in the embassy." Batiushkov slandered the riding master of the horse guards, Steigers, who supposedly was plotting with his comrades to put the grand prince on the throne. Paul allegedly knew of their intentions through Panin. Steigers invited Batiushkov to participate in the conspiracy and convinced him to recruit others. Batiushkov spoke with Major Patrikeev and Opochinin. Batiushkov, according to Opochinin's deposition, stated: "Fedor Khitrov wished to depose the empress but he failed. They exiled him to the countryside and tied Zakhar Grigorevich (Chernyshev) into the affair for which they made him retire. But later he evidently straightened himself out, and they took him back into the service as before. But it's all for nothing that he reformed, he'll be with our party because he's not the son of Grigory Petrovich but of Peter the Great."

Batiushkov confessed all. Steigers placed all the blame on Batiushkov, who said: "I am more annoyed at the Counts Orlov for not remembering the kindness of my father, turning my sister, Kropotova, out of the palace and removing me against my will from the service." Batiushkov admitted that he first began to talk about his intention to make the same sort of change as the Orlovs had done. His crime was attributed to drunkenness and insanity. He was sentenced to deprivation of his rank and nobility and to exile in Mangaza with two copecks a day for his room and board. When his sanity returned, he would be forced to work. Because of his youth, his repentance and his father's service, Opochinin kept his rank and was sent to a garrison on the frontier.

II

RELATIONS WITH POLAND, PRUSSIA, SWEDEN, DENMARK, BRITAIN, UKRAINE, WAR WITH TURKEY 1766, 1767, 1768

RUSSIAN RELATIONS WITH POLAND – PONIATOWSKI AND THE CZARTORYSKIS

At the same time that the deputies from eastern Russia were listening to the Instruction and deliberating means of bettering their lives, the population of western Russia awaited with trepidation the end of the struggle in Poland. It had begun with the decision of that same compiler of the Instruction not to rest until the Russian people "arrive at a lawful position with respect to rights and justice." Thus the problem was the same in east and west and was being resolved simultaneously but by different means.

We have seen that the argument over the dissidents had disrupted the old connection between the Russian court and the Princes Czartoryski, who long had been considered the leaders of the Russian party in Poland. On January 2, 1766 Repnin[1] wrote to Panin: "While out on a hunt I chanced to talk with his majesty about the pretensions of the Czartoryski princes to rule and the dire need that he try himself to be a real king and not remain dependent upon them forever. I have already written so much to your excellency on this matter that I am almost ashamed to repeat it in view of the fruitlessness and baselessness of all the promises made to me by the king. Knowing his weakness, I do not dare have faith in him. I report this to you, not in the assurance that he will follow my advice, but only by way of information. In this conversation his majesty gave me all sorts of assurances that he will take steps to free himself from dependence upon his uncles. He said that already he has told them to their faces that he intends to maintain direct correspondence with the most important nobles living in all of the provinces. He will thereby have a picture of the state of affairs in each province. All who wish to be appointed to provincial offices will have to address him directly. In general anyone who wants some sort of favor from him will have to come to him and not to the Czartoryskis as has been done up to now.

"Such a move of course quickly would disrupt the power of the Czartoryskis and would attract their partisans to the king in the hope of receiving various favors from him. However, his resolve in such cases is so weak that I do not dare hope that he really will put this plan into action. Unfortunately, he has managed to get into his head the hope that he will convince his uncles to act within the limits of proper subjects by using reason and flattery. Having an interest in holding him in their claws so that they can remain independent, they will not give way voluntarily—a fact which I have not hesitated to report directly and repeatedly to his majesty. His weakness is so surprising that people will not recognize what an unusual man he used to be. I know for certain that Rzewuski[2] himself speaks with wonder in extreme confidentiality that he would not recognize the king as the same man. Had he known the king would be so weak, he would have advised him not to take upon himself this lofty position. Rzewuski himself has become very zealous for our own court, as if he were one of our subjects. He tries in every way to urge the court here into good conduct towards the king of Prussia, in order always to be friendly with him, as long as he maintains friendly relations with us.

"I spoke about this with the king. He affirmed that the Prussian king does not want a prosperous or activist Poland. I explained to him that on the contrary the king of Prussia would agree to that if Poland wished to demonstrate to him that its welfare might be useful through an alliance with him, in which Poland might render him aid in many matters. All this of course depends on how much and how long the king of Prussia remains friendly toward us.

"Finally, in this conversation, his majesty promised me to undertake all that seems useful and necessary for Russia and assured me that he will never deviate in the slightest from our system. I do not know whether his majesty will remain firm in these intentions. I do not doubt his complete loyalty to us and his straightforwardness. I almost dare to vouch for them, but his weakness in the face of his uncles is unspeakable, and they always interfere and will interfere in affairs so that they will always be needed by the king."

The opposing families wanted to take advantage of the growing coolness between the Russian court and the Czartoryskis and began to seek the favor of the sovereign, whose authority had been shattered. The lord high treasurer, Count Wessel, had been assuring Repnin that the governor of Kiev, the bishop of Cracow, the high chief hetman,[3] the governnor of Cracow, the lord high marshal of the court, and many others wished only one thing—to be part of the Russian party independent of the king. They would undertake no obligations with other courts if the Russians would become their patrons. In return Russia must defend them firmly and strongly against the Czartoryskis. Above all, the general confederation on which the Czartoryski· party chiefly depended must be annulled at the next meeting of the Diet.[4] Wessel asked Repnin to give him an answer as swiftly as possible so that he could take the necessary measures before the forthcoming sub-Diets, if they were given hope of Russian protection.

Repnin answered graciously but in general terms. He said that the Russian court never refused people who sincerely sought its protection. Justice and the observance of Polish rights always had guided Russia's policy. As for a decisive answer, Repnin asked him to wait and allow time for consideration and consultation with his court.

Reporting this conversation with Wessel, Repnin wrote to Panin: "If, *contrary to every expectation,* we find ourselves in such an extremity as to form our own special party independent of the king, we can accomplish this without great difficulty due to the great number of discontented magnates here. In that event it will be necessary to obligate them in writing so they cannot fly as easily to other quarters as our previous friends here have done. I must acknowledge that I speak of such a tactic with the greatest feelings of regret since it will cause untold discontent to a king who is, of course, loyal to us. However, it is not possible to rely upon that loyalty because of his excessive weakness, of which we already have ample evidence."

Repnin used the expression *contrary to every expectation* in vain. The necessity of opposing the Czartoryskis and relying upon their enemies was obvious if the matter of the dissidents was to be settled successfully. Still seeking justice, Bishop Konisski[5] was living in Warsaw. Repnin submitted two memoranda on Konisski's behalf to the Polish ministry. He did so, remarking that the ministry did not wish to give him satisfaction and that the chancellor of Lithuania, Michael Czartoryski, was behind this reluctance. Czartoryski insisted that it was not necessary in this case to issue a royal proclamation but merely to circulate ministerial letters instructing the Uniate bishops to cease harassing Greek Orthodox believers. But it was known that similar letters had had no effect. This same Czartoryski opposed confirmation of the privileges of Orthodox subjects. The king, who previously had wished to give Konisski full satisfaction, began to waver.

In view of the king's vacillations, which Petersburg attributed to Czartoryski, Panin wrote Repnin that the proposal of the Potockis to enter into direct contact with Russia deserved full attention. One had to conclude from the conduct of the Czartoryski family that they cared little about fulfilling the Russian demands, especially those concerning the dissident and border questions; they were concerned solely about influencing the king, turning everything to their advantage and settling matters according to their ideas and interests. The time was coming when the king might display by his acts how far he intended to facilitate the views and aims of the empress. The cause of the dissidents was inextricably connected with the well-being of our fellow believers and therefore of prime interest to the empress. It would serve in this instance as a prime example of the sincerity of the Polish monarch, or of his weakness should he remain subject to his uncles. If the former is presumed, it is essential to presume a break between the king and the Princes Czartoryski. Therefore one had, first, to attempt beforehand to assure him of another source of support and, second, to demonstrate to the Czartoryskis how much they could lose were they deprived of Russian patronage. If the king remained in the clutches of his family and dependent upon them, Russia must have other means to attain her desired ends. "Therefore," Panin concluded, "I recommend that you align the Potocki family with our interests."

SALDERN'S MISSION

Repnin constantly wrote of the loyalty and weakness of the king. This might arouse suspicion that the ambassador himself was displaying some weakness as a consequence of his loyalty to Stanislaw Augustus. Therefore a decision was made to send to Repnin's aid a man whose character would enable him to express the demands of his court with sufficient force. Could he not force the king and the Czartoryskis to accede to these demands, at least he could make clear the relations of the two countries.

This man was the native of Holstein, Saldern, who has been mentioned already.[6] He appeared first during the reign of Peter III when, bearing the title conference councillor, he was named plenipotentiary to the Berlin Congress on Denmark. At that time he appeared to be completely devoted to Prussia, but after June 28, 1762[7] he was responsible for dealing with Holstein and was very close to Panin who called him a close friend. Saldern was adept at ingratiating himself with the powerful, taking their interests closely to heart, and appropriating and developing their favorite ideas. Thus he represented himself to Panin as an ardent advocate of Panin's favorite ideas, the Northern accord and the cession of Holstein to the king of Denmark. But Saldern did not abstain from other means of acquiring the favor of powerful figures. In letters to Panin he called Panin his father and protector and wrote of his inexpressible joy at the sight of Panin's signature and the heavenly feeling which he experienced in Panin's presence. But, as usual, this man hurried to reward himself when not in the presence of a powerful man. When he himself was in a position of power he gave rein to his irritable nature.

People obliged to deal with him did not experience a heavenly feeling in his presence.

Saldern set out for Warsaw. On April 17 he wrote Panin of the pains he had taken in his attempts to set the king and members of the various parties on the correct path. Saldern expressed the hope that because of the serious tone in which he had warned the king of a terrible future, Poniatowski would act carefully, adhere to principles which had been recognized as true and remain steadfast in carrying them out. The king promised not to fall into the grasp of his uncles but at the same time recognized the necessity of restraining his own brothers and friends who were agitating against the Czartoryskis.

Saldern also transmitted the reply of the Czartoryskis to the proposals and demands he had conveyed with both flattery and threats. "Up to now," the Czartoryskis stated, "we thought that being young, indecisive and unsure of his own capabilities, the king needed us, his old friends and relatives, as advisors at least in domestic affairs. We think our view both just and moderate when we see that the king has surrounded himself with new friends and young people and has acceded blindly to their ideas and advice. We often have had occasion to oppose people whose principles seemed suspicious to us and whose counsel harmed the real interests of the king and the fatherland. Our age, position and wisdom do not permit us to seek the scornful title of royal favorites. Let him have as many bosom friends and favorites as he wishes, let him give them posts and shower them with wealth and favors of every kind, as long as it is not against the laws. Let him amuse himself with them. It would be ridiculous for us to be insulted by this. But when we see that these young people are blinded by favors and supported by ruses which they employ to arouse the sensitivity and impetuousity of the king, we consider it our duty to oppose them, although we have never thought of forming a special party or separating our interests from the true interests of the king and the nation. As soon as we see that our petitions are without avail and the evil so strong that it will determine the present and future, we are prepared to abandon government activity and remain peaceful spectators. We are certain that such a decision and such conduct will not please the Russian court since, sooner or later and especially in the coming Diet, all the blame might fall on us. The intrigues and strategems of our enemies and rivals will never cease to ruin matters in order to magnify the accusations against us."

Transmitting the Czartoryskis' statements, Saldern wrote: "If the princes sincerely wish to remove themselves from affairs of state, a means for full success without them can be found, although it would prolong matters somewhat. But if they do not wish to retire by themselves, should they draw others after them at the wrong time out of bitterness, misfortune will be unavoidable. Their conduct will ruin everything at the coming Diet just as the last Diet was wrecked by the question of the dissidents, which they would not deal with in good conscience. It seems to me that they must be spared at present and kept in power until such time as their conduct is revealed at the coming Diet. If their conduct proves to be bad, we can take our own measures and precautions."

Repnin wrote Panin that Saldern's presence in Warsaw was a boon for him, and he praised Saldern's actions with all his powers. Nevertheless, it was apparent from his words that Saldern, despite all his ardor, could do nothing. Repnin was fully vindicated and should well have exulted at Saldern's dispatch and indefatigable activity. "I daresay," wrote Repnin, "that if Saldern's presence does not correct the conduct of the court here, then nothing in the world will. There has not been a day on which he has not offered the sharpest admonitions to the king for the weakness and lack of consistency in his conduct. He has done the same with the Czartoryski princes in order to place a limit on their boundless vanity and have them understand what sorrowful consequences their incorrigibility will have. Like me, he flattered himself with the hope that he could reconcile them with the king and his brothers, but this turned out to be completely impossible. Saldern received many promises and pretty words from all sides. Time will tell what will come of this since, knowing the extraordinary weakness of the king, I cannot hope that he will act firmly in anything, just as I cannot offer assurances that his uncles will not get hold of him again."

Meanwhile the king decided to bypass Repnin and deal with Petersburg directly. He decided to send Count Rzewuski, a man considered totally dedicated to Russia. Repnin learned that Rzewuski was instructed to lobby for the withdrawal of Russian troops from Polish territory, especially at the insistence of Prince Michael Czartoryski. In a conversation with Rzewuski, Repnin touched on the subject without revealing that he knew of the envoy's instructions. Rzewuski admitted that he actually did have such an order. Repnin looked surprised and told him that this contradicted the agreement they had made, namely, that the troops were needed to restrain the nation and prompt it to fulfill the Russian demands in the cause of the dissidents. Rzewuski agreed that this was correct but that the king was merely maintaining a facade because he did not have the power to oppose the proposal of his ministry which was based on requests from every corner of Poland.

On this occasion Repnin wrote Panin: "Wishing complete success at the coming Diet, I am full of hope but dare not deceive myself. In case of failure I think that it will be necessary to deploy our forces in the villages of the opponents of our proposals in order to weaken their pride, stubbornness and credibility in the country. For when their supporters see that their chiefs cannot protect themselves against this course, they naturally will begin to desert their chiefs after losing hope that the latter can defend them any more than they can themselves. I have in mind here the two elder Czartoryskis, who alone can help or harm our purposes in the present circumstances. If matters are resolved against our wishes, then we will see, given the circumstances, how they can be straightened out: a special Diet, a new confederation or some other means." Catherine wrote Panin on this dispatch: "I think it possible to incline even these elders to support our wishes at the coming Diet; speak with me about this."

Panin answered that the empress approved of all that Repnin had done along with Saldern. He ordered Repnin to watch with extreme care the conduct of the Czartoryskis and to restore as much as possible the agreement between them and the adherents of the king for the approaching Diet and successful resolution of the question of the dissidents. At the same time Repnin was to win over the Potockis and other opponents of the Czartoryskis in the interest of solving the dissident question. He was secretly to give them to understand that since this matter was of vital concern for the prestige of the empress and the well-being of their fatherland, their cooperation would win the favor of the empress and in consequence greatly influence the affairs of Poland. Panin then ordered that all French diplomats be kept away from matters dealing with the Diet.

POLISH OPPOSITION TO THE DISSIDENTS

If all Russian efforts aimed at successful settlement of the dissident question in the coming Diet, the opponents of the dissidents were not asleep. In Lithuania the Masalskis, who had been ardent adherents of Russia, now declared themselves bitter enemies of the dissidents, and Repnin ordered an officer dispatched to them with a warning to restrain themselves unless they wished to suffer some unpleasantness. In Poland itself Soltik, the bishop of Cracow, was an opponent of the dissidents. He stated forthrightly in a letter to the king that at the Diet he would use all his influence to see that the dissidents received no rights whatsoever.

At the end of July Repnin wrote to Panin: "I think that his outburst cannot be disregarded unless we want to teach the Poles impudence and give them grounds to ignore our words when not backed by deeds." Repnin requested permission to deploy Russian forces to Soltik's villages prior to the Diet. "This example, of course," he wrote, "will lead to respect for our demands here. Everyone will be wary of thwarting us. Meanwhile this troop movement will bring our forces closer to Warsaw. This will serve as some restraint on the deputies to the Diet in Warsaw. I judge that some forces also must be left in Lithuania in order to make a similar example of the Masalskis if they too continue their perverse actions."

Panin answered that the empress had approved this proposal. Furthermore, Repnin was directed to announce openly that the dissidents' cause was inextricably linked to the welfare of the republic and that quite dire consequences would befall those who opposed it. The empress made her friendship and good will toward vital Polish interests contingent upon the position the Diet assigned the dissidents. If the matter of the dissidents were not settled successfully, the consequences could easily be seen from what had befallen Soltik and the Masalskis. If they and their cohorts learned nothing from this first lesson, they could be sure that 40,000 troops were on the border. They would be sent immediately into Poland and Lithuania, quartered in the villages of the opponents and maintained at their expense because the empress considered the matter of dissidents to involve both her own glory and the fundamental welfare of the republic. She was firm in her desire to succeed by all possible means, even the most forceful, in order to eliminate obstacles at their source, that is, the estates and persons of those who raised insurrection and unrest and thereby made themselves the true malefactors of their fatherland.

Stanislaw Augustus wrote in a completely different tone to Rzewuski in Petersburg: "The more I think about it," the king wrote, "the more I find it a bad idea to solve the dissident question by force of arms. First, to make the measure effective, a large army must be deployed. Second, when affairs are conducted in such manner they become for me the seed of Ravaillac and for the dissidents the foreshadowing of a St. Bartholemew's night.[8] The dissidents' cause is difficult but not impossible. God grant that there be no Russian forces in Poland and no phrases suggesting foreign hegemony."

Meanwhile the Czartoryskis sent Panin a letter filled with complaints against the king and Repnin. They wrote: "We must admit that with the greatest sorrow we see the disappearance of our best hopes, the disappearance of the means given, it would seem, by Providence to lift Poland from the depths of the evils into which it has been plunged. Instead of a happy future, we now foresee only turmoil if the king is surrounded constantly by youths who lack experience and discipline, and are guided solely by their passions. Ruining the most important matters of state for the most petty motives and not possessing the qualities needed to obtain royal favor, they daily misuse the mind and heart of the king with every kind of trick. They irritate him and make him irritated with those who might lead him toward a stable system.

"The people surrounding the king would never have dared to act so openly and boldly had they not flattered themselves with the hope of Russia's support. This is a result of the public, completely open patronage and reception they receive daily from Prince Repnin, the ambassador, and of his completely undisguised aloofness to us. We are forced to inform you that such conduct on the part of Prince Repnin has reversed the ideas of the majority of our people. They are forced to think that mere ties of friendship and the amusement of your nephew could not move him to such partisanship if the political structure of Russia were against it. The prospect of the next Diet fills us with horror. Of course the empress wishes Poland well and wishes to give us proof of her good will in standing firm on the dissidents' cause. Along with us not one educated Pole doubts the importance of this question for the welfare of the country. But similar questions at all times have been subject to popular preconceptions and should be entrusted to skilled hands. Here it is necessary not to use alien power, always degrading for a people, but gentleness and tact to acquire the trust and esteem of each prominent man in the country. Despite our efforts and the intentions of the empress, the affair doubtless will be unsuccessfully resolved should the mainsprings of gentleness and persuasion not be employed artfully and persistently. Neither the empress nor you will witness our actions, and it will be easy to accuse us from 200 leagues distance. If people aiming toward a common goal cannot come to precise agreement among themselves and do not help one another, success is impossible even with the best of intentions. But what kind of agreement can there be when there is no trust? And yet there is no trust for us in Prince Repnin's heart although we have spared nothing to acquire that trust since his arrival. We would observe happily a rebirth of that trust thanks to your suggestion."

Panin sent Repnin a copy of this letter and his answer. The Czartoryskis were given notice in the gentlest and decorative phrases that the empress held full right to suspect their conduct during the coronation Diet.[9] Foreign courts informed the Russians that they, the Czartoryskis, had helped the dissidents' cause least of all. And, indeed, this news was confirmed by their removal from the Diet. If Prince Repnin has added some sort of personality to all this, he will be restrained. But the empress demanded that they cooperate as befitted them in attainment of her goals. These goals were three: an alliance of Russia with Poland, restoration of the rights of the dissidents and demarcation of the border. The empress looked upon the matter of the dissidents as a test revealing their leanings. The only time that this affair can be resolved in a gentle manner is during the next Diet. At that time they must demonstrate their loyalty to the empress and to their fatherland by using the wisdom of their counsel, their high position in the state and their experience to contribute to successful resolution of the question. As for determination of the borders between Russia and **Poland**, the empress did not raise at all the question of enlarging her own possessions only that those living along the border finally might escape that primitive condition in which people do not know what is theirs, what is someone else's, and can defend their property solely by force and violence. Once the borders had been settled, nothing would prevent a close alliance between the two states.

Panin wrote Repnin that he should restore his confidence in the Czartoryskis and assure them that the Russian court wished to see their advice preferred by the king to that of the younger people, who were striving to attain personal goals. At the same time he should let them know directly that the empress thought that the king was attempting immoderately to further his own interests, that is, to expand his power. This would frighten people who loved freedom and arouse distrust among his neighbors. Should the question of increasing the armed forces of the republic arise, Repnin should offer the opinion to the Czartoryskis that they, as wise and skilled senior men, should know that an increase in the size of the army occurs either in war with weak neighbors or during the decline of the latter. Poland found itself in neither position in relation to its neighbors, and of course had no wish to begin a war to enlarge its army. Therefore Poland had no other means of regaining its power except by alliance with powers whose own political requirements demanded an increase in its strength.

Repnin was to deal with the Czartoryskis kindly, for whatever one thought, the Czartoryski family still represented the best tool for successful advancement of Russian interests in Poland. The heads of the family, the chancellor of Lithuania and the Russian viceroy, unquestionably enjoyed more skill and influence than any others. Except for them, no one could be found who could be entrusted with leadership and formation of a new party.

On August 21 Repnin replied, "Of course the cooperation of the Princes Czartoryski is necessary at the coming Diet, not because one can rely on their sincerity or ardor, but because their credit is very great. Although their hearts are foul, their heads are healthier than anyone else's in this land. Their remonstrances to your excellency concerning the conduct of the king are not all just. I agree fully that he is exceptionally weak and impetuous, but I cannot agree that anything, however minor, has been done without their knowledge. As for my relations with them, amusements alone were not the cause of my estrangement from them; rather, it is their ambivalence and ingratitude to our court. Their conduct has not changed since receiving your letter. They still limit themselves to their previous cold civility. Apparently they were waiting for me to take the first step. This I did."

Repnin went off to the Russian viceroy with assurances of the restoration of his accreditation and the good will of the empress in the hope that Czartoryski's diligence and loyalty would correspond fully with this favor. Czartoryski replied with assurances of his own ardor, loyalty and gratitude. After mutual compliments, they got down to business. Repnin asked the viceroy to make available all means which might bring success in the matter of the dissidents. The viceroy assured him in reply of his devotion but did not vouch for success in the affair. "Who will speak first about it in the Diet?" Czartoryski asked. "I at least do not dare to do so." Repnin was powerfully offended by these words. He pointed out to the viceroy the important consequences of failure and added that if the leading men of the country avoided open cooperation in resolving the question, the lesser men would of course not speak. Czartoryski replied that everyone has his limits.

Then Repnin began to speak of the outrageous pronouncements of the Masalskis, the bishop of Cracow and the bishop of Kamenets, Krasinski, who lately had joined them. He asked whether Czartoryski would find it useful to deploy Russian forces in their villages. Czartoryski answered that this would upset, offend and alienate everyone from the Russian side and could disrupt completely the Diet. Czartoryski added that in his opinion it would be useful to withdraw all Russian troops while the Diet was in session for the troops always could return later. Repnin noted that since the confederation still existed so did the cause for Russian troops to be in Poland. Repnin ended his report of this conversation with: "It remains to be seen whether their conduct at the Diet will be energetic and honorable. If kindness and invitation do not win us our desired end at the Diet, there are no means left except force." Catherine noted: "If they gave him their word, they will keep it."

On August 21 Repnin also wrote Panin that in greater Poland all leaders had promised to support the dissidents but that friends of one of the Czartoryskis, the bishop of Poznan, were blocking such support. When Repnin complained of this to the Russian viceroy, he replied that he knew nothing about it and had received no news from his brother. Repnin concluded his letter: "Truly, fulfillment of this task is so difficult, confused and onerous that I often lapse into despair." Again defending the elder Czartoryskis, Catherine wrote of the bishop of Poznan:

"He is a fool whom his brothers will never be able to set straight. Fools have more influence over him."

Repnin wrote that Soltik was dealing with foreign sovereigns and demanding their help in the matter of the dissidents. Thanks to his influence at the Cracow sub-Diet, the Catholic nobility had expelled all dissidents. But Soltik wrote to Count G.G. Orlov that he was not at all persecuting the dissidents, and that Repnin had threatened him in a conversation with his representative that he would be sent to Siberia and his estates sequestered. Repnin objected that he had never said anything of the kind. As for the dissidents, he referred to their deputy, Holz, who had set out for Petersburg and could testify there that there had been no injustice which the bishop of Cracow had not visited upon them and that they were not dealt with as fiercely in any other bishopric.

Repnin was vindicated in his comments on the Czartoryskis best of all by a dispatch sent by Stanislaw Augustus to Rzewuski in Petersburg. "You know," the king wrote, "that I have demanded long and constantly of my uncles that they explain to me their orders about the preliminary Diets, out of the fear that their agents and mine might oppose one another by being kept in the dark. You witnessed how they always avoided an explanation. And now precisely what I feared has happened. At many preliminary Diets the elections were twofold. It is important for me that Count Panin knows about this before my uncles tell the Russian government that the affair was not resolved because of my unwillingness to come to an agreement with them and give them sufficient influence. It is important for me and for the course of affairs that they learn from others and not from me. That is, that the empress order someone to write them that Russia will attempt to weaken their influence in the country and with me if they do not start to help me and satisfy me instead of opposing me as they do now. I entrust this to you as a matter of extraordinary importance. Request of Count Panin in my name that he do this as quickly as possible. I would not want to open the Diet without this warning to my uncles. Prince Repnin is now treating them better than ever."

RUSSIAN PRESSURES ON POLAND

The admonition was made. On September 10 Panin wrote the Czartoryskis that they should spare no concern or labor for the success of the dissidents' cause for this was the decisive opportunity for them to show their intentions. "I do not conceal from you," wrote Panin, "that only your indifference in this matter and in others, where the empress knows and approves of the disposition of the king, will destroy in principle all of the good which was expected from the revolution. This event, which was seen as a source of happiness for your fatherland, will produce only a series of misfortunes for it, the king and you personally."

The Czartoryskis were admonished, but the king also should have received a strong admonition. On September 1 Repnin reported that the king had sent him the draft of an edict on the dissidents for the coming Diet. Repnin found many harmful and unseemly things in this draft. That which was said in favor of the dissidents was vague, and in generalities, while that which opposed them was expressed clearly, in detail. The dissidents' churches were not mentioned at all, nor was the preservation of their estates and the right to repair or rebuild them. The religious rights guaranteed by treaties were not detailed. A clear law was necessary here in view of the slanders spread by the Catholic clergy and a significant portion of the population. Finally, the draft included a provision that dissidents never be allowed to hold government posts and civil service ranks. At Repnin's insistence, the chancellor of Lithuania, Czartoryski, undertook the revision of the draft which, however, had been sent without change to Rzewuski in Petersburg to show to Panin. Repnin wrote to the latter: "I think that the draft might surprise your excellency a bit."

The result of this surprise was a letter from Panin to Repnin on September 18. "I entrust you to express our feeling to the king that sovereigns, when close and trusted friends, do not act among themselves as his Polish majesty has done. This forces us to suspect unbounded ambitions, a lack of frankness and trust and an attempt to win time. He seems to be leading us along with various statements and ambiguous hopes while reaching only his own one-sided views. Such conduct has become more and more apparent and might finally lead the present court to dissolve the general confederation and join with those who want to place the Diet on an ordinary legal basis, in order that, having annihilated the majority in the Diet, all the king's paths to strengthening himself further to our detriment be blocked.

"It would then be more convenient for us to establish a confederation of dissidents and act through it with armed force. The new brand of friends and intimates of the Polish court are aiding in just that; while they flatter the king and prepare to protect him, we will succeed in finishing everything and resolving forever the fates of our false friends, who will repent their lack of gratitude, but too late. The king of Prussia is urging us strongly to discontinue the general confederation. Therefore, the king of Poland should consider it an inescapable rule that if he does not conclude matters as desired by the empress, he cannot even think of any new advantage for himself, not to speak of attempting actually to achieve such. The sovereign empress has perceived already all the intricacies of the Polish court. She is now painfully touched and insulted by its new ruse, woven so artfully. While they tempted us with the hope of achieving all that we wanted, when a draft had been sent for approval by the Diet granting free exercise of religion by the dissidents, they did not await the answer of the empress, who alone should have instituted the measure, and they thought to make things more difficult for us by another draft of a constitution for the Diet. This draft impudently repudiates solemnly and forever that which her majesty is trying most to achieve. From such offensive duplicity the empress can conclude only that they wished to forestall a formal demand from our side for civil rights for the dissidents.

"You must adhere strictly to the rule that until the dissidents' cause has been brought to complete resolution, the king cannot receive anything important which furthers his interests. Thus, until the conclusion of the matter, he must remain in thrall to us, all the more so since his own and his uncles' clear aversion to the restoration of the civil rights of the dissidents has begun to appear most clearly. But the empress will never retreat from this demand. Try to gather about you as many dissidents as possible, including some of our Orthodox Christians, if there are capable people among them. Deal with the best of both openly, and prepare and strengthen their hope for strong protection from the empress. Have them present a memorial to the king and Diet in which as free citizens they demand the restoration of their rights."

In Petersburg, the desire to grant the dissidents civil rights was unshakeable. In Warsaw, no one had any hope that this could be achieved in any ordinary, peaceful fashion. The king wrote to Rzewuski: "Repnin's orders to win the dissidents' involvement in the legislative progress of the republic are thunderous blows for the country and for me personally. If there is any human possibility, impress upon the empress that the crown which she won for me has become the cloak of Nessus.[10] I am burning in it and my end will be horrible. I foresee clearly the terrible choice awaiting me if the empress insists on her orders. Either I will have to reject her friendship, so dear to my heart and so necessary for my rule and state, or I will have to be a traitor to my fatherland. If Russia is firm in wishing dissidents in the legislature, then let there be a few, ten or twelve, and yet that will still be ten or twelve leaders of a legal party which views the Polish state and government as an enemy against which it must constantly seek outside aid. I know that this affair might cost me my crown and my life. I know that, but I repeat that I cannot betray my fatherland. If the empress retains even the smallest grace toward me, there is still time. She can order Repnin that if the Diet should yield to the dissidents on their other demands but exclude them from the legislature, he should not move the troops now in Lithuania and not introduce new forces into the territories of the republic. Might can do anything—I know that. But will they really use force against those they love to force them to do that which they see as the greatest of misfortunes? I could not bring myself to write this directly to the empress. I feared that my sundered heart and agitated spirit would have filled my letter with words which would have irritated instead of softened her. But you do what you can. To perish is nothing, but to perish at the hands of one so dear is horrible."

Repnin was also horrified. "The decrees issued in the matter of the dissidents are terrible," he wrote Panin. "My hair literally stands on end when I think about it. I have almost no hope, except through force alone, of fulfilling the will of the most merciful sovereign as to the civil liberties of the dissidents." But Catherine was not horrified and ordered an answer sent to Stanislaw Augustus. She said that she certainly did not understand how the dissidents, once permitted legislative activity, would in consequence be more inimicable than before to the Polish state and government. She could not comprehend how the king could consider himself a traitor to his fatherland for doing what justice demanded and which would bring glory to him and lasting good to the state. "If the king views the affair this way," Catherine concluded, "I retain eternal and heartfelt regret that I could be so deceived as to the king's friendship, feelings, and manner of thought."

Repnin continued to repeat his previous warnings. "I cannot report otherwise about the inclinations of the public on the dissident question than I have reported previously. Everyone is against granting the dissidents even civil ranks, and they will not even hear of the possibility that they might be elected deputies to the Diets. There are many leaders who are so insane and in such confused despair that they say that it is better to go to extremes and suffer complete ruin from Russian troops than to agree to this."

Repnin announced to the king that Russia demanded full civil rights for the dissidents, except the right to be a senator or hetman. However, if Russia had to achieve this by force, perhaps she would not even agree to the latter exception. "But the nation can never be convinced to do this!" the king objected. "The will of her imperial majesty is firm and will be fulfilled in every respect," answered Repnin. The king turned every which way and importuned him whether this was really the last word from the Russian side and whether Russian troops really would invade Poland if the dissidents' cause was not settled at the Diet. Repnin assured him that this was so. Then the king asked him: "Can you assure me that if all your demands are met the empress will be completely satisfied and will not carry this affair any further?" Repnin answered that he could give such assurance. The Czartoryskis stated that they saw hardly any means of forcing the nation to accede to Russia's demands, but that they would attempt to do what was possible, without answering for results which were beyond their powers.

THE FIRST CONFRONTATIONS

On September 19 Repnin and the Prussian, Danish, and British ministers went to the cardinal's, where the entire Polish ministry had gathered. The representatives of the four powers announced an agreement among their courts to cooperate in the defense of the dissidents. Consequently, they, the ambassadors, formally demanded restoration to the dissidents of all their ancient rights and freedoms, and asked that this be reported to his majesty before any action was taken. The cardinal answered that he would carry out their wish, and that in a matter of days the king would call together all the senators present and announce it to them. "Fanaticism is growing to such a degree," noted Repnin, "that people are avoiding me as they once avoided those excommunicated. They toast the health of the defenders of Catholicism, and the hotheads say that they would sooner perish than allow any improvement in the position of the dissidents. No one from the dissidents' side is here yet, and I am greatly dissatisfied by this. That is inexcusable negligence! I have written to many of them, and I have their replies that they will be here. Meanwhile, they are not coming."

Repnin soon had to report to Petersburg that the lines of battle had been drawn. The king and the Czartoryskis announced openly that they would not agree to have dissidents not only in government, but even to grant them civil rank. They were prepared to ask for toleration only. Repnin told the Czartoryskis that if this was the case, he would deploy Russian forces in the villages of the bishops of Cracow and Wilno. This would make an example of them and others would see what awaited opponents of the dissidents. The Czartoryskis answered that they would face ruin and every travail, but that they could not satisfy the Russian demands in this matter.

The threat had to be carried out. On September 24 Repnin wrote Petersburg: "This date I have ordered Major General Saltykov to enter the villages of the bishops of Cracow and Wilno with his army corps. They will be maintained at the bishops' expense. Nothing could be worse in the dissident affair than the present situation. Perhaps this act will make an impression and straighten things out somewhat. There is no hope of success in this matter without the use of force. One can rely only on force, for not just a part of the Diet but all of the leadership will be in opposition. Besides the entire clergy and its influence, the king and the Princes Czartoryski and their partisans have joined the opposition, which includes everyone."

The empress answered this report with the rescript of October 6. Were the dissidents' cause not considered in the Diet in formal negotiations with the ambassador and the dissidents, from which reasonable fruits might be expected, and if the loss of all hope again should be attributed solely to the intrigues of the Czartoryskis, Repnin should determine precisely the state of affairs and use all his powers to break up the general confederation and the Diet. The Czartoryskis wished to use the confederation, in which matters were settled by majority vote, to bring about reforms. From the very first, Repnin should address himself directly to those of the opponents of the Czartoryskis who most envied the advantage which that family had gained. *"One cannot doubt* that such a change in our preferences will produce an important reversal in their spirits and that many of the opponents of the Czartoryskis who now oppose the dissidents will think better of the matter."

But Repnin had serious doubts. Before using force and making a final break with the Czartoryskis, he attempted one last time to facilitate the course of the affair by relinquishing a part of the Russian demands. Seeing "Strings drawn so taut that they must break in two," he gave the king some personal advice. To avoid more serious consequences, he should propose to the empress that the dissidents receive only civil rights without the right to serve as deputies to the Diets. The king evidently took this advice and shortly showed Repnin his letter to the empress. However, in this note he proposed only religious toleration, with exclusion of the dissidents from all civil ranks. "I did not advise this," said the stunned ambassador. "But I cannot propose anything else," the king answered. Repnin grew furious. He stated: "Her imperial majesty will always desire the welfare of the Polish republic. But she sees in those who oppose the dissidents miscreants who are harming this very republic, its tranquility, and her own person. It is clear from this how these people should be dealt with. I will begin with the bishops of Cracow and Wilno as the prime offenders and disrupters of the local peace." "You will only insult and hurt me with this," the king said. "I am very sorry, if that is so," Repnin answered, "but I must finally make clear the fury of her imperial majesty about this affair with those people who ignore their own welfare." This ended the conversation.

"I cannot understand the causes of the Czartoryskis' opposition," Repnin wrote to Panin. "How did they determine to suffer all the baleful consequences without any hope, in my judgment, of opposing our might? The thought of resistance could occur only to frivolous minds who think to find firmness in desperation. As for a dissidents' confederation, which one might turn to in extremity, the Holzes are inclined to one. They speak for the other leaders of the dissidents, but they demand not only troops in the areas where the confederation would be formed but also money to attract and support the poor nobles who cannot manage it with their own resources. The confederation should be established all at once, in one day and in four places: Prussian Poland, greater Poland, little Poland, and Lithuania. The Greeks (that is, the Orthodox) should be united with the latter. The Russian troops here number three battalions, two grenadier companies of the Kurinsk regiment, one regiment of carabineers, and a regiment of Chuguev Cossacks. I do not expect formal resistance to these forces, but I do not dare answer for the fanaticism of private persons, combined with irrational rage and drunkenness, which cannot be held in check. I have assembled as many dissidents here as possible. They will submit a petition, but of all the Greeks only one Belorussian archbishop has signed, since there are none of them here, and unfortunately there is no one to be brought here. Almost all of the Orthodox nobility are so poor that they till the land themselves. As for seeking out other leaders of our party in case of need, I must admit that this is very difficult. I do not now see one capable man for our side; of the opposition families, all persons of any significance whatsoever, always have been inclined to Austria and France. They have always opposed us, and now they fight us even more over the dissident question."

ATTEMPTED CONSTITUTIONAL CHANGES

Meanwhile, the king and the Czartoryskis hurried to pass at the Diet changes important for them. In the first days of October a draft presented by the king and the ministries, in agreement with the Czartoryskis and their party, was read in the Diet. The draft concerned the manner of resolution of financial matters in the Diet. The draft stated that all financial measures always should be approved by majority vote, including the levy of new taxes. Repnin and Benoit[11] visited the Czartoryskis and demanded an exact specification of the measures subject to such approval. In the opinion of Repnin and his Prussian colleague, such measures necessarily included only orderly and advantageous distribution of already approved revenues, and not the imposition of new taxes, since this was not a domestic but a national matter, which should be subject to unanimous approval at the Diet. The Czartoryskis remonstrated that even the imposition of new taxes was a matter of finance and consequently belonged to the class of measures which were assigned to the treasury committee when the Diet was convened.

Repnin replied that Prussia and Russia could not agree to such an interpretation. They began to argue. The chancellor of Lithuania grew
heated and stated that the Poles had the right to issue whatever domestic
decrees they deemed best. "You are empowered," Repnin answered,
"to do what you wish domestically, but we are empowered to accept
only what we want to. You can sign your draft and enter it in the constitution of the present Diet, but you will meet our resistance in implementing it. Because we are neighbors, we must assure that the form of
government here is not altered." Czartoryski proclaimed: "I would rather
see the republic completely conquered than exist in such a state of
dependence."

"At the Diet," Repnin continued, "it has been decided that measures
in the military committee as well as the treasury committee be approved
by majority vote. Do you mean by this that you can increase the size of
your army by majority vote?"

"Of course. Exactly," Czartoryski answered.

Repnin replied: "No, it cannot be. Such an interpretation is in opposition to your greatest freedom, the *liberum veto*.[12] We cannot allow this
to be destroyed. Indeed, increase in revenues and armed forces are the
chief matters in national affairs."

Czartoryski stated: "We do not now intend to enlarge our army, so
that we will not provoke any doubts in our neighbors."

"Excessive revenues," Repnin said, "provoke the same doubts, since
enlargement of the army can be achieved only in this way."

Repnin went from the Czartoryskis to the king, who gave the same
interpretation as his uncles. This forced Repnin to inform the party
opposed to the court that Russia and Prussia in no way agreed with the
king's proposal and desired that the rule of unanimity and the *liberum
veto* remain in full force. Catherine noted on Repnin's report: "It's bad
that they are trying to deceive us, but they will not gain anything from
this conduct."

TURMOIL OVER THE DISSIDENTS

Petersburg nonetheless allowed the Poles some gains in the matter of the
dissidents. On October 2 Panin wrote to Repnin: "In view of the extreme tension, I could do nothing else in so short a time except to react
somehow to the strong assurances of Count Rzewuski without losing
time. I told him my own idea for directing the matter somehow toward
talks or negotiations, that it was absolutely necessary that the Poles
offer us some means of allowing our fellow believers and dissidents who
are nobles at least civil ranks. We can leave alone all ranks which in essence concern government or legislation."

Repnin answered that he had suggested already that the dissidents be allowed at least civil rights, but all Poles were against this and spoke of religious toleration only. Soltik stated in the Diet: "We must start from the basis on which our rights, freedoms, and welfare rest. This basis is the holy Roman Catholic faith. A handful of our fellow citizens refuse to obey the statutes of the republic and accuse us of oppression, persecution, and violation of their rights and freedoms. They make these accusations not before our king, nor officials of the republic, nor legally appointed judges. No, they carry their complaints far abroad. They seek the aid of our neighbors through presentation of baseless pretensions. They call down fearful threats against government figures of our republic, and they cause the entire fatherland countless difficulties. Children carry complaints to their neighbors against their own mother!

"As God is my witness, I am forced to oppose their pretensions not by vengeance, personal hatred for anyone, or fanaticism, but by the obligations of a good Catholic, a bishop, and a senator true to his king and fatherland. As a Catholic, I am learning from the dissidents themselves zeal toward the faith of my ancestors. If they choose to propagate sects which we barely tolerate, how can I be ashamed or fear to defend the dominant religion in a free country? As a bishop, I feel obligated to defend the lambs of Christ against the infection of heretical teachings. As a senator, I observe my oath to offer the king and the republic only good counsel, and to reject what is harmful. Being convinced that religious unity is fundamental to any well-regulated state and that a variety of religions with equal rights is endlessly pernicious, I cannot allow the extension of greater rights to the dissidents without betraying my king and fatherland. If I saw the doors to the Senate, the ambassadors' chambers, and various tribunals opened to the dissidents, I would block these doors with my own body—let them trample me. If I saw a place prepared for construction of a non-Catholic church, I would lie down there—let them place the cornerstone on my head." In conclusion Soltik read the draft of a decree of the Diet under which no one in any future Diet would dare to raise the question of the dissidents under threat of cruel punishment.

At the same time Soltik launched rumors that he had received a pleasant and kind letter from Count Grigory Orlov and that the Russian demands in the dissident question were not so firm. "I am convinced of the contrary," wrote Repnin, "and I am assured of this by the fact that the words Pole and liar are synonymous. In devotion to duty, I must report that the use of force becomes more necessary from hour to hour, not only to resolve the dissident question but also to end all the deceptions being employed. We must issue a formal decree specifying the limits of all these matters of state and the force of the *liberum veto*. Polish laws are insufficient for this because they can be changed at any Diet. We absolutely must demolish all this trickery once and for all if we are not to have unstable and at times even dangerous neighbors."

The difficulty of the situation and the irritation arising from it prompted Repnin to make the following admission: "I must make the demeaning admission that all intrigues of the court here stem from our permissiveness in the Diet, and that my inexperience in these affairs is at least in part a cause of this, since I highly esteemed the penetrating mind and knowledge of the late Count Keyserling. I relied totally on him and gave him complete liberty to act. Unfortunately, as is now apparent, he was deceived by the duplicity of our friends and the two-faced rules of this Diet."

On October 11 Repnin had a conversation with the king in a neutral house. Stanislaw Augustus excoriated the ambassador for the latter's opposition to majority-vote decisions on financial and military questions. The king then asked: "Where is that hope which you offered, to help Poland become a better country than before, when you made that impossible dissident question a prerequisite for this?" Repnin answered that he did not see the dissident affair as impossible. The hope of rectifying Polish affairs lay just where it was earlier; that is, in reaching agreement with its neighbors and placing limits on everything. People should not be allowed to take unlimited advantages if they wished to avoid harm. This is the fundamental law in all political systems.

THE ATTACK ON THE CZARTORYSKIS

Petersburg also was well aware of the mistake, which was not just Keiserling's and Repnin's. It was understood that when Petersburg had tried to use the Czartoryskis and Poniatowski to attain its ends, the latter had attempted to use Russia, and Russian power and influence, as weapons to achieve their respective goals, namely, alteration of the Polish constitution. Now there were no bounds to the indignation against the *cunning* Czartoryski princes, although not so long ago Petersburg had spared them.

Panin wrote Repnin that above all, in consultation with the Prussian ambassador, it was necessary to dissolve the general confederation in order to deprive the Czartoryskis of their power. Panin ordered that Repnin and the dissidents spare the king in all declarations and place all blame on the Czartoryskis. A rescript from the empress herself to Repnin stated: "All of their relations with us have been duplicitous. In this, they have sought step by step in an unconscionable manner only to consummate the plot in which they now have been exposed. They thought, perhaps, that what they alone did to us would not lead to actual destruction of their plan. We repeat to you our previous order to destroy as fast as possible the general confederation and the entire Diet so that our nephew and his uncles might have palpable proof that we will not be deceived by their cleverness but, recognizing their ingratitude, intend rather to convert it into the means of their own disgrace and injury."

The king asked Repnin to disburse the 50,000 rubles designated as his subsidy. But Repnin replied that because of the change in circumstances he could not relinquish the money without receiving new instructions from his court. In this matter, the rescript read: "We approve of your reply to the king and we direct you to announce to that sovereign in our name that it is with great surprise that we discern an unexpected change in his conduct. We now perceive the futility of his promises, which were made not in the expectation of fulfillment, but solely to take unnoticed what he needed in his own sole interests. Let him judge himself whether such intentions and conduct can prompt us to aid him. We would have sinned against ourselves had we delivered into his hands new means to be used against us. We cannot be sufficiently amazed at how he could deliver himself so blindly into the hands of his crafty uncles, who deflect his every act to their own advantage in order solely to preserve and entrench forever their complete domination of him and all affairs of state.

"To the Czartoryskis themselves you may say in our name that it might seem cleverly conceived to them that they have formed a conspiracy against national liberty, decided to eliminate it gradually, grasping at one and another phrase of their constitution. They have of course not succeeded and will not succeed in preventing us from seeing through their duplicity. We began to sense it long ago, but we tried to the very extreme to convince them by our sincerity and candor. We know perfectly well the essence and importance of the rule which they have tried to introduce of majority vote in fundamental national affairs, which concern general freedom and state policy. It is vain for them to flatter themselves with the hope that they can attack this subject in such a way in the present confederation and take up arms against us over the question of the dissidents. No, they could not have taken such deceitful measures against us, for every neighbor of Poland would agree readily to the composition of its entire government by dissidents, but would not agree that duties, taxes, and increase of its armed forces should depend on forty or fifty people loyal to the Czartoryskis. Yet, once we received this impression of their deceitful enterprise, they can easily understand how the interest of our empire, our own duty and position, and that disinterested and constant care which we have for the true welfare of the Polish republic and the secure welfare of each of its inhabitants, will force us to act against their scheme."

Sending Repnin this rescript, Panin wrote to him: "The time now clearly has come for us to break all ties with the Czartoryski princes and expose them to the world as intriguers, in whose hidden plans and intentions we never wished any part. The present confederation must be destroyed, naturally with the result that all innovations introduced by the Czartoryskis in the Polish government be buried under its ruins. I am impatiently awaiting a courier from you with news of what more has happened in this affair, what sort of success your new activities have met, and what the status is now of the matter of the dissidents. I pray, my friend, God help you. Describe to me in greater detail all your conversations and consultations with each of the new people with whom you enter into contact, their minds, characters, positions, so that I can get to know them myself."

But at the same time that Petersburg turned its rage upon the Czartoryskis, Repnin wrote that the king's brothers, a lord high chamberlain and a general, were supporting the king's bias against the dissidents much more strongly than the king's uncles, the Czartoryskis. In further dispatches the ambassador reported that he had made new contact with the Czartoryskis in furtherance of the goals assigned to him. As he put it, he was following the path which the Czartoryskis themselves offered through their doubts and discontents with the king, his brothers, and their party. The king and his brothers proclaimed that they would sooner die than retreat from upholding the confederation and preservation of the rule of majority vote in financial and military affairs.

The Czartoryskis acted completely differently. They saw the impossibility of implementing the changes, not only because of the opposition of Russia and Prussia, but also because of the resistance of a majority of the Poles. On the other hand, they wished to show the Russian empress their loyalty and their willingness to serve her in any way possible. Therefore, they refused to institute majority vote on the matters in question. This is why Repnin altered his comments about the Czartoryskis.

RUSSIA REACHES A DECISION

On November 3 he wrote: "The chief members of the party against the court here are: from Poland, the bishop of Cracow (Soltik) and from Lithuania, the bishop of Wilno and his father (the Masalskis). However, they have no people, or at the least, very few dependent upon them. Now they are united solely in their stubbornness and discontent with the court, which I am using as much as possible in my own endeavors. The former (Soltik) is vain, arrogant, and impudent, and the latter (Masalski) is quiet but deceitful. There is no firm basis in the one or the other. Time will tell whom we shall be able to choose as leaders of our party, for the matter of the dissidents now is turning everyone against us. Meanwhile, I think that the Czartoryskis ought to be managed."

Finally even the king told Repnin that he was abandoning the rule of majority vote. He asked naively several times whether Russia really would use force immediately were the Polish government not to abandon majority vote. Of course Repnin answered affirmatively. Stanislaw Augustus then began to speak as if he wished to restore the trust and complete agreement between Russia and Poland which now had been ruined by unfortunate circumstances. Repnin replied that everyone is satisfied by what he needs, and there is no other way to acquire friendship. The king asked whether Russian troops would be withdrawn from Polish territory after the conclusion of the Diet. Repnin replied that the dissident question might still keep the previous force there and cause new troops to be brought in. The king stated as before that although he was convinced personally of the need to grant the dissidents civil ranks, no one dared to make such a proposal. In fact, the conferences of the ministries with the bishops on the dissident question had not led to anything. Repnin argued in vain that the point about the secular rights of the dissidents did not concern the clergy. The king told him that the matter could not be resolved without the bishops. (Catherine noted opposite Repnin's report on this: "It might be necessary to try to buy some bishops; they are accustomed to piling up gold pieces.")

The chancellor of Lithuania informed Repnin that the ministry deemed it necessary to appoint a commission to study the dissidents' claims and that the bishops had agreed to this. But Repnin understood that they merely wished to prolong the affair by this and he answered that a commission could be charged only with a review of legal affairs: for example, which churches to take from the dissidents, and so on. But as concerned religious and civil rights, a decisive answer must be given at the present Diet. Meanwhile, Repnin wrote to Panin that the latter should react kindly to Count Rzewuski and, if possible, the Czartoryskis, and the king's marshal, Prince Liubomirski, in view of their cooperation in eliminating the majority vote rule and destroying the confederation. He especially cited the services of Prince Adam Czartoryski,[13] who had acted as chief agent in inclining the elder Czartoryskis to the ambassador's side. The meeting of the Diet on November 11 rejected the rule of majority vote. Repnin wrote Panin on this occasion in response to the latter's congratulations on this success. "I admit that I am very content to have rectified that which was corrupted at the convocation Diet." Catherine added, "I also congratulate him for this."

But at the same time Repnin commented on the difficulties of the dissident question. "Successful resolution is not within the powers of the king or the Czartoryskis. The best evidence of this is the rejection of the rule of majority vote which they introduced. It is indisputable that this latter measure was much more important and necessary for them, but, seeing the open chasm, they themselves carved up what was most valuable to them. They would do the same with the matter of the dissidents were they able, all the more since they are much cooler toward this question than the other. The fervor and mindlessness engendered by the urging of the clergy and the desire not to share royal favors with the dissidents are extraordinary. The king is in a state of despair which I cannot portray. When I approached him to thank him for his cooperation in eliminating the majority rule, he burst into bitter tears in public and was not in any condition to make a reply. Such grief shows how attached he was to this measure. If he could abolish it, he would satisfy our wishes in the dissident question as well, if he only could."

The king grieved, but the Czartoryskis clustered around Repnin, announced their loyalty to Russia, asked for return of their former favor, and slandered the king. "The chancellor of Lithuania told me," Repnin wrote, "that hour by hour the king distrusted him more, since their disagreement had mounted at this last Diet because of the opposition which the Czartoryskis had shown the king in favor of us, something the king would not have accepted except out of necessity. The chancellor added that, being assured of the king's agreement, however forced, it was necessary to establish all elements of a new alliance (with Russia). Through this they badly wished to diminish the demands of the king, since he asks so much that is superfluous."

The Diet adjourned on November 19. The pay of the armed forces was raised, a military school was ordered to be founded, but the demands of foreign powers in favor of the dissidents remained without satisfaction. All Warsaw impatiently awaited the courier from Petersburg with the reply to the decisions of the Diet. Repnin implored Panin that the answer be sent as quickly as possible. He wrote that "haste is highly necessary for the sake of secrecy and success in the matter of the dissidents, if we wish to make a beginning on it."

"Our dignity and the true interests of the empire entrusted to us by God demand that we at once carry to the desired conclusion this clear and solemnly begun affair," was Catherine's answer. The matter could be completed solely by means of a confederation of the dissidents. While the dissidents must be supported by Russian forces, in Petersburg they wished through this to attempt "to separate at last the king from the Czartoryski princes and draw the latter to our side. We should make them chiefs of our party, which they will constitute, and see if thereby we get what we desire with less work and fewer troubles." This is what Panin wrote to Repnin. In Panin's opinion, the Czartoryskis, the most prominent and richest people in Poland, ought to fear civil strife more than anyone. Since they were discontented with their nephew the king, one might propose to them as the sole means of averting all of the coming calamities the convocation of an extraordinary Diet at which the dissidents' demands should be satisfied and a form of government under the protection of Russia established with freedom of voting to control the power-hungry king and his henchmen. Panin also demanded that Repnin ascertain whether another confederation besides that of the dissidents might be formed, and whether the hetmen, especially Count Branicki, because of his well-known vanity, might be induced to take joint measures with Russia. Whatever the answer of the Czartoryskis, Panin wrote that the Russians already had determined to take extreme steps. Russian forces were ready to march, and at the end of February 1767 they would actually cross Poland's borders, three corps moving to Sandomir, Sluck, and Torun. As early as July the British ambassador in Petersburg, Macartney, had reported to his court Panin's words to him: "I would sooner sacrifice 50,000 men and abandon everything else than allow failure in our Polish affairs."

THE ROLE OF FREDERICK THE GREAT

Apparently Russia acted as one with its ally, Prussia, in the question of the dissidents. In reality Frederick II did not wish to grant the dissidents any advantages except religious toleration. First, he did not want to allow Russia greater influence in Polish affairs through equality of Poland's Orthodox subjects. Second, he foresaw great difficulties, the intervention of Catholic powers, and war. Frederick wrote to Benoit: "Keep it as a complete secret that in essence I will not be grieved if the dissidents are not successful. Do not reveal this to the Russians. Act as if I were very angry that all the labors devoted to the resolution of this affair have come to naught. It would be good and profitable if you could make some well-known people work against the dissidents, if they can just do it secretly, so that no one can find out who is prompting them. Tell Prince Repnin politely from me that I am sure that the intentions of the empress incline to tranquility and peace. I flatter myself with the hope that she will not carry the dissident question too far and will not ignite a new war on such a paltry pretext. I am ready to join my friendly proposals and declarations with the Russians in this matter, but I cannot countenance aggressive measures, which might upset social stability."

Benoit supported the king in his notion that the Russian intentions for the dissidents could not be realized. He wrote: "The Poles are beginning to see that they will be obliged to yield to force. But they speak with one voice that Russian forces will not remain in Poland forever, and as soon as the troops leave, the means will be found to make the position of the dissidents a thousand times worse than now. They will exterminate them or drive them out. The Catholics already secretly are swearing each other to this."

Aside from Poland, Frederick II was very unhappy with the Russian cabinet because it had tied him to its northern system, an alliance of the northern powers against the southern: France, Austria, and Spain. He was especially discontented by the fact that Russia wished to include Saxony in this alliance. Saxony was a state whose existence he could not tolerate with equanimity. In April, Count Solms [the Prussian envoy to Petersburg] presented the following note: "His majesty the king of Prussia, supposing it indisputable that a system of states united by family agreement (Austria, France, Spain) could be dangerous to the peace of Europe, would consider it very useful to accept in the Russo-Prussian alliance all sovereigns who propose to act together with Russia and Prussia against the schemes of the houses of Bourbon and Austria. However, it seems to his Prussian majesty that in the present situation few states and sovereigns are disposed to take such a view. Saxony is fully dependent upon the Viennese court. Bavaria is connected with Austria through the emperor's marriage. The electors [Kurfürsten] in the clergy are committed to the Austrian court because usually they are chosen from Austrian families. The elector of Westphalia is dependent upon France. As the elector of Hanover, the British king has his own party. The duke of Braunschweig is loyal to England. The people of Hesse incline to whomever pays them the most. It is dubious that the Dutch republic will wish to participate due to the extensive trade which the city of Amsterdam conducts with France. The Danes are in no condition to act unless they are given a healthy subsidy. As for the Swedes, one cannot count on them because of their well-known situation. His majesty concludes that only Poland can unite its interests with the interests of Russia and Prussia."

Frederick wrote to Solms: "I see that you do not fully agree with my policy. The Russian alliance is sufficient for me. Even if I do not receive any aid from them in case of war, I will still gain from the fact that Russia, as my ally, will not declare against me. This is enough for me. As for the English, they ought now to fear the French and Spanish. To conclude an alliance with them would mean entering into a new war, from which Prussia could gain no advantage. If I remain allied with

Russia, no one will threaten me and I will preserve the peace. These are the general ideas from which I do not at all wish to stray. I can agree to an alliance with England only on condition that this alliance would not obligate me to anything which might disturb the peace in Germany."

But Petersburg steadfastly hoped to dissuade Frederick from these ideas. In order to incline the Prussian king to the northern system, Panin sent Saldern, to whom the king had been very well disposed since the time of Peter III. Saldern was supposed to stop in Berlin en route from Poland to Denmark, ostensibly to inform the king about the progress of Polish affairs, especially about the customs question, which interested Frederick more than the dissidents. The king set May 8 to receive Saldern. On that day Saldern went to Charlottenburg together with Falkenstein.[14] Entering the king's study, Saldern found Frederick II standing in the middle of the room and began his speech: "Her imperial majesty of all Russia has ordered me to assure your majesty of her unbounded esteem (de son estime san bornes) and her unshakeable friendship (á toute épreuve). She also has commanded me to recount to you the state in which I found the king and Republic of Poland in relation to Prussia, and especially to present to you her views concerning many questions important to your majesty and to her."

"I am very grateful," the king replied, "for this new assurance of friendship on the empress' part. I desire nothing so much as preservation of that friendship. Now, without ceremony, let us get down to philosophizing and practical politics." Having spoken, Frederick began to pace around the room, in which one could hardly move six steps in a straight line. Saldern had wished to remain standing in the middle of the room, but the king ordered him to walk along with him.

"Well, how are they disposed to me in Poland?" Frederick inquired. Saldern answered that the king and all the ministers could not be better disposed to him; he offered as proof that the chief customs agency had been reduced to inaction and would be abolished completely at the next Diet. The king smiled and said: "You finished up that affair quickly in Poland, but it's all the same to me." Saldern replied that in his opinion, Poland could not show more respect for the advice of the empress and the wishes of his majesty. "That is looking at it as you interpret the affair," the king said, and expanded on the fact that it was absolutely necessary to leave Poland in its present situation. Nothing good would ever come of any sort of fundamental change; one had to think about the future. Although the present king was nothing to worry about, Poland's neighbors ought to have as a general rule that any change in the form of the republic could be harmful in the future.

"By the way," Frederick said, "are you still thinking about allowing the Poles to eliminate the *liberum veto*?" Saldern blushed and answered: "My lord, we have never considered that."

"What do you mean you never even thought of it?" Frederick interjected.

"I venture to assure your majesty," answered Saldern, trying to remain as calm as possible, "that neither the empress nor her ministers ever have thought seriously of permitting the Poles to do away with that distinguished custom. If the ministers of the empress spoke secretly with your majesty's ministers about this question and other Polish wishes, this was done with the intention of demonstrating great trust in your majesty and not hiding from you any of the proposals made then by the Poles, and only to gain the views and thoughts of your majesty on such an important question."

"If that is the case, then this is an entirely different matter," the king stated. Then he launched into a long monologue, stating that Russia and Prussia needed no other alliance than the one they had now and that he did not wish to be allied with anyone but Russia. Saldern countered with the opinion that Russia and Prussia needed to draw other powers into their alliance to affirm the northern system as completely independent. This was the sole means of insuring themselves against outside strife and doing a service to other states, which naturally ought to quail before the fearsome alliance of the Houses of Bourbon and Austria.

Frederick interrupted here: "I have said to you that there is nothing to fear from this alliance, which seems so fearsome to you, because they are all beggars without any money (ce sont de gueux)." Saldern continued to advance the necessity of the northern system, which naturally would include both active and passive states. The goal of this system, he stated, was the long-term preservation of peace in Europe, maintenance of a balance of power, and support of the Prussian monarchy, so necessary and valuable.

"All of this is well and good," the king noted, "but what do you want to say with your active and passive states?" Saldern answered that in the North there were three active states: Russia, Prussia, and Great Britain.

"Great Britain?" Frederick laughed. "You can count it out at present! The king is the weakest man in the world. He changes his ministers like shirts. What can you count on the British ministry for? Don't you know that the ministry already has changed and that the duke of Grafton has left his post? It may be that Count Egmont, the most ardent adherent of the Austrian house, will take his place. I ask you not to count on Britain."

Saldern replied that if one could not now count on Britain, there would come a time when the British government would assume a different look. Besides, in addition to Denmark and Sweden, where French influence had weakened significantly, one had to turn one's attention to Germany, to the states of Hesse, **Braunschweig**, and Saxony, which one could view as passive powers.

At these words, Frederick's eyes lit up. "Saxony," he said. "How can you rely on it? Saxony has close connections with Austria and the House of Bourbon. Is there any possibility in such an idea? Please tell me if there are emissaries from the court of Saxony in Russia who are dangling such chimeras before you."

"The feelings of the empress," Saldern answered, "are guided by wisdom and love for humanity, and have never been altered by illegal or suspicious means. The empress considered it necessary to be completely open with your majesty, especially in the case when views are involved completely in accord with the close alliance existing between Russia and Prussia, an alliance which should instill as much respect as trust in other states. The empress thought that the most reliable means of making the Russo-Prussian alliance the basis of peace and well-being in the North is to deal amicably and indulgently with the weaker powers and in this way to inspire their trust. As a result of this trust, we can draw them into the alliance peacefully and quietly. My sovereign presupposes that Saxony will make haste to turn away from the various interests of Austria, as soon as it finds it possible to do so safely."

Frederick listened to all this with his eyes fixed on the floor of the study and then said: "You have mentioned friendship and indulgence. This doesn't concern you. Let me deal with the Saxons, because affairs there involve my interests."

On May 13 Saldern had a second conversation with Frederick in the same study in Charlottenburg. The talk lasted three hours. "If you wish," the king began, "we shall review all the states and sovereigns of Europe and see whether we think alike. Let us begin with Austria, which is in a sorry financial position. Her debts must amount to 230 florins."

"But they say that the Austrian army is in very good shape," Saldern noted.

"This is more so on paper than in fact," answered the king. "They pay their generals half in specie and half in paper money. I don't fear the Austrians at all. They will abandon their old prejudices against me. The present emperor is my friend, I know this for a fact. He is grateful that I did not agree to the cession of Tuscany to his brother. This is a good ruler, peace-loving, and he hates the French. He never runs afoul in dangerous or duplicitous schemes. I answer for him."

"Might I dare to express my doubts," said Saldern, "whether the Austrian royal house can forget so easily the loss of Silesia? Sooner or later the Austrians may submit to the temptation to renew their claims."

"What will be, will be," answered the king, "but the Austrians will think twice before they do this."

"Quite true," noted Saldern, "the Austrians will think more than once before they try this for the fourth time. But there are means which will force them never to consider it."

"What means are these?" asked the king.

"Very simple," Saldern answered. "Your majesty, in alliance with Russia, ought to establish together with it a northern system with the sole aim of preserving peace. You should acquire friends, as the empress has done, and by this force Russia itself and its other friends to vouch for the preservation of the integrity of the Prussian monarchy."

"This is too complicated for me," said Frederick. "I need only the Russian alliance and I do not want any others."

"All this is fine for the present, but one must think about the future," Saldern objected, "especially when Russia, despite its awareness of its might, never will disregard peaceful means to try to win friends for itself, eliminate distrust, and attract to itself sovereigns forced out of fear to enter into alliance with other powers, who make them feel envious of the Russo-Prussian alliance and thereby win more friends for themselves."

"I am sure that others envy us," said the king, "but what does that matter to us? I repeat that neither Austria nor France nor Spain will cause us the least bit of trouble. Who, in your opinion, would wish to unite with them and increase the number of their friends?"

Saldern replied softly: "Some states, perhaps insignificant in terms of power, and all the ruler of Germany."

The king burst out laughing. "If there's no money, there's no German (point d'argent, point d'Allemand)," he said. Then with great eloquence, according to Saldern, Frederick expounded on the situation of Spain and France with the aim of proving that the Bourbon and Austrian allies were so weak that nothing need be feared from them. France, in Frederick's words, had not been able to straighten out its finances for ten years. His speech concluded with the notion that it was best of all for Russia and Prussia not to bother with any other alliance, to stand firmly together, and to *laugh* at everyone else.

"All this," Saldern remarked, "is completely just at the moment, but there are no assurances for the future. The Seven Years' War ruined the finances of the [southern] allies for the present, but they still had some means left. I do not presuppose that a new war could flare up in the course of the next ten years, but I am obliged to assure your majesty that the empress, my sovereign, sees the unification of the entire North into one system as a matter of extreme importance and necessity for the peace of Europe in the present and future. The empress is decisively inclined to demonstrate to Europe that the path of peace and moderation is most capable of restoring trust among all rulers who might find it to their advantage to join this system. The interests of Russia and Prussia, always inseparable, find here their strongest support. Russia looks upon this plan as the sole, most reliable means of preserving the integrity of the Russian and Prussian monarchies, and this integrity is the natural basis of the Russo-Prussian alliance. A sovereign so esteemed, so victorious, so covered with glory as your highness, will find the ways to success laid out and prepared by the generosity and kindness of my sovereign. The successes of heroes are always facilitated by their ability to acquire the good opinion of people and nations."

The king replied: "I still do not see any cause to hurry in such a complicated matter. I must admit to you that I do not like to deal with the English, because of the weakness of their present government and especially because I fear that they soon will be at war with France and Spain."

Saldern remarked that now was the most favorable time for concluding alliances, when all Europe was fully at peace. Those same causes which motivated the Austrian and Bourbon monarchies to unite and form the southern system forced the northern powers to insure themselves with a similar alliance.

"Solms writes," the king stated, "that you imagine the possibility of an agreement between Austria and France to divide Bavaria in case of the death of its elector. I admit frankly that I don't believe this." Saldern commented that in all probability the Austrian monarchy would not have divided its Italian possessions to the advantage of Archduke Leopold had France not wooed them with other hopes. The king answered: "No, I don't believe it! Impossible!" Then he abruptly turned to the subject of Holland. "You have a better opinion of this republic of merchants than I do. I know them too well. Trade is their god, their all. The stadholder[15] will never give them firmness or that exaltation of spirit which they lost long ago, for the last time in the battle at Fontenoy."[16]

Saldern noted that while the extent of their trade might force them to be careful in European political affairs, it was still true that the person of the stadholder usually gave much more power to the republic. "True," the king answered, "but we should await the succession of the new stadholder."

"Only don't lose time waiting," Saldern said.

The king again suddenly changed the subject and stated: "As for Denmark and Sweden, I understand that you can do anything that suits you. But one must have money. If you could only force the British to give some money! Why, you have an alliance with the Danes—force the British to give them a subsidy. Of course, you need Herculean labor for that." After saying this, Frederick bent over and whispered in Saldern's ear, as if someone were listening to the conversation: "The British are rubbish! (Les Angliais [sic] sont des miserables!)"

Saldern sang his own tune: "In order to make the British pay sub- sidies, one must show them the foundation of a firm northern system in which they find advantage for themselves."

"This is a *pia desideria* [sic] ," the king answered. "You have too high an opinion of them. I know them better than you do. Sweden is in the same spot as Denmark. The alliance between Sweden and England serves as the best proof that the British do not wish to do anything. It's true that Russia has done much so far and that it will have to continue on the same course to destroy French influence, if it wants to gain anything from what it has begun. Meanwhile, Sweden does not deserve to be considered as a real state. This nation has fallen so far that intelligent Swedes themselves recognize the fact. As for Poland, I will agree to any- thing that the empress does there. I want royal revenues to increase, for one must live on something. But I ask you with all my heart that there be no changes in the Polish constitution. All that would be harmful."

Saldern began to assure the king that the empress never had thought of making any substantive alteration in the form of the Polish govern- ment and more than anyone would assure that the laws of the republic were never violated. But along with this, Saldern requested Frederick to take into account the fact that it was very important for Russia that Poland replace Austria in its relations with Turkey. Austria had become more distant from Russia as a consequence of the Prussian alliance.

Looking attentive, the king asked: "But how do you wish to do this?" Saldern answered that he did not know for certain *how*, but he thought the most reliable means to be restoration of the rights of the dissidents and granting to the king some power on the basis of a *pacta conventa*. In this way the small Polish army would be disciplined in a respectable manner and could render aid in case of need.

"Both points will be extraordinarily hard to carry out," the king replied.

"I find no difficulties here," Saldern noted. "Many good things can still be done in Poland."

"I know this very well," the king stated, "but it is necessary to leave Poland in its lethargic state."

"Lethargy," Saldern replied, "is good and even necessary where the Poles might harm their neighbors. However, there are cases when a state becomes absolutely useless if one does not allow it certain powers in order to render aid to its allies. Russia and Prussia are capable of crushing the Poles at any minute if they attempt to use for ill that power given to them momentarily."

"I must admit that I do not know of these instances you speak of," stated Frederick.

"Here, for example, is one case," replied Saldern. "While I was in Poland, I found the king and all his chancellors predisposed to eliminate the Main Customs Office. However, because of a lack of power and activity both the king, with all his good inclinations, and his ministers, with their good intentions, could promise only to lobby for the elimination of the customs at the next Diet. The establishment of a permanent council in Poland during those two-year intervals between Diets would be useful not only to Poland but also to its neighbors."

"This seems to me a rational measure," the king stated, "but before it is permitted it must all be worked out quite well."

After this the king began to discourse on Saldern's departure to Copenhagen. Saldern noted that the king desired to be rid of him and meanwhile had said nothing about Saxony. Saldern resolved to ask him what to relay to the empress concerning her desire that the Prussians be less harsh in relations with Saxony. "Truly, I forgot," Frederick replied. He paced around the study twice and then answered. "The Saxons are a foul people. They wish to control all trade, which I cannot countenance with equanimity. My subjects suffer from that. Our commissioners are now conferring about this matter. I must have the liberty to deal with them as advantageously as possible for my country." Saldern said to this that the empress would be overjoyed to see that his majesty wished to convince Saxony by kindness, and that this would all the better draw Saxony completely away from Austria. Frederick then said with some irritation: "Let me work now. I will answer this evening." Saldern bowed and asked no more about Saxony. He noticed that this subject was very unpleasant for the king.

Frederick ceased to talk about politics and began to inquire about the health and capabilities of the grand prince. Then all at once he asked: "Is the empress really so busy with so much, as they say? I have been told that she works more than I do. True, she has fewer distractions than I. I am too much taken up by the military. You wouldn't believe how the smallest trifle bothers me."

"Lord," Saldern replied, "habits turn into obsessions. As for the empress, she works a lot and, perhaps, too much for her own health."

"Ah ha!" said Frederick, "ambition and glory are the mainsprings that move sovereigns to action." Saldern did not say a word about *so delicate a matter*. Frederick gazed at him intently and began: "There are many roads that lead to everlasting glory. The empress is on the main highway, to be sure." Saying this, he never took his eyes off Saldern. The latter understood that the king wished to hear something from him and offered: "Of course, the empress is consolidating the happiness of her own people and a significant proportion of humanity. She has a broad perspective, which encompasses the past, present, and future. She loves the living, without forgetting posterity."

"This is a great deal, this is worthy of her," the king noted and ended the conversation.

This conference irritated Frederick terribly, and his full fury fell upon the unfortunate Saldern, who had the temerity to appear with unpleasant proposals and support them. Frederick's earlier predisposition to Saldern turned to hatred. "The court of St. Petersburg," Frederick writes in his memoirs, "is discontented with the conduct of the Polish king and still more with the Czartoryskis, his uncles, who direct him. They sent one Saldern to Warsaw to watch over them, offer them proper counsel, and force them to conduct themselves with more moderation and wisdom. From Warsaw this diplomat came to Berlin armed with wide-ranging projects. Count Panin composed them and plays on his own vanity with them. Saldern has neither good manners nor a subtle mind. He took the tone of a Roman dictator to force the king to agree to the addition of England, Sweden, Denmark, and Saxony to the Petersburg treaty. Since this project was opposed completely to Prussia's interests, the king could not accept it. How could one really think that the king would enter into an agreement with England, after all the trials he has suffered at its hands? The help of Sweden, Denmark, and Saxony is equal to nothing, because one could not force them into action except with large subsidies. Besides, since they would be aligned with Russia, the king would have to share with them the influence which he hoped to acquire in Russia. Therefore, it was necessary to hold them off for a time, all the more since one should not multiply alliances without need. All these factors caused the king to refuse Saldern's proposals. This minister grew angry, considering himself a praetor of Popillius and taking his majesty as Antioch, ruler of Syria.[17] He wanted to issue laws to the sovereign. The king, who did not see himself as Antioch, sent the minister on his way as coldly as possible. He assured Saldern that he would always be a friend of Russia, but never its slave."

Rumors of the talks between Frederick and Saldern and the fact that both had parted dissatisfied reached Vienna. Benoit reported to Frederick that from the conversations of La Roche, an agent of the Moldavian *hospodar*, it was apparent that Austria had not lost hope of winning out in the battle for influence in Russia. They hoped to win Count Chernyshev to their side with gifts. Finally, they would separate the empress from the king of Prussia, for a certain coldness on her part toward Frederick had been noted as a result of his refusal of many of Saldern's proposals. But Solms pacified the king on this count. He wrote that the lack of sympathy which Catherine always had nurtured toward Maria Theresa now was being fortified in consequence of the suspicion and that out of Roman Catholic fervor the queen of Hungary and Bohemia was thwarting the plans of the empress of Russia in Poland.

However, Frederick could not calm down for a long time after Saldern's proposals. There were other annoying factors joined here: Russia's intervention in favor of Saxony; the luring of the famous mathematician, Euler, from the Berlin academy to the Russian, something which Frederick did not at all desire; the discontent which Russia had expressed that Frederick had raised postal rates; and, finally, the inattention of the Russian court to his propositions about the dissident affair. Frederick wrote Solms about the postal question: "The yoke which they wish to lay upon me is beginning to chafe terribly. I will happily be allied with the Russians, but until my eyes are closed I will not be their slave. You can say this to anyone who wishes to listen. I remain of the opinion that the Russian alliance is more advantageous to me than any other. On this basis, I have been more compliant with the projects of the empress than any other ally ever has been. But now I am changing and holding back because of the effrontery with which these gentlemen want to dictate laws to me within my own jurisdiction. I announce to you as my unshakeable will that I will never suffer this first step to be taken in Russia. Let God's will be done. You see how they treat Sweden and Poland. Should I, born an autocrat and remaining one to this day, fall under the yoke of a state to which I am allied but not subject? No, this will never be! I will preserve my independence until my eyes are closed. If these gentlemen wish to enslave me, it is better to quarrel with them now than tomorrow. If I yield once, Russia will start to poke into my most minute affairs, decide everything, and treat me as the Turks treat the hospodar of Wallachia."

Concerning the dissident question, the king did not cease to insist that one must be content with religious freedom. To attain rights for the dissidents equal to those of the Catholics was the kind of nonsense that was not worth provoking such strong movements. Frederick continued also to proclaim his apprehension about Austrian intervention. However, Solms had heard a curious report about Austria from Panin, who requested Solms to take his words as emanating directly from the empress. "If the Viennese court wishes to fight, the empress is not at all afraid. She is ready to wage such a war that Austria will repent. If Austria intervenes in Polish affairs under the pretext of protecting Catholicism, Russia will arouse all the non-Catholics in Hungary and other Austrian provinces."

THE TURKISH THREAT

Besides Austria, Turkey might also intervene in Poland. We have seen with what joy the empress learned of the possibility of fulfilling an old desire of the Russian government to have a consul in the Crimea. It is easy to understand that the necessity of recalling Nikiforov [the Russian consul in the Crimea] as a result of events must have caused great disappointment in Petersburg. Obrezkov[18] received instructions to lobby with all his might for permission to send a new envoy to the Crimea. But all efforts came to naught. The Porte maintained that the presence of a Russian consul in the Crimea was impossible because of the extreme opposition of the Bakhchisarai clergy. The Porte could not force the khan to receive a consul because the khan was an independent ruler in domestic affairs. Even were they to decide to force the khan to accede, no good would come of it, for the khan and especially the clergy would find means for undermining the new consul. This might produce unpleasant results for both courts.

Panin noted on Obrezkov's report of the Porte's answer: "Of course these last objections from the Turks have a rational basis. It is evident that they believe in good faith the statements here of the Crimean khan, and harbor no pretense or evil intentions. I can see that now, as before, there is no great need to force them. However, we must insist that in not receiving a consul from us, a neighboring power, we cannot countenance, without doubting their sincerity, the fact that the Crimean khan permits at his court a consul from France, which has no other interest there than making trouble between the neighboring states. Obrezkov was written about this earlier, but surprisingly he makes no mention of what use he made of this argument or why he did not use it." The empress appended: "Add to this that if the intrigues of the French consul are to be tolerated, we need our own consul to counter them. They quarrel easily, as is evident from the khan's report on Mozdok, where, I expect, there never were as many cannon (on which I will demand a definitive report) and were not as many people as needed for so many weapons."

On the other hand, the men of Zaporozhe complained that the Tatars were cutting timber in their lands and were moving Tatar settlements closer to the Russian borders. Obrezkov inquired whether he need demand satisfaction from the Porte on the basis of the article of the peace

treaty which stated that if something occurred which was not mentioned in the treaty both sides should seek swiftly a means of eliminating
the harm. Obrezkov added that the Turks were taking advantage of this
article in many instances often having nothing at all to do with treaty
matters.

"Except in extremity," Panin noted, "it is best not to act in a way
that will give the Turks, those extreme and proud ignoramuses, unbridled
in all their caprices, any grounds to refer to this article and demand
new conditions and decrees. As much as the encroachment of these
settlements and the present wood-cutting discomfits and harms our men
of Zaporozhe, one must all the same not take their complaints literally,
for they are usually exaggerated without limit, especially from such a
crude lot as the people of Zaporozhe. In this case it is necessary first of
all to send a loyal representative to the spot to investigate and obtain
accurate and reliable information. In this way one can judge and order
that which is more useful: whether to curtail the settlements, even if
they are in truth large and important for us or whether not to legalize
the custom of the Turks to demand something in return from us for all
new decrees." On her part, Catherine noted: "The dispatch of an unquestionably loyal man is highly necessary, since I still doubt whether
there is anyone besides artisans there. I have not heard about the timber."
Whereas these small conflicts did not herald serious consequences, the
conflicts over Poland were difficult to foresee. Events on the other side
of Europe seemed more deserving of attention.

OSTERMANN AND THE SWEDISH DILEMMA

In Stockholm Ostermann[19] was lobbying for the most rapid conclusion
of an agreement with Sweden and England. He wrote: "No one more
influential than Senator Rudenschild has fought against acceptance of
the British treaty. It is highly necessary to dissuade him for he, one
might say, passionately has defended French interests in the Senate like
a half-wit. It is too bad only that we cannot separate him alone from
the other two prominent opponents, for his downfall might then be
effected more easily."

"Well-intentioned" people[20] also agitated for a quick marriage of the
heir to the Swedish throne, Prince Gustav, with a Danish princess. The
king, queen, and the French party opposed this marriage. This had to
make Ostermann favor the union all the more strongly. On the other
hand, the Danish envoy, Schack, requested him to aid in achieving the
union, and argued that the Danish court would act in complete concord
with Russia in respect to the Swedish Diet. Panin informed Ostermann
"in extreme confidence" that the Danish court was quite satisfactory to

Russia. Panin wrote: "Since you have in your hands our principal views on the direction of affairs between our neighbors Denmark and Sweden, you have no more to do than to arrange the marriage as speedily as possible and thereby display to them both that the primacy of her imperial majesty serves and henceforth will serve them as the greatest hope for the maintenance of peace and quiet. You can strengthen still more the intention expressed among our friends that the crown officials demand from the king only designation of the time of the wedding. You should state that the marriage already has been agreed upon by treaty between the Danish and Swedish courts. If the leaders of our party want you to appeal directly to the crown prince about this wedding, this is how you can do it. Tell him that while her imperial majesty leaves him to his own inclinations in such a delicate affair, she views it as useful for both himself and Sweden. Therefore she hopes that it is in agreement with the predilections of his highness."

Having spent up to 10,000 in Swedish coin, Ostermann managed to achieve a decision in favor of the English alliance in a secret committee. Ostermann revelled in the fact that the French ambassador and his informants, Fersen and Sinkler, had been mistaken in their hope to bribe the secret committee. But Ostermann asked the leaders of his party not to count in any way on his triumph in the secret committee and to be careful, because the French party hoped to receive additional financial support from the Spanish court. The king was much more calm than before, and in those still waters there lurked some hidden scheme.

The treaty with England was concluded and the marriage postponed, although on the night of February 24 a notice was affixed to a column. It stated that now was the time for all true patriots to come together and not to allow Russia and Denmark to place a yoke upon Sweden, since there was no lack of leaders or money. Petersburg was disturbed greatly by the continuing session of the Swedish Diet, on which much Russian money was being spent. But Ostermann demanded new funds and in April received 100,000 rubles for a conclusion of the Diet in accordance with Russian desires. Besides this, Sweden was counting on Russia for some unpaid subsidies, and the "well-intentioned" people inquired of Ostermann whether this debt might be paid in grain, namely by sending 50,000 rubles worth of grain over six years. Catherine wrote to Panin on this report from Ostermann: "Nikita Ivanovich, this year we have shortages ourselves. I gave the grain that was ready last year in Riga to the military stores."

Meanwhile, the hatred of the king and queen for the Russian party rose to the extreme. At an assembly at court they refused to look upon Senator Kaling or invite him to dinner because he had received the

Russian Order of St. Andrew. The crown prince also turned his back on him, but he let it be known to the "well-intentioned" people that they should not think him discontented with them. He acted in this way only toward Kaling, with whom his father was displeased. One of the so-called "well-intentioned" group noted to the prince that such conduct might cause the people to turn cold toward him. Therefore, he should not follow the example of his mother. The prince replied that the queen had indeed chosen a dangerous course.

Ostermann suspected that the queen had chosen yet another path to reach her goals. In May a peasant rebellion flared up in Westergota province and Ostermann detected some signs by which one might guess that the French party had a hand in it and that the revolt might serve as a means for the restoration of autocracy. Ostermann turned to the Danish emissary, Schack, and told him that in a similar situation he, Ostermann, enjoyed plenipotentiary powers to act in concert with Schack. However, the Prussian envoy, Cocceji, confirmed that his court was against the restoration of autocracy in Sweden, but did not announce any intention of cooperating with Ostermann. He stated only that, in his opinion, matters would not proceed that far. To this, Catherine remarked: "Nevertheless, the secret article of the treaty obliges his Prussian majesty to cooperate with us in assuring that nothing be done to alter the form (of the Swedish government) of 1720."

Ostermann continued to send news of the growth of the revolt and its aims. It was rumored that the rebels intended to march on Stockholm, kill the nobility, depose the king because of the weakness of his administration, and raise the crown prince to the throne with autocratic powers. Another rumor made the rounds that the insurgents wished only to eliminate the arbitrary rule of crown officials and give more power to the person to whom it belonged. Ostermann acknowledged the latter as probably true, since he thought he discerned the work of Sinkler in the popular indignation. The chief agitator among the peasants, one Hoffman, was caught and the troubles subsided.

But the trial of Hoffman gave rise to a new struggle between the parties in the Diet. The "well-intentioned" people wished to establish a statutory judicial commission of three ranks. The French party opposed this strongly, in the fear that their opponents, now stronger, would take advantage of the situation to conduct personal persecutions. Ostermann wrote: "I am not in a position to report all the threats, impudence, and militancy of the opposing side not to allow the formation of a commission. In the entire session of the Diet I have needed money at no time so badly as I do on this critical occasion."

Finally, Count Fersen[21] recognized that the opposition was stronger. He entered into talks with the heads of the Russian party, and agreed not to hinder the formation of a commission, as long as no individuals were persecuted. On the other hand, the French ambassador spoke about this several times with Ostermann "in a manner of particular openness." Ostermann assured him that now, as before, all measures would be taken to assure that no individuals were persecuted, if Breteuil[22] would only persuade his friends to stop their "impudence." The ambassador vowed that there would be no "impudence." The king and especially the queen were greatly irritated by all this. They wanted nothing to do with the "well-intentioned" party, and they were not very happy with the leaders of the French party, for the queen was adamant in her wish that they oppose the foundation of a commission to the last extremity.

In the middle of July Ostermann sent word to Petersburg that the French ministry had adopted an entirely new policy toward Sweden. The French no longer wished to rely upon any Swedish party, which was subject to the constant danger of subversion and, therefore, could give no consistent assurance of carrying the cause it supported. France therefore decided to effect a basic change in the form of the Swedish government, namely, to restore the autocracy. If the autocracy were restored, it might well be that the king could not be forced to act in agreement with France's views, but this future and merely potential evil was far preferable to the real tyranny of the present system, which forced one to depend upon legislative parties. To implement this decision, the French were just awaiting a plan which Breteuil was supposed to send from Stockholm.

Forwarding this information, which he had acquired from the British ambassador, Ostermann wrote to Panin: "I do not think that they wish to implement this pernicious plan in the current Diet, which would really be desperate and, in fact, doubtful. But according to my most reliable information, it could easily happen that the French ambassador will entice the court here with such alluring prospects for the future and attempt to consolidate more and more his influence over the king and queen. Meanwhile, he and his band will whip up hatred for the present form of government in the nation. To this end, they will scatter money all over the provinces. From the following, one can see that Sinkler truly intends to cooperate with such a plan. After the banquets given at Hermanson and Landingshausen, Sinkler insisted that Count Fersen and his creatures should get rid of the name 'hats' for his party because this name is not in public favor. Instead, the new party should be called 'the land party.'[23] Fersen objected at first, but then agreed. 'Call it what you like,' he said, 'just as long as we are saved from the tyranny of the present ruling party.'

"They also decided there to tell the people how Russia along with Denmark and England had bought up half of the Swedish nation, in order to administer Sweden like one of their provinces. England had ruined prominent Swedish merchants to increase the market for its own manufactures. Russia and Denmark had subverted the previous ministry, which had guarded Swedish independence so zealously. They wish to publish a book to this effect and spread it about the provinces. In order to thwart such a malicious plan, I agreed with our friends that they should describe in print their own actions for the good of the state and all the harm which France has done Sweden from the very start of their alliance."

In August Ostermann reported that the constitution which had been drawn up by the "well-intentioned" party in agreement with Russian wishes had passed without obstacle in the chief committee of the Diet. Panin wrote on the report: "This is a deed which resolves once and for all the stability of the Swedish form of government. Your majesty's predecessors were never able to achieve this, even though, of all our previous worries about Sweden, which sometimes truly alarmed us, this has been the most important." But Catherine added: "I propose to congratulate you when all the estates agree to it."

The constitution passed a full assembly of the estates. The boundaries between the three branches of the government were defined precisely. In the future, national legislators were not to interfere in conferrals of ranks or appointments. If the king rejected a nomination of the Senate three times, the nominee would be confirmed without royal approval. The power of appointment of the chancellor of justice was granted, however, to the legislators of each successive Diet " . . . because," wrote Ostermann, "the present chancellor of justice, Stockenstrem, is a creature of France. If he remains in his post he can take revenge on many of our party and block the implementation of measures taken at this Diet." It specified that henceforth no clarifications, amendments, or emendations to the fundamental laws could be approved in the same Diet which proposed them, but only in the next Diet. Ostermann found this point most difficult of all to carry, because it deprived the opposition of the possibility of changing the constitution in the coming Diet.

The king and queen repaid the party favoring Russia on the occasion of the wedding of the crown prince. Ostermann informed his court of the special favors which their majesties showed the entire French gang and their clear distaste for the "well-intentioned" party, especially the land marshal, whom the king, queen, and crown prince would neither look at or speak to. When the land marshal greeted the crown prince on behalf of the Senate and the legislators, the prince did not honor him with an answer. The queen attempted to demonstrate that she was very pleased with the marriage. She treated the bride kindly, in order to *surround* her completely with French creatures, as Ostermann put it, and keep the well-intentioned away from her. The Spanish and especially the French ambassadors were shown unusual favor.

Despite the triumph of the "well-intentioned" party at the last Diet, Ostermann sent Panin disturbing news in early November. The opposition was using all means to force the convocation of a new, extraordinary Diet. They spoke of this Diet as an undoubted fact, and when the Russian party showed them that the newly-passed financial edicts completely precluded the necessity of an extraordinary Diet, they laughed in reply that they had other means besides finances to place the Senate in such difficulties that it would have to resort to convocation of a special Diet. Ostermann finally learned what these means were. The king would fasten upon some dispute with the Senate and tell that body that in view of the weakening of his prerogatives he intended to cease attending the Senate and considering any matters. He demanded a special session of the Diet. Meanwhile, he intended to isolate himself. Catherine wrote on the report: "Well, God go with him." The French party hoped that upon convocation of the Diet the representatives, out of pity, not only would not allow the king to abdicate his administrative responsibilities, but would return to him all the rights and powers taken from him and grant him even more than he had possessed earlier. Catherine wrote here: "To give in pity cela est bien commun (is very trite) [sic]." The king cited the limitation of his powers and refused to sign the new constitution.

DENMARK AND THE HOLSTEIN QUESTION

As Russia's struggle in Sweden against France grew more intense, the relations of the court of St. Petersburg with Denmark became more important. These relations were very good, but Denmark could not be at peace while Holstein remained in Russian hands and the Holstein question remained unsettled. Denmark had been calm during the reign of Elizabeth, but what was not threatened during the brief tenure of Peter III? Now Denmark breathed easier with Catherine's accession to the throne, but who could be sure that Paul would not look upon Holstein just as his father had? Panin gave the following report on this situation: "The construction of a special general system in the North is and should be the prime question of current Russian foreign policy. While the small principality of Holstein remains in its present position, there can never be a sound peace in the North. Consequently, in the future there must be constituted there the kind of system independent of outside powers which alone might preserve complete balance in Europe. Denmark cannot and will never rely on Russia with complete trust as long as there remains the slightest hint of a stumbling block in Holstein affairs. Until

then Denmark will of course remain with France and Austria and tune
its strings to their pitch in order to seek protection and aid at these
courts every time the question of Holstein is raised. Surely France and
Austria will try always to maintain this obstacle in order thus to keep
Denmark forever dependent upon them, just as it has been up to now. If
it is therefore necessary that the special Northern system sometime reach
perfection, the time now has come to lay the basis for it. The youth of
his imperial highness the grand prince can serve now as a basis for taking
preparatory measures regarding all sources of discord. This can be ordered
provisionally by her imperial majesty and then will be put into practice
when his highness reaches maturity. One can say almost without error
that now the basic foundation of that illustrious Northern political edifice which I deem useful and necessary for the fatherland is being laid.

"True, Peter the Great considered the chief item of his policy some
sort of acquisition in Germany. To this end he directed all his deeds,
but times and circumstances are changing the rules. In leading his people
out of ignorance, Peter the Great considered it a tremendous achievement to make them equal to powers of the second rank. These powers
derived their influence in general European affairs more from member-
ship in the German community, for there they are the strongest among
a multitude of small princes and they can play a special role in Imperial
affairs, connected with general European questions, something which
their real power otherwise would not allow them to do. With this in
mind, Peter contemplated and attempted to prepare for union with the
duchy of Holstein. Although the duchy itself was small, under Russian
rule it would give Russia a voice in the German Empire. Peter could
make use of this in the course of affairs according to his own interests
of spreading his fame, power, and influence, which only then had begun
to grow through his efforts.

"In subsequent times the glory and importance of our fatherland obviously outgrew such narrow bounds and Russia rose by itself to full
equality with the leading powers in Europe. Nevertheless, this established
preconception remained unchanged, in full force, and guided all our
enterprise. This point of view naturally was reinforced by all the abilities
of the Viennese court in order to keep Russia somewhat dependent upon Vienna in German affairs. But now, under the wise and beneficial
rule of her imperial majesty, when Russia is esteemed by all of Europe
for itself and a real and firm foundation of our own independent system
has been laid (a system which gloriously and beneficially produced the
selection of the king of Poland), we should not consider seeking issues
to affirm our prominence, but should be governed by the course of
events and preserve peace and order in our empire. Her majesty herself

has recognized and determined that nothing can facilitate this so much as gathering the Northern powers into a general union and alliance under Russian guidance. Remaining silent about all other circumstances relating to this subject, I find only that I must note that, although through Holstein we might draw Denmark into a permanent alliance with us, Holstein itself can hardly be considered an important acquisition, given Russia's estimate of its status and its present level of power and renown in Europe.

"It is of much less use to equate possession of Holstein at any time with a general Northern alliance. The value of the alliance is obvious, real, and indisputable, while the advantage of holding Holstein vanishes completely if you properly construe the small size of that part of the principality which belongs to the grand prince, along with its inconvenient location, so far from Russia. One must add that in the past Denmark has proposed to exchange the duchies of Oldenburg and Delmenhorst for the grand prince's portion of Holstein. Such a proposition is in conflict with the most basic principles of Russian foreign policy. Such a great empire, with its power now thoroughly established, of course should never need to take such poor little scraps of land in any exchange. For the Russian realm to possess such crumbs in Germany, and to suffer the feudal domination of the Austrian court, its supremacy, or even the bounds of the justice of the Imperial court in the mixed-up body of the German Empire, would mean to get into endless disputes over borders and competition for power and jurisdiction with our strongest neighbors. According to the present principles of our foreign policy, Russia does not need a single inch of land in Germany to increase its might. It is more illustrious for us to have nothing there, but to swing the balance of power in Europe as well as in the German empire in every instance through our strong alliances, especially the general Northern alliance. For these reasons the exchange of the duchies of Oldenburg and Delmengorst proposed by Denmark would serve the Russian empire only in that it would turn it to the use and satisfaction of the relatives and lazy servitors of his imperial highness the grand prince."

Catherine agreed with this opinion and Saldern was sent to Denmark and Holstein to settle the matter. He did not go, however, in the capacity of an ambassador, a post taken first by Korff and then General Filosofov.

On January 4, 1766, in his first report, Korff relayed news of the death of King Frederick V, who was succeeded by Christian VII. At first everything remained as before. The most influential personage under the late king had been Chief Marshal Count Moltke. The new king reconfirmed him in all his positions, but it was rumored that the queen, the grandmother of the young Christian VII, would have a great influence upon him. "Consequently," Korff added, "the future of many individuals here remains obscure." On March 27 Korff died and was replaced by Major General Filosofov. Until his arrival the secretary of the embassy, Baron Fersen, was to inform Panin of developments in Copenhagen. On July 8 Fersen reported that Count Moltke would have to resign all his posts because he had not pleased the old queen during the previous reign.

Filosofov did not arrive in Copenhagen until the end of the year. He learned from Saldern that the Danish court was in a sorry state. The only man with whom business could be done was Bernstorff, but even he was not in a secure position, and Saldern was lobbying for support for him. "I have been here two weeks already," Filosofov wrote, "and my comrade a bit longer, but no one—not the king himself, nor his ministers, have held any substantive conversations with us. When we wish to draw them out on a serious matter, one can see from their answers their complete ignorance. Therefore, it seems that necessity demands support with all our powers of Bernstorff as the only reliable instrument capable of cooperating with us in achieving all of the advantages which we desire from this court. Although the confidence of the queen in Bernstorff has been restored completely, thanks to the initiatives of my colleague and my own presentations in the matter, since the extraordinary, immoderate frivolity of the king and his daily altering relationships to everyone without exception do not permit reliance on his present predisposition to Bernstorff, I find it necessary to make a precautionary report that in case of Bernstorff's fall, if our other means and approaches through other people do not suffice to restore him, I think we should politely tell the king himself that if he doesn't place all his trust in Bernstorff during negotiations that we will be forced to break off negotiations and demand new orders from his court. We know that our sovereign has counted on a great success in these negotiations in view of the acknowledged capabilities of Bernstorff."

RELATIONS WITH BRITAIN

In London, the elderly Gross died even before Korf. He was replaced by Count Aleksei Musin-Pushkin. Until the latter's arrival affairs were handled by a relative of the late embassy councillor. On the basis of the talks still dragging on about a trade agreement and alliance between England and Russia, Gross wrote Panin that given its present domestic circumstances, England could offer only weak assistance in the establishment of a strong northern system. The present ministers encountered hardships at every turn and were subject to constant danger of loss of their positions. There was no agreement among them, and they enjoyed the trust of neither the king nor the people. In the words of British historians, ". . . the excellent intentions and generally excellent measures of Lord Rockingham's administration did not suffice to avert the evil stemming from the personal failings of Lord Rockingham. For want of a great center of control, the entire system was subject to disruption." Finally the expected change came. The noted Pitt, Lord Chatham, entered the ministry. Meanwhile, Lord Macartney[24] sent Panin one tearful note after another begging him not to delay conclusion of the trade agreement, although its confirmation already had been announced in Britain.

The treaty was stalled on one article. In the Russian text a passage concerning new regulations on trade stated that British merchants would enjoy the same benefits from such new decrees as did the empress' subjects. The British demanded that this article be worded as follows: "Any new law shall in no manner restrict or limit the trade of British merchants in Russia, nor alter the substance and nature of that trade." The imperial cabinet would not agree to this change. Panin listened attentively to all of Macartney's speeches and arguments, and replied: "I see that we shall never have a trade agreement."

Macartney then presented a note. "In our country," he wrote Panin, "political and mercantile interests cannot be separated. Britain's might is founded on trade. Do you really wish to demonstrate before the entire world your lack of respect for this basis of our greatness just out of formality? Is it possible for anyone to believe that the statement which we demand could injure the dignity of the empress? Her imperial majesty possesses not only heroic virtues, but also gentleness and moderation. She will not refuse this special favor which the king, my sovereign, will perceive as shown personally to him. The constant aim of Britain's policy consists of satisfying the empress. To this end the king sent a minister to Stockholm, despite the insult visited on him there. In the cause of Russian interests, he overlooked the insult. To please the empress, he befriends her friends. For example, not long ago he made an overture to the king of Denmark. To please the empress, once again he is sending a minister to the court of Berlin. This minister is instructed to cooperate in furthering all Russia's interests. Should the empress remain immovable, what shall I report to my sovereign? That she prefers a minor point (*un punctilio*) not only to the ardent desire of the king to acquire her friendship but also to the happiness of humanity? The establishment of the northern system will assure peace and happiness not just in our century, but for distant posterity. Are we just mildly degraded as a consequence of the empress' repeated refusals? Does she really refuse to uplift us and to appear so much the greater in her magnanimity as well as attention to maintenance of her dignity and renown? We trust her completely and would be content with a verbal promise from her. But who will vouch

that all Russian sovereigns will be like her and that her life will be as
eternal as her glory? I pray you take heed of the difference between the
British constitution and the constitution of your grand and awesome
empire and the fine borders which separate the power of the sovereign
from the privileges of the people in our system. If, to our good fortune,
your excellency were a minister in England, you would penetrate the
genius of our constitution and forgive us our deficiencies. You would
look lightly upon our weaknesses. Your exalted rationality would penetrate the secrets of our policy and you would see what we are able to do
and what we dare not do. Do I not know how much we are obligated to
the abilities of the man who was able to overcome Swedish prejudices
and Danish envy, and make Russia the judge of the destiny of the North?
And yet at that very minute when a brilliant future has opened before
our eyes, when one small concession on your part would suffice to
glorify the empress' reign and the wisdom of your counsel, out of pure
formality (insignificant for you and necessary for us) you will abandon
this great system which holds Europe in a balanced position, a most
beautiful system, which a political genius thought up and will make the
era of Catherine the most illustrious in the annals of world history. Do
you really wish to lose the chance to subordinate Great Britain to your
conceptions, to force it to join with your allies and cooperate under
your leadership because of such a trifle?"

"When we were working to renew the trade agreement," Panin answered, "our chief aim was the restoration of complete mutual equality.
The British statute (the Navigation Act) limits the participation of
foreigners in British commerce. An article must be included as a coun-
terweight to this act. That is why we have reserved the right to make
some subsequent domestic regulation which will strengthen and spread
Russian maritime trade. This right cannot be denied without clear injustice and infringement upon the independence of our government. If
a government is deprived of the power to act in its domestic self-interest,
what is left of an independent government?

"Can an existing constitution be more sacred than the liberty to
establish a similar constitution elsewhere, if the new one is deemed advantageous? One state would begin to dictate laws to another if it stated
that 'we have laws which long have brought us great profit; you do not
have similar laws; the present state of affairs favors us, so support it in
all its inviolability!' Trade might be the basis of British policy, but trade
is not destroyed solely because there is no treaty specifying the conditions under which it shall be conducted. Our mutual needs coincide and
give rise to the distinction which we make between British and Russian
subjects and subjects of other powers. We support with all our power

the political relations which unite us. The difficulty which has been encountered in ratification of the trade treaty cannot change the relations
between the empress and the king or violate the system which both
courts envision to keep the peace in the North. An alliance presupposes
the same unity of interests as a trade treaty. The obstacles encountered
in concluding the trade agreement should not dispirit us. On the contrary, we should attempt ardently to conclude an alliance which will
demonstrate to Europe that no obstacle can separate Russia's political
system from Britain's. We will demonstrate this first by how we deal
with English merchants in Russia in the absence of a treaty. By this conduct we will demonstrate that we are able to distinguish our friends."

In conjunction with his unsuccessful struggle Macartney wrote to his
ministry: "I must note that both states are lost in dealing with one another. In Petersburg they imagine that the court of London can force
the British nation to embrace their ideas as easily as the Russian empress
can force her subjects to submit to her decrees. Although I exerted un-
common effort in order to explain to them the difference between both
governments, they cannot or will not understand. Our mistake with them
lies in the fact that we view them as a civilized people and deal with
them as such, when they do not at all deserve such an appellation. I
daresay that the Tibetan state or the holdings of Prester John deserve
the same consideration. Not one of the ministers here knows Latin, and
few possess basic literary knowledge. Pride is the child of ignorance and
therefore it is not surprising that the actions of the court here sometimes
smack of vanity and arrogance. To introduce Grotius and Pufendorf to
the Petersburg ministers is the same as to discuss Clark and Tillotson
with the Turkish Divan.

"I have been told that the usual ceremonies and formalities employed
in other courts have been introduced here only during the present reign.
Both Panin and the vice-chancellor have assured me that during the reign
of the Empress Elizabeth, Bestuzhev[25] signed all treaties, conventions,
and declarations without authorization from the sovereign. It is under-
standable that international law can make little headway in a country
where there is nothing resembling a university.

"Since they are barbarians and ignorant in everything which might
facilitate intellectual development and discovery, I hardly fear their successes in trade and navigation. Like children, they are enticed by every
new idea, pursue it for a while, and then abandon it when a new one
captures their imagination.

"The decrees of Peter I in 1718 were based on our Navigation Acts,[26]
but I do not think that any seafaring power has experienced any harm
from the former. Their passion for the sea vanished so rapidly that under

Peter II, Prince Dolgoruky[27] issued a decree which halted all shipbuilding. Under the Empress Anna they altered their opinions once again and
renewed their previous system. Despite this, all their subsequent commercial ventures have been accompanied by loss, misfortune, and embarrass-
ment. Their stubbornness in the present instance stems purely from
arrogance. It is much more difficult to overcome a Russian in a matter
of pride than in one where real interests are involved. It is my ultimate
understanding that it is completely impossible to persuade them to
accede to our demand. Therefore, I think that it is necessary to ratify
the treaty, for otherwise we might lose a great deal."

When a foreign envoy began to abuse Russia and the Russians in
strong terms, such as accusing them of barbarism and ignorance, it was
usually a sign that the Russian court had been able to preserve its honor
and interests. Angry with Panin, Macartney informed his ministry with
pleasure of the weakening of Panin's influence. He stated that Panin had
fallen passionately in love with Countess Stroganov, the daughter of the
former chancellor, Vorontsov; she was seeking a divorce from her present
husband. As a result of his unfortunate passion, Panin had grown careless
and disorganized; his affairs had come to a halt, and he himself had lost
the esteem of polite society, which could not forgive such infatuation in
a man of his years and position. His enemies pointed to the bad example
set by the minister and, more important, tutor of the heir to the throne.
The Orlovs were Panin's chief enemies. Upon Saldern's departure, Panin's
chief friends were the Chernyshevs.[28] Unfortunately for Macartney,
these relationships did not alter the status of the trade treaty, and he
was forced to sign it in the form which Panin demanded.

The trade treaty was concluded, and only the treaty of alliance remained, which England also would have signed gladly. London liked the
northern system, opposed to the southern powers but, as before, there
was a stumbling block: the absolute refusal of England to mention
Turkey in an alliance; that is, to be obligated to aid Russia against
Turkey. In early 1767 Macartney wrote to his ministry that the sole
basis of an alliance acceptable to the Russian court would be agreement
in the event of discontent in Sweden or disturbances in Poland where
France openly aided the former or Austria the latter. In either case,
Russia would find the British alliance essential.

RUSSIAN SUPPORT OF POLISH DISSIDENTS

Macartney's expectations appeared to be realized when uprisings broke
out in Poland. In early 1767 Repnin asked Panin whether it was necessary
to restore all old rights to the dissidents, excluding only the instances

of the chief hetman. Repnin also inquired whether the number of dissident deputies in the Diet should be limited or made equal to the number of deputies from the Catholic nobility. Panin replied that this matter should be raised with the Poles in various ways, depending upon who asked him about it. Those who were indifferent and belonged to no party should be told that the dissident question essentially involved two separate questions: ecclesiastical and civil. Therefore Russian concerns were separate, and addressed each question.

In reference to the ecclesiastical question, the truth was clear and had been recognized at the last Diet even by the Polish clergy. The dissidents were oppressed unlawfully and unjustly. Consequently, the Russians demanded the elimination of established unjust practices and restoration in the future of full freedom of worship to the dissidents.

As far as civil rights were concerned, the Russians from the beginning had advanced them as a topic for negotiations. Thus, the Russian intention was to settle the matter amicably along rational lines. The Russians would not alter their intentions even now (although the matter had gone to extremes due to the intransigence of the Polish court) were the opposing party to recognize its mistakes, wish to avoid the dangers threatening the republic, and set out to settle the affair openly and peacefully. If it were wished sincerely to preserve peace in the country, the dissidents would not present excessive demands and would be content with anything that assured them a specified equality with their fellow citizens.

"But those who, being unhappy with the court, have sought the protection of her majesty, who have constituted a special party, and even have tried to form an open and formal confederation, should be given another reply. It should be suggested to them that her majesty harbors no harmful intentions against Catholicism. On the contrary, she allows its preeminence over other faiths. We will agree willingly that Catholics exclusively shall hold the higher offices of state, for example, those of chief hetman and minister. Catholics also should comprise a majority in the legislature and judiciary, with a designated number of places for the dissidents in the Diet and the courts.

"Given these advantages, the Catholics may remain calm and secure vis-a-vis the dissidents. In addition, the distribution of offices and favors will depend solely on a Catholic king. Can it be supposed, without offending common sense, that in these circumstances the dissidents will dominate or even challenge the Catholics?

"I hardly think it necessary to recommend to your radiance," wrote Panin further, "that you accustom the Poles, with these and similar explanations, to view with equanimity the measures we take to aid the dissidents. If only the film of fanaticism and prejudice can be pulled from their eyes they cannot help but recognize that restoration of the dissidents' rights will restore the legal entity of their damaged constitution, assure peace in their homeland, exorcise the roots of mutual enmity and hatred, and make Catholicism the dominant religion not by force but by amicable agreement with other faiths. Catholicism's present preeminence could disappear through force just as easily as with force it gained and now holds its sway."

Panin appended to this response a postscript in his own handwriting: "All of that which has been ordered should be moderated with perspicacity. Some curtailment in the equality of religious observance and civil rights is necessary for the dissidents to prevent greater interventions and for the fastest conclusion of this matter by us alone with affirmation for us of the new right of influence in the Polish government. But restoration of this equality as much as possible always will remain the basis of our interest, and, therefore, these two subjects always should be argued among ourselves."

In order to arrange finally his relations with the Czartoryskis, Panin wrote them that they should give him a definite reply as to their agreement to support Russia's views in the matter of the dissidents. The Czartoryskis answered evasively, assuring Panin of their devotion to the empress and their unshakeable desire to see their fatherland closely allied with Russia. Repnin told them that their letter was very vague and that nothing of their intentions could be fathomed. They must prove themselves by acting as Russia desired.

"You maintain that the dissidents endanger themselves by forming a confederation, but you do not say what else could be done. Danger will threaten not the dissidents but those who permit themselves the use of any force on the dissidents. Russia will take terrible vengeance upon such offenders. You say not a word about whether you will act in agreement with us at the coming Diet in order to bring the matter of the dissidents to its full, desired conclusion. In your letter, you intimate that Poland should be granted some benefits for alleviation of the dissidents' situation. Please be more specific, for we do not wish to waste time talking."

The Czartoryskis answered that they could not undertake to support the dissidents themselves or propose a basis for successful resolution of the problem. During the conversation, one of the Czartoryskis let slip that they sooner would chase the dissidents out of Poland than allow them to hold government offices. Repnin rejoined: "Those same states that now request the restoration of the dissidents' rights will invade, use force, to return the estates of the dissidents, and sooner will overturn all Poland than desist from their demands."

Repnin showed the Czartoryskis' answer to the leaders of the dissidents and inquired when their confederation would be ready. They set March 9 (O.S.) of the current year [1767]. Repnin relayed this to Petersburg so that Russian forces might be prepared to invade Poland by that time.

Meanwhile, Podoski, the crown secretary,[29] completely loyal to Repnin, set out to visit all the chief enemies of "the family" [the Czartoryskis]: the Potockis, Ossolinskis, Mniszeks, Bishops Soltik and Krasinski. He was to sound out their intentions and promise Russian protection to enable them to gain ascendency over the Czartoryski family on condition that they agreed to cooperate in resolving the dissident question. "Podoski is a clergyman," Repnin wrote, "but he is not at all a fanatic and he thinks far more of the blessings of this world than of the martyr's crown. He is a bright and very rational man. He will persuade the higher nobles to write a collective letter to the empress with the request that she use her power to restore and insure for all time the laws which have been violated during the present reign. He will convince them to form a confederation as soon as our troops enter Poland, for these troops will protect them." This same Podoski wrote to Prince Radziwill,[30] who was in exile, and invited him to join the Russian side.

Initially negotiations had been conducted with the Czartoryskis. In view of the unsatisfactory nature of their answers, the Russians turned to the enemies of the Czartoryskis. It was as if the king were forgotten. No one paid him any attention or made any advances to him. At the end of January 1767 Stanislaw Augustus decided to approach Repnin himself, and made a jocular and not very fitting start of a serious conversation. "The French actress Cleron," the king began, "offers me her services, and I would like to avail myself of them. Will the shaky situation this year preclude me such pleasures?" Repnin replied that he was surprised that his majesty mixed serious matters with such trifles. But the king continued to talk about the actress and ended with a question: "Are you going to war with us?"

Repnin answered that this depended upon the Poles, since war occurred only where there was resistance. Those who offered no open or covert resistance while seeing the justice and power of unity and attempting to meet them *in a decent manner,* looking patiently on the deeds of others, such persons need not fear a war. "I hold the same opinion," answered the king. "I assure you that, in the event your forces advance here, I do not wish to offer direct or covert resistance. But, aside from this, what would you advise me to do?"

"Satisfy our demands," Repnin replied. "If that satisfaction is accompanied by careful and judicious conduct, your majesty cannot fail to regain your previous friendship with Russia."

THE PRO-RUSSIAN CONFEDERATIONS

The leaders of the dissidents, who had taken 20,000 gold pieces from Repnin, kept their promise to him. In March, at the appointed time, they formed a confederation of Protestants in Torun, and named Count von Holz as their marshal. At the same time, another confederation was formed in Slutsk under the leadership of General Grabowski. This confederation was joined by the Orthodox population of Nowogorodek and other, neighboring regions. The conversations with Radziwill, conducted through the mediation of the Saxon agent Alois, ended in success. Radziwill was promised that he could return home with his old rights and position restored under the following conditions: he must act in the interests of the Russian empress; he must especially support her plans in the dissident question; he must not persecute them on their estates; he must return their churches, return Russian defectors, and behave himself. This last condition was considered necessary because this renowned official, especially at jolly hours (and these were hardly rare) often indulged in outrageous pranks.

Radziwill rejoiced at the Russian propositions. On February 28 he answered Repnin from Dresden that he was possessed of extreme gratitude to the empress for her preferred favor. He declared himself subject to her magnanimous will for the good of the republic. He promised that he would abide always by the Russian party and always would receive with respect and obedience any directions the Russian court saw fit to give him. He would carry out these orders without the slightest resistance, either open or hidden. So that there should be no doubt as to his actions, so that his enemies would not have the slightest possibility of maligning him, and as a token of the empress' favor, Radziwill requested that he have a Russian official at his side at all times, who would pass on directly to him the empress' will. In conclusion, Radziwill promised to use all his powers to cooperate in resolving the matter of the dissidents, and to use his influence to whatever measure the Russian court might deem wise in this matter.

Podoski also returned from his travels. He reported that Potocki, Ossolinski, Welgurski, Soltik, and several others were willing to beseech the empress' protection in a collective letter. With this protection they then would form a confederation and settle the dissident question as Russia desired. However, they first wished an audience with the Russian ambassador. Repnin announced that they should come to Warsaw no later than April 10, new style. "It seems that this is as good a start as one could wish," Repnin reported to Panin. "Nevertheless, already I have been deceived here so many times in so many ways that I do not at all dare answer for the success of this endeavor. I will not fail to attempt to carry it through truly."

The break of the Russian court with the Czartoryskis, the inflexibility of the king in the question of the dissidents, and the movement of Russian troops into Polish territory, all gave hope to Prince Charles of Saxony that important changes would occur in Poland, which he could exploit. Charles' agent, Alois, received orders to ingratiate himself with Repnin and find out all that the latter was seeking. This was advantageous for the Russian envoy because Alois had relations with all the old Saxon party, with which Repnin wished to act in unison. Alois had been the intermediary in the talks with Radziwill. With the aid of Alois and Podoski, Repnin drafted a project for a Lithuanian Catholic confederacy without royal participation.

When the dissidents' confederation had been formed and Russian protection announced, Repnin told the Czartoryskis that now they could aid him more freely. Their fanatical blindness should lessen as a result of the letter shown to them in which Russia announced its intentions and demonstrated it meant no harm to Poland and Catholicism. The Czartoryskis replied that they would cooperate as much as possible. They would attempt to change their convictions and hoped for success in the entire matter. When Repnin told them that the deputies of the dissidents' confederation should meet with the king, the Czartoryskis requested that this not happen. They claimed that such a visit would be of no importance, for only the Diet, and not the king, could render any decision in this matter. This would only greatly harm the king and give substance to the arguments of the opponents of the dissidents. The confederation could not be considered legal until it was embraced by the country and approved in all provinces. Therefore the king held no authority to receive its deputies.

"I see," Repnin wrote, "that the Czartoryskis are attempting to squirm about and as far as possible avoid frankness. They fear to oppose us openly, but they equally fear to show agreement with us in this affair." But he could not say anything immediately to them about their opposition to sending the dissidents' deputies to the king. He consulted the members of the confederation and they told him that it was necessary for them to gain a royal audience for their deputies. Refusal would be a mark of scorn for their confederation; such a gesture could be made only to enemies of the republic.

During the days after March 20 the Senate council met in Warsaw, where the charter of the dissidents' confederation and the declarations of the Russian and Prussian envoys on the dissidents were read. The council ended by deciding to call a full session of the Senate on May 25. In this instance, Repnin wrote: "His majesty spoke to me about this and intimated to me that he purposely had postponed the convocation of the Senate until the above date in order to give our forces more time to penetrate the country and take up necessary positions. I do not see any further evidence that he will submit and cooperate with us. He simply assures me, as before, that he will take no measures against us. The Czartoryskis say the same thing, and assure us that they will co-operate as much as possible. Nevertheless, they limit this as much as possible and meanwhile remain as stubborn as before about receiving the dissidents' deputies. They deflect the king from a settlement, toward which personally he would be inclined, were they not restraining him. He has given me to understand this several times. I am still standing firm with the Czartoryskis over this."

Stanislaw Poniatowski expressed his view of the progress of the dissident question in a letter to Geoffrin.[31] "The empress has asked too much in the question of the dissidents, and the Diet has refused too much." He wrote this at the very end of 1766. In March 1767 he wrote: "Do not rush to judge me; have patience, and I will be vindicated. Patience and fortitude—there is my motto. A tempest nears, and it will be terrible. From moment to moment I await the news that Russian troops have invaded my country. I will not tell you what I shall do. This is impossible; you are too far away. I will tell you only that I am attempting to keep a very cool head and that I repeat to myself fifty times a day that to chase after glory is stupidity." As for the Czartoryskis, he wrote: "Attic and Cicero (the Czartoryskis) see themselves in a difficult position between the Compass (Catherine) and the Square (public opinion) and they wish to place Telemach (the king) in their own position through their advice, which would ruin him before both. To this, Telemach said to himself: 'service of public opinion is one well-recognized obligation, but service of the real interests of the state is a higher duty. It is fortunate when the two coincide; when they do not, one must hold to the latter.' Telemach to this time has gone consistently against his own opinion, but has seen that many times it would have been better to follow his own counsel. From this time forth, in order to evade the traps set for him, he will follow his own opinion; already he has begun to perceive the advantage of this."

On April 4 Repnin reported that formation of a Catholic confederation in Lithuania was going well, thanks to the activity of Count Brostowski, the elder of Bistritsk, brother-in-law of Prince Radziwill. However, the ambassador complained about the nobles at court, whose slowness and cowardice were hindering developments in Poland. He wrote to Panin: "Your excellency, I think, in fact, often consider, that I am too ardent, but I truly wish that an angel were in my place. I am sure that even he would lose his patience with such laggards. You know that many of the local notables opposed to the court and the Czartoryskis wished to assemble here to meet with me and take some decisive measures about current affairs. Aside from the governor of Wohlynia, who sent his son, and the crown treasurer, Wessel, who came himself, none of these lords have arrived, all claiming illness. I see clearly that they are temporizing; they want someone else to rake up and quench the fire, but only when the affair is finished. They hold to their chimera that our court is secretly in agreement with the one here and opposes it only as a front. They spend their time in such dreams, no matter how much I importune them. There is hourly evidence of lying and cowardice. These opponents fear the court and the Czartoryskis, while the latter fear the former. Their fear is fed by idle speculation; and they just scream and complain about the court and the government, and do not dare to stir from their bondage. Such is the make-up of the Polish nation. One may conclude from this how unpleasant it is to deal with them and how impossible it is to rely upon them."

Pouring out his annoyance in his letters to Panin, Repnin did not fold his hands. He summoned the king's councillor, Count Potocki, a young man, but reliable, stolid, and wealthy. Repnin dispatched him to induce the nobles to come to Warsaw for an audience. According to Repnin, Potocki also was supposed to prepare the actors in the confederation in Galicia. The envoy intended to make Prince Radziwill himself marshal of the royal confederation "in order to throw a scare" into the Czartoryskis, and to avoid any setbacks since Radziwill was beginning to stand on his own, and to display clearly to the party opposed to the court that there was no agreement between the Russian and Polish courts. Repnin also wanted to assign Colonel Kar with a detachment of men, ostensibly as escorts for the confederation, in order to keep the marshal in hand and to make sure that Radziwill committed no stupidities.

To do this it was necessary to settle the matter of an audience of the dissidents' deputies with the king. Repnin summoned a nobleman, one Ogrodski, the director of the king's cabinet, and demanded of him an immediate and direct answer to the question: would the king receive the dissidents' deputies? The ambassador ended his conversation with Ogrodski with the threat: "If the king and the ministry do not wish to receive the deputies properly, his majesty risks the loss of the friendship of our most merciful empress." These words had a magical effect. Ogrodski returned with the reply that "the king, cherishing the friendship of her imperial majesty and wishing always to prove his devotion to her, intends to receive the dissidents' deputies, although his council opposes it." The audience took place on April 28, new style. After presentation of their wishes, the deputies were allowed to kiss the king's hand. This was a symbol of affirmation of the legality of the dissidents' confederation.

Finally, at the end of April, Repnin awaited the arrival in Warsaw of the governor of Kiev, Potocki, the bishop of Kamenets, Krasinski, and the lord high marshal of the court, Mniszek. The first two had supported warmly the formation of a Catholic confederation, while Mniszek himself had visited the provinces of Poznan and Kalisz in the same cause. During this time Repnin constantly experienced "labor pains," as he put it, since he had so many concerns, exhortations, flatteries, disputes, and curses to endure in his dealings with the magnates. Each wished to have the lead in the affair and envied the others. Finally, Repnin was forced to tell them openly that "no one had succeeded in flattering him so as to gain leadership in a matter that he alone wished to manage; whoever did not like this could discontinue dealings with him."

"This short answer," added Repnin, "seems to have returned them to proper limits and suppressed their internecine squabbling. Now I hope that all will go properly. By the way, these new arrivals had some dreams that the king would be deposed entirely. But I gave them strict instructions against this and totally rooted out all such schemes. He (the king) has recognized his own frivolity in a state of great sorrow and despondency, but he realizes that this repentance has come to him too late. I must acknowledge that I do not look upon his grief without pity. He has been misled either by swindlers or by hot-heads, and his greatest guilt has come from them. Show him a bit of kindness."

When the rumor arose that a Catholic confederation was to be organized, the king began to advance every argument against this to Repnin. The latter rejoined that without such action the Russian court no longer could avoid dependence solely upon the Princes Czartoryski in the coming Diet. Russia did not wish to rely only on promises; it desired to be assured of success. The king objected that success was sure even without this, in view of the force which was being used by the Russian side. "Then would it not please you," Repnin rejoined, "to answer in advance, in writing, for the resolution of the dissident question as well as to assure that the form of the republic will remain in full force on its prior basis, and that for affirmation of this you will request the intercession of the empress in the interest of the inviolability of the rights, laws, and freedoms of the republic."

This forced the king to be silent about the confederation, and he began to ask only that Repnin inform him of the nature of the act of confederation. Repnin told him that the first goal of the confederation would be restoration of the dissidents' rights and the second a request for the protection and aid of the empress in preserving and guaranteeing forever the established form and strength of the government. Prince Radziwill was to return home and regain all his former holdings. As concerned the king, nothing would be done against his dignity. The confederation would speak of his person with appropriate respect.

''And why shall Prince Radziwill be marshal of the confederation?'' the king inquired. ''Because I am more certain of his dependence upon us than of anyone else,'' Repnin answered. "I want to have obedient people. I do not wish to trust strangers to carry out my business, for I have already been deceived so many times by false promises." The king was about to start arguing against a guarantee of the constitution by the empress, but Repnin said that this was the central issue. Stanislaw Augustus ended the conversation with a promise that he would countenance all this with grief, but quietly and patiently. Repnin stated that this type of conduct would regain him the kindness and friendship of the empress.

After this conversation with the king, Repnin received a visit from August Czartoryski, the Russian governor, who told him: "The confederations are beginning, things are so delicate now. I do not know how to act with my family and friends. I fear that out of ignorance I might do something unpleasant for the imperial court, to which we are so devoted." Repnin ruminated and said: "I know the force of your words. These confederations have been aimed against harmful innovations which have been introduced into the government. They are directed against violation of the ancient laws and governmental structure. Consequently, they are in agreement with the useful views of her imperial majesty on the present republic. Above and beyond this, since these confederations are turning to the protection of the empress and ask her to guarantee the unswerving preservation of the rights and freedoms of the republic, this most gracious protection will be granted along with eternal affirmation, according to their wish, of the present government and the privileges of each. But generosity and humanitarianism are the very bases of the empress' just conduct, these confederations consequently should not force anyone to unite with them. They will deem villains only those who dare to act against them. Therefore, you are completely free, my lords, to join the confederations or to remain peaceful and neutral observers."

Czartoryski was profuse in his thanks, praised the moderation of the Russian government, reluctance to use force, and in conclusion offered whatever services he could. But now the Czartoryskis' services could merely make difficulties for Repnin. To cooperate once again with the Czartoryskis meant to alienate his new allies, who had come over to the Russian side solely because Repnin had broken with "the family."

Having been forced to resort to so strong a measure as a confederation, Repnin nevertheless worked to avert the disorders and upheavals which were the usual results of a confederation. According to old custom, as soon as a confederation was formed and received recognition, all previous authorities at once ceased to operate. All subordinated themselves to the will of the confederated nobility. The king, the senate, and all high officials and judges must be responsible to it. Repnin did not wish this. "It would only insult the king, in vain, since we do not deem this necessary. It also would lend more power to the confederation to perpetrate injustices while gaining revenge on district judges for previous cases. Beyond this, in banning all jurisdictions the confederation thereby also would dissolve military and treasury commissions. Although these certainly need reform, their complete destruction does not seem advantageous to me. I will restrain as much as possible and oppose this abolition of jurisdictions; yet at the same time I will use it to make things easier and more pleasant for the king. I wish to draw him to loyalty to our court, for I find it better here when things are not always accomplished by the use of force. Aside from this, I must recognize in all fairness that his majesty has shown no opposition to us, even if he has not cooperated openly with us. Sometimes he is insulted and sometimes he naturally requests that his friends protect him, but he has allowed the execution of almost all my domestic measures here and restrains his subjects from senseless passion."

The king soon was given an opportunity to demonstrate his obedience. In June, the cardinal of Poland died. It was extremely important to Repnin that this post be filled by a man loyal to Russia, and he insisted on his choice of the crown secretary, Count Podoski, "who had served him more than anyone else." The king did not like Podoski, who always had been opposed to him. Therefore Stanislaw Augustus preferred to give the post to his brother, Abbot Poniatowski. Despite this, when he heard from Repnin that the choice of Podoski would serve to demonstrate his friendship and loyalty to the empress, he ceased to object.

"The elevation of Podoski to cardinal," Repnin wrote, "greatly increases our influence here. He is openly devoted to me and has worked as my secretary in all of the present circumstances. Through his rise the entire nation will see how generously we reward those who serve us faithfully. The nation will witness that it can have complete confidence in the protection of our most exalted court. After all, the king could not refuse the highest office of the state to the man who was the chief, foremost actor in the formation of the confederation so insulting to the king, all to satisfy Russia. We can have no doubts about the loyalty of this Count Podoski, for he is a strong, rational man who sees that he owes everything to us. When he was not in our party he had nothing, not even the hope of being one of the lowliest bishops. That is how much the court opposed him! In a word, I can report in strict justice that I trust him completely, and that this matter is very important for the growth of our credit here."

On June 11 Repnin received news from the Radom confederation via Colonel Kar, stationed there with the Russian troops. The tenth had been set as the date of election of a marshal of the confederation, and Kar was given to understand that the newly-elected marshal must swear an oath of loyalty to all provisions of the articles of confederation. Kar did not know the procedures observed in confederations and thought that this oath should be one of them, all the more since Crown Secretary Podoski confirmed him in this opinion. Radziwill began to protest and stated that he would not accept the post of marshal until he saw the articles of confederation. He told Kar that the latter should be careful; they would be deceived if Kar did not order the act of confederation read first. Radziwill said: "There is some sort of trickery there."

In truth, at the opening of the conference the friends of the governor of Kiev, Potocki, shouted "We won't allow it" to every point of the articles of confederation, upon Potocki's orders, and demanded that each be amended. When the portion about the dissidents was reached, they scarcely allowed the article to be read. Kar approached the governor and Marshal Mniszek and stated that he considered this meeting to be invalid. If they wished to rewrite the articles of confederation, they should know that he would not allow it. If necessary, he would use the troops at his disposal to settle the matter. The assembly dispersed. Kar also announced to Potocki that the empress had promised protection to their confederation on condition that she should direct all its actions through her envoy in Warsaw, and that the same articles of confederation adopted in Lithuania would be adopted in Radom, word for word. Potocki replied quite dryly that he would attempt to observe these conditions, although he had no hope of success. Were the articles of confederation amended to include the discontent with the king, he could answer for the success of the rest of the plan. Kar answered to this that it was not Potocki's place to conclude treaties with the Russian court.

If he did not wish to get down to business now, Russia would demand that he perform very well when he left Radom. Kar concluded his letter about this to Repnin with the following words: "I do not know how to thank your radiance for the commission to preside at the confederation. From morn to night, I either lie or remonstrate. And worst of all, there is much talk but no action." Action finally was taken on June 12; Prince Radziwill was elected marshal and the required articles of confederation were signed.

CONFLICT WITH THE CHURCH

Things worked out in Radom but difficulties concerning Podoski were encountered in Warsaw. A papal nuncio visited the king on June 14. Stanislaw Augustus told him that he had given his word to raise to cardinal the choice of the Russian empress. Since it was obvious from Repnin's words that his choice was Crown Secretary Podoski, Stanislaw was forewarning the nuncio of this in order that the Papal See would raise no objections to the consecration. The king was doing this at the pleasure of the power to which he owed everything, and therefore he should turn to it to request protection against intrigues so offensive to his prestige. The nuncio answered that Rome could not look with equanimity on a man heading the Polish clergy who was so well-disposed to the dissidents. The Pope would refuse him consecration.

The successful establishment of a confederation meanwhile offered grounds for strengthening Russian demands concerning the dissidents. Repnin received instructions to build for the dissidents a position as nearly as possible equal to the Catholics. Panin wrote to him: "You would attain the pinnacle of glory if at the coming Diet our archbishop of Belorussia were seated in the Diet together with a recommendation from the republic to the king that several of the earliest senatorial vacancies be filled by dissidents. I feel and understand all the difficulties involved in consummation of such a plan. The lack of personal qualities of our Belorussian archbishop, I think, may well be enough to prevent this. Therefore, of course, I do not intend to order you to do this, but I only wish to give you my thoughts as a friend."

Panin also wrote of the Czartoryskis: "When matters are brought to a close, do not stint in trying to exclude them totally from dealings with you and to deprive them of all influence in the government. Thus, not just they themselves and all Poland, but also other courts will be assured that they have no significance. If they enjoyed any measure of power before, it was due solely to the patronage of our court."

As for Podoski, Repnin was to intimate to the nuncio that if the Papal See intended to act contrary to Russia in this affair, it would quickly subject its faith to the same disadvantages in Poland which now so unjustly and maliciously were attributed to Russia by ill-wishers.

Repnin held a curious conversation with the king concerning the conflict with the Papal See in the Podoski matter. "If a Papal Bull is withheld, as in some other instances, and the causes are enumerated, what do you advise me to do?" Stanislaw Augustus asked the ambassador. "Create a synod and confirm Podoski as cardinal in this way," Repnin answered. Poniatowski relates that the reply was that Repnin also confirmed that he said: "We will find some way to support our case, for example, convocation of a synod." The king countered "Do you think, Prince, that even one bishop will heed my summons to a synod? Do you not think that they all will see in this defiance of papal authority, as in England under Henry VIII?" Repnin: "But I know that the clergy here are very discontented with the Roman yoke. This is a happy opportunity for emancipation of the Polish church."

This is the king's version whereas Repnin claims that he said: "Among the clergy, as always, some will be for, others against. Part of the clergy is indeed very discontented with the Roman yoke, which perhaps they would wish to be rid of, given this opportunity." The king: "Prince! The same priests who grumble sometimes when they are fleeced in Rome will support Rome strongly when it speaks loudly and clearly. The priests cannot forget that the moment their dependence upon the pope is removed, their power, wealth, and status will depend solely upon the good disposition of secular authority. Even the laity will stand behind Rome the moment it raises the alarm!" Repnin: "Hah! Didn't they join a confederation which recognized the wrongs inflicted on the dissidents, even though the nuncio delivered a pompous speech against the dissidents at the last Diet?" The king: "Yes, the confederations were signed by such frivolous or ignorant people that one easily could assure them that they were signing a document diametrically opposed to the content of the act of confederation. A great many signed and added that they wished to support the constitution of 1717 against the dissidents. True, the nuncio gave a pompous speech at the Diet, but at the direction of his court he told the bishops to exercise the greatest wisdom. Why, after the Diet it was practically intimated from Rome that it was necessary to accept the circumstances. But if Rome takes another tone the people who up to now have submitted to your leadership will rush just as quickly to the opposite side. I am beginning to think that this is what Rome will do, given the statements of the nuncio, who otherwise is an intelligent and moderate man. If Podoski is forced into the Senate with bayonets, and if you find it necessary to shed blood for him, Poland and I will pay for it. This is what makes one stop and think—at least me. Even you cannot remain indifferent to the prospect of the Pope turning to other courts with fire and thunder, lending the matter a religious and political color."

But Repnin remained inflexible. He answered that things would not come to bloodletting and other courts would not act out of fanaticism. They had not interfered in the dissident question, and they would not intervene in the choice of a cardinal. In truth, the king did not wish to appoint Podoski and exaggerated his own danger to intimidate Repnin. The Papal See bowed to circumstances and Podoski was consecrated Cardinal.

PREPARATIONS FOR THE DIET

The king, at least in his letters to Geoffrin, looked calmly upon the impending events. "The confederation of the so-called discontented is almost complete, throughout the entire kingdom," he wrote. "The members of the confederation would be ashamed or hard-put if one forced them to enumerate exactly what they are dissatisfied with. But since one must seek good in evil itself, the fruit of this fever in the state, when it passes, will be that I will be in a position to evaluate people according to their true worth, having found out the frivolity of the majority, the immorality of the leaders, the black ingratitude of many of them, and the virtue and wisdom of some good citizens. Every reign has its crisis, just as everyone is exposed to smallpox and gets greater or fewer scars. I will emerge greatly scarred from this bout with the pox but, having escaped once, I will have greater hope for longevity. I have to suffer my full measure of grief, unrest, irritation, and silence, which is sometimes more burdensome than all the rest. Do not despair, for I do not. I will reach the harbor—with difficulty, no doubt, and not without losses, but I will get there. My despair would be base and the gravest evil for my state."

The dissident and Catholic confederations were formed, but it remained to get the matter through an extraordinary Diet. The king agreed on the two chief points: guarantee of the Polish constitution by the empress and restoration of the dissidents' rights. The king forced all of his friends to join the confederation. Even the young Prince Adam Czartoryski joined and agreed to be its representative to the Diet. This was important, for the elder Czartoryskis subsequently could not claim that the dominant religion had been subverted without their participation, and turn popular fanaticism to their benefit. Finally, a delegation was sent to the empress to express the thanks of the confederated republic. It consisted of four members: the frontier commander of Lithuania, Potsei, the Lithuanian Master of Provisions Welgurski, the crown councillor, Podoski, and the Sendomir elder, Ossolinski.

Repnin wrote Panin to inform him of this delegation: "The first member is connected with the governor of Kiev. The second is partial to Mniszek, his troublesome wife, and the bishop of Cracow. Consequently, both may harbor thoughts of limiting the restoration of the dissidents' rights and injurious sentiments on the king's account. The third is a good man; the fourth may be young, but is adroit and opposed to the king. In addition, he has bound himself to marry the daughter of the governor of Kiev. Therefore, allow me to observe that not too much faith should be put in their evil, whispered blandishments, but outwardly, I beseech you, please receive them with exceptional politeness. The Poles have already ventured some bargaining in the instructions given the emissaries, and they also are clarifying their opinions on changes in the commissions and other matters. It was difficult just to keep the confederation from writing like that about the dissidents in their letter to her imperial majesty. This point approaches resolution, but grows more difficult by the hour. I had to use a great many measures to keep the matter out of the mission. There were also some difficulties in requesting her majesty's protection. They are starting to think twice about that. Nevertheless, I will not let all these perverse thoughts turn into anything, as far as is possible with the powers given me."

"This point (that is, the dissident question) approaches resolutions, but grows more difficult by the hour," Repnin wrote. The difficulty was revealed at the sub-Diets held in preparation for the extraordinary Diet which the troubled state of the republic demanded. At the Poznan sub-Diet the delegates nearly cut up Gurowski and Count Poninski, staunch supporters of the Russian cause. Count Apraksin saved them by surrounding the mob with his troops. Repnin feared that artillery would be needed at the Diet, even though he hoped to have a majority. Soltik, the bishop of Cracow, Potocki, the governor of Kiev, Mniszek, a lord high marshal of the court, and Branitski, a high crown hetman, fanned the flames. Repnin forbade the reading of circular letters at the sub-Diets, but these gentlemen published their messages.

"I repeat," Repnin wrote Panin on August 17, "that if we desire success in the dissident matter at the coming Diet it will be absolutely necessary to arrest the bishop of Cracow and similar fanatics. Otherwise we will never work out anything with them. About the domestic situation here, I can answer that, except for fear and foreboding, such an arrest will produce no other movement. I do not concern myself with what appearance this action will present and what will follow as a result in relation to the neighboring powers."

Repnin's tribulations were increased by the slowness of the mails. Panin answered his message of July 14 on August 14. In this answer Panin laid out the chief principle concerning the dissidents. "The dissident question must be settled, not in order to spread Orthodoxy and Protestantism in Poland, but to acquire through our co-religionists and the Protestants once and for all a strong and reliable party with a legal right to participate in Polish affairs, not just because of the present request of the republic for her imperial majesty's guarantee of the inviolability of the Polish constitution, but also as a result of protection of the dissidents, which right we will appropriate for ourselves forever. As the weakest element of the future government of Poland, the dissidents will find it possible to remain in the government only with our help. The Protestant religion curbs superstition and limits the power of the clergy. Its excessive growth easily might lift the Poles out of the ignorance in which they are now mired. Liberation from ignorance might lead step by step to a new order which would concentrate all Polish domestic power in one place and make it much greater than it is now. This could turn quickly against the interest of Russia, the protector of the Protestants at present and Poland's chief competitor in the future. Between political societies neither hostility for harm suffered nor thanks for aid can have any place.

"As far as those of our faith are concerned, this inconvenience cannot arise. But on the other hand, should we strengthen them too much and they gain stature in the republic and share the power of governing it alone, independent of us, we will subject ourselves to inconvenience in our relations with them. Even without this, there will be more frequent and larger flights from Russia when freedom of religion is allied with the benefits of a people free in all other things. Then we will have cause to worry about our border provinces, which are similar to Poland in the manners and customs of the people.

"The king demands that four bishoprics which have left the union be left unconditionally in their present state. This demand is in agreement with our basic principle and therefore should meet no objection from our side. But it would be all the better to treat them and the entire union both at the Diet and in the coming mandate with complete and unrelieved silence, as a sect which cannot be considered directly connected with either faith. The dissidents, of course, will pester you to fulfill their every wish, especially concerning free return from Catholic laws to their own. For this we have dictated our political rules to you, and you can say to them that there are insuperable difficulties in this matter and that we never intended to conduct a war to proselytize their faiths for them.

"Besides, it seems to me that it will be absolutely necessary to frighten the Poles not just with words but with direct action, by billeting our forces in villages which hold intransigents or intriguers. I think that it is not even necessary to relieve the king himself completely of the fear of losing his throne." Accordingly Panin authorized Repnin in case of extreme need to arrest those who would most oppose the resolution of both matters—the dissidents and the empress' guarantee of the constitution.

SOLTIK LEADS THE OPPOSITION

The clouds grew thicker. The previous papal nuncio departed for Vienna. The scheming nature of his successor, Durrini, promised Repnin nothing good. He was an intriguer and a fanatic. Pope Clement XIII sent a pastoral letter opposing the dissidents. On the copy of this sent by Repnin to Panin is written in Catherine's hand: "There are certainly enough tales about what the Pope will do!" But what were tales in Russia were received with reverence in Poland. Soltik had fifteen secretaries writing day and night on his instructions to his congregation. "Dearest sons, given into my care," his messages read. "Strive for the good in all you do. Call with a contrite spirit to the throne on high that the Holy Spirit be sent down to uphold the sacred Catholic faith, to repel the pretensions of the dissidents manfully, and to preserve the basic rights of freedom. During the entire session of the Diet there should be daily prayers before the holy mysteries and psalms sung to the Lord in all the Catholic churches in Poland."

Soltik appears before us as a Catholic bishop in this pastoral letter. But in a letter to one of his friends, Welgurski, he is revealed as a politician. "The empress," he writes, "is soliciting two things: a general guarantee of the constitution and restoration of the dissidents. The king of Poland guaranteed the liberties of Courland and affirmed the privileges of the Prussian lands. By this, both countries were drawn into dependence upon the republic. The chief means of escaping the guarantee is to raise the point that Turkey will not allow it. As for the dissidents, the peace of the nation depends on the condition that the dissidents—namely, the non-Uniates—not be allowed in the Senate or ministries. It is sufficient to recall that there are thirty families in Russia of Polish extraction, and that distribution of ranks in Poland is within the power of the Russian empress. Will it be good when the Moscow Senate is transferred to Poland and we are sent to Siberia? The chief policy of the Polish opposition should consist in prolonging the Diet for these reasons: (1) so that the confederation might reach perfection; (2) to give foreign courts time for negotiations; (3) so that the elector of Saxony might come of age; (4) to explain our position better with the Petersburg Court through our emissaries, and not through that despot (Repnin); (5) because of the infirmity (poor health) of the king of Prussia—if he should die what would hinder Saxony's armies from entering Poland?"

The enemies acted forcefully, the ally [Prussia] feebly. On August 24 Repnin wrote to Panin: "I should report that although Benoit does not openly refuse to act in agreement with me, it seems to me that their court does not wish the success of the dissident movement as strongly as we. Perhaps the cause for this is hidden in a certain jealousy that the Prussian king is playing a subordinate role here, not equal to ours. I do not think that it would be bad, without making any complaints about Benoit's weak cooperation, to assure ourselves of the Berlin court and to prod it a bit."

A messenger, Lieutenant Azanchevsky, arrived in Warsaw and related the scenes he and Cavalry Captain Soleman had witnessed at the Podolian sub-Diet in Kamenets. When the reading of Repnin's letter commenced, the delegates raised an unseemly noise and laughter. Rzewuski, the elder from Dolina, said that anyone who did not swear to prevent the dissidents from free exercise of their religion would be damned. He, Rzewuski, would sooner allow himself to be chopped to bits than to allow any improvement in the position of the dissidents. The delegates hurled a note at the marshal on the dais which alleged that the archpriest of Pereiaslavl was writing to Uniate priests in the border regions that they should submit to his authority. Hearing this, the Poles at the assembly began to swear at Soleman and Azanchevsky and the marshal told the Russian officers to leave, since he could not vouch for their safety. Repnin ordered Major General Krechetnikov to post Cossacks on the estates of those nobles who had disturbed the Kamenets assembly.

But these events would not have so aggrieved Repnin had he not discovered the duplicity of the leaders of the Catholic confederation. He found this out from the secret correspondence of Soltik with Welgurski, who was sent as one of the confederation's emissaries to the empress. The ambassador learned also that the formerly loyal secretary of his new Cardinal Podoski was acting in concert with Soltik, Krasinski (the bishop of Kamenets), Mniszek, Potocki (the governor of Kiev), and Crown Treasurer Wessel. Acting as one, these men approached Repnin and God knows what they said to one another. "Please see," Repnin wrote Panin, "with what honorable people I deal and how pleasant my speech and conduct must be. I truly fear that I myself will end up a swindler after dealing with them in this fashion." But the ambassador's greatest tormentor was Soltik. "In truth," he penned, "I would give him anything I could to make him disappear; I am sick to death of him."

The prominent people acted craftily, pushing lesser men forward. Of the latter, one Czacki was the most disturbed and disturbed the other nobles most, so Repnin ordered his arrest. Soltik came to Repnin on this pretext and began a speech about the dissidents with a question: what did the Russian court ultimately desire for them? Repnin answered that the dissidents should have all their former rights restored. Since everyone knew that the dissidents formerly had enjoyed full equality with Catholics, it followed that now this status should apply. Soltik objected that previously they had enjoyed this equality not as a matter of right, but through force.

Then he moved to the arrest of Czacki. "We are a free people," he stated, "and consequently we are entitled to speak and act as we please. No one can forbid us these rights. The empress has assured us in her declarations that she will protect our freedom."

"Our imperial court," Repnin answered, "of course always will protect and strengthen Polish freedom. But it is necessary to distinguish freedom from outrageous actions, and Czacki is guilty of the latter. All those who contemplate disruption of domestic tranquility will be subject to the same fate, for the republic itself requested her majesty's protection."

"We are not your subjects," Soltik countered.

"True," stated Repnin, "but the proximity, alliance, and very desires of the republic force the empress to concern herself with order here, and to restrain those who would violate that order."

"We are willing to die for our freedom," Soltik continued.

"Freedom and insurrection are two different things," Repnin replied. "If any one of you thinks of raising a revolt against his fatherland and its protectress, let him arm himself, so that he might receive his just deserts all the more quickly for such conduct. But I advise you to look at matters attentively first." This ended the conversation.

Repnin assigned Podoski to intimate to Soltik that if he conducted himself at the coming Diet as he had at the last, the same might happen to him as that had happened to Czacki. To the Russian empress he was no more important than Czacki; in fact, he would be shown such esteem that they would never let him out of confinement. But Soltik replied to Podoski that he would not be silent when the cause of the faith demanded defense. "He (Soltik) is not the kind of man in his ravings who can be deterred by threats or ruin," Repnin wrote Panin. "Actually, it is necessary to use against him the extreme measures with which the cardinal threatened him for me. He will ruin me with his unalterable stubbornness in the dissident question. I have already told him privately that he should not go to the Diet if he does not wish to participate in restoring the rights of the dissidents and if he cannot restrain himself from speaking out against them."

In respect to Podoski, Repnin wrote: "I know that the new cardinal would like a good sable fur. I ask you to send me one, if you deem it wise, so that I can present it to him in the name of our court, for of course one must flatter him and hold him in line. I hope to do this fully, although the dispatches of the bishop of Cracow make Podoski out to be our foe. But Soltik very often resorts to lies in his empty schemes, and I have begun to notice that the cardinal is distancing himself from Soltik."

At the beginning of September Repnin moved Russian forces to Warsaw and stationed them three, four, and five miles[32] from the capital. The Third Grenadier Regiment entered Warsaw proper and a number of Chuguev Cossacks made camp in the courtyard of the building where the Russian ambassador lived. To obtain provisions more easily, Repnin stationed several small detachments in the outskirts of Warsaw: one opposite Zakrochim on his side of the Vistula; another between Rava and Warsaw; a third at a little place called Gura on the Vistula; a fourth opposite Gura on the other bank of the river; and a fifth at the junction of the Bug with the Narev, on his side of the rivers. This was done so that these detachments might surround Warsaw in one day's march and cut off all exits, including those by water, from the city. Soltik exclaimed that soon he would have 60,000 Polish troops to face these forces. "But these troops exist only in his empty head," Repnin wrote. "It has gone so far that he has invoked the spectre of the Sicilian vespers[33] against the Russians in his ravings to the cardinal. In his feverish delirium he slanders himself gratuitously."

Repnin wrote Panin more than once that of all the Czartoryskis only the young Prince Adam, general of the Podolian lands, was distinguished by an attachment to Russia. But something else was found in the purloined correspondence of Soltik with Welgurski. According to Soltik, Prince Adam told his friends that he had to be surprised at the cowardice of his father, who had such wide holdings, so much money and standing among the people, but did not use them to annihilate Muscovite dominion in the name of the faith and freedom.

Soltik wrote of himself: "Prince Repnin tells everyone that he will make me Duke of Siberia. I asked the cardinal whether he meant this, or if he was just threatening me. I received the reply that, in truth, he is being forced to do this by the king himself, who states that if we do not conceal the leader of our party our work in the matter of the dissidents affair will be unsuccessful. The cardinal and I have spoken with others about how they would take me and where they would send me. They will not keep me under arrest here because the patriots and the common people might revolt. They will not send me to Moscow or Siberia. Prince Repnin would fear that there I might report in detail about everything to the empress. It is more likely that they will send me to some remote corner and watch over me and my people to make sure that I write nothing and speak to no one."

"I cannot portray the fanaticism here adequately," Repnin wrote. "Women pray daily for deliverance of the perishing faith. The monks and priests speak in their sermons in accordance with the orders of the bishops of Cracow and Kiev, and instill fanaticism everywhere they can. The nuncio was not satisfied that the bishop of Kiev published the papal pastoral letter in a Polish translation, and published it in the Latin original, too, and distributed it to the public.

"When people encounter dissidents in public parks or out walking the women, who have great power here, leave at once as if the place were defiled by the presence of heretics. In a word, there is such public irritation that if I did not know the cowardly nature of the people I would expect at any hour some sort of desperate act. Although I do not foresee any such open attempt, some hidden evil-doing might occur. We shall lead the poor king to the point where they will cut his throat."

But there was no danger to anyone, only jeering. Soltik let Repnin know that he desired to reach agreement with him and guaranteed the conduct of the bishops and his entire party. Repnin answered that he could conduct formal negotiations only with those whose rank in the republic entitled them to that right. The bishop of Cracow and the other bishops did not have that right. If he wished a friendly agreement, he should come personally without ceremony. Above all, it was necessary to agree on the chief point, namely that the dissidents should receive equal rights with the Catholics, without which no arrangements might be made. In reply Soltik sang his same old song that he would sooner give his body to be cut to bits, and sooner die with all his friends, than to allow equality of the dissidents with the Catholics. Wishing to demonstrate that he was willing to submit to the fate with which Repnin threatened him, he began to collect presents for those who would come to place him under guard, so much so that, in Repnin's words, his room began to resemble a Nürnberg shop.

Even so, Soltik again let Repnin know that he was undertaking to convince all true Catholics to satisfy the dissenters, if the Russian ambassador would allow him to continue his previous activity to maintain his standing in his party. Repnin answered him through Podoski, saying that such conduct could only harm the course of events. Such misunderstanding did not do justice to his intelligence, or he was intriguing in order to wreck the dissidents' cause and then turn around and lay all the blame upon others while maintaining the appearance that outwardly he was in agreement with the Russian ambassador. "I ask of the bishop," concluded Repnin, "that he act clearly and honestly in word and deed in the interest of complete equality between the dissidents and Catholics."

The Orthodox demanded that the Belorussian bishop receive a seat in the Senate. But the king insisted that two Uniate bishops should accompany an Orthodox bishop into the Senate. Panin did not agree to this. He wrote to Repnin: "Although placing two Uniate bishops in the Senate is essentially in partial agreement with the chief principle set out above (that the spread of other faiths at the expense of Catholicism should not be a motive), in assessing present circumstances this would be prejudicial to the glory of her majesty. Would not such inclusion of Uniate bishops seem to the world to have been done intentionally to annoy her majesty, when, to the contrary, the very essence of the matter demands fulfillment of all her wishes?"

Panin did not agree either to Stanislaw Augustus' demand that some punishment be fixed for those abandoning the dominant Catholic faith. It bothered Panin that Uniates long since had been allowed to convert to Orthodoxy and, therefore, "it is necessary," he wrote, "to preserve in the eyes of the public the purity of our intentions concerning our own faith." Repnin did not agree with Panin. "I have doubts," he wrote, "if in fact you do not intend to attempt to unite the Uniates with the Orthodox church. If not—if you hold the opinion that the spread of Greek Orthodoxy and Protestantism here is harmful for Russian interests, why do you not yield on the two points which will pacify the nation here and acquire thereby for yourself lasting assurance that these faiths will not spread any more than is necessary for our interests? This precaution is especially necessary against the Uniates, since one soon might find among them some who wish to convert to our faith. This would increase the number of our runaways, and kindle such a flame in the nation here that would truly be difficult to quench. Then one truly must expect Sicilian vespers at any hour. I really do not know whether foreign courts would remain calm at the sight of such events, which they might attribute to our desire to seize Poland imperceptibly. On the other hand, should we allow the aforementioned points, the second will demonstrate to the whole world that we do not intend to expand ours or the dissidents' faiths here. The first will prove that we are supporting religious equality here and attempting to assure that no one is persecuted for reasons of faith."

Aside from this, Repnin's difficulties were increased by the position of the Russian Orthodox population in Poland, where representation was granted only to the nobility. Persecutions had eliminated the Orthodox nobility or left the poorest and least capable and educated to take major posts. Panin agreed to the wish of the king that the number of dissidents in the Senate and Diet be fixed exactly. Panin agreed to this, all the more since without a definite figure being set the Catholic king and Catholic nobility constituted a majority and easily could exclude the dissidents completely.

But the dissidents submitted a request that a quota not be set on the number of government posts they could hold, for they were not in a position to take on these posts. The Orthodox nobility was unable to advance a single man who could be nominated to any office. "I have already searched and sent out couriers to bring me someone who has just a bit of ability," wrote Repnin. "But up to now I have found no one, for they all simply work the land and lack education." Konissky could not be a senator because of his family background and therefore had to be left in the diocese of Belorussia if the title of bishop of Belorussia were to be combined with that of senator. Repnin wrote: "Through the bishop of Belorussia I wrote to all the centers of our faith here, to find out if there are Polish nobles among our monks, in case it is decided that the bishop of Belorussia shall become a senator. I have no hope that this will be the case, or at least there are very few. On the other hand, the present bishop of Belorussia (Konissky) thinks that in our part of the Ukraine there are Polish nobles among the monks, and therefore I humbly request you to find out about this there. Are there such people and what sort are they? Their qualities should correspond to senatorial dignity."

On September 21 Repnin reported *turmoil* in Warsaw to Panin. A public outcry arose that the Diet should not be held in the presence of Russian troops. Repnin convinced the marshal of the confederation and the king himself that the confederation should issue a manifesto in which the Russian troops would be portrayed as friendly and helpers of popular freedom. Besides this, Repnin demanded a resolution from the confederation repudiating all oaths sworn by the delegates at the local sub-Diets opposing the sense of the act of confederation. Otherwise, the delegates who had given these oaths would be considered improperly chosen and not allowed to participate in the Diet. The confederation desired to do neither. The chief protestor was the nobleman Kosziuchowski. Repnin ordered his arrest, but then released him. As soon as it became known that Kosziuchowski was free, the papal nuncio visited him, followed by mobs of Poles, deifying him as a hero and martyr and getting portraits of him. Repnin ordered Kosziuchowski to say that he was going to his estate, if he did not wish to be arrested again. Kosziuchowski did not go voluntarily, and had to be transported to his estate under guard.

THE DIET MEETS

The Diet was supposed to open on September 23. On that day, when the delegates assembled at Prince Radziwill's to go to the first session together, the nuncio arrived and stated that the faith was perishing, their duty was to defend it to the last drop of blood, and they should not grant equality to other religions. In the name of the Pope he announced that no agreement could be given to the naming of plenipotentiaries from the republic to negotiate with the Russian ambassador, for the consequence inevitably would be the demise of the faith. The meeting was electrified. The calmest sobbed, while others swore loudly that they were ready to die for the faith. A minority—the king, cardinal, marshals of both confederations, and some fifty delegates—did not know what to do, or how to open the Diet, fearing carnage at the very beginning. At the climax of these scenes Repnin suddenly appeared at the assembly. Several moderate deputies ran up to meet him with exhortations to go back; otherwise they could not answer for his safety. But Repnin did not heed their advice and went straight into the middle of the crowd, which greeted him with the cry that all were prepared to die for their religion.

"Stop yelling!" Repnin said loudly. "If you continue to make noise, I will make noise, too, and mine will be louder than yours." The marshals of the confederations also came up and began to speak to the delegates, who ceased their shouting. When quiet reigned, Repnin began: "I only came to visit Prince Radziwill, and not to dispute with you, because none of you can have that honor, not being plenipotentiaries of the republic. But privately, I will say to you as a friend, that I am surprised and chagrined to see you in such a rebellious state. You have forgotten how much evidence you have of the good will of her majesty; you have forgotten that only under her protection could you confederate to preserve your rights and freedom."

Here Repnin's speech was interrupted by a shout: "We also united ourselves to preserve the Catholic faith!" Again Repnin told them to stop shouting, or else he would do the same. When the cries died down, he continued: "No one is taking from you the right to be firm in your belief. Of course, this ardor is praiseworthy. But really, who wishes to violate the rights of the Roman faith? If you are really true to your religion, you should obey its just dictates that no one should be coerced in matters of belief, be unshakeable in preservation of your obligations, and render justice to all. If you want good, neighborly relations with Russia and wish to enjoy the protection of her majesty, then observe the treaties. Only some troublemakers, who want to make a name for themselves in civil war, tell you that restoration of the dissidents' rights concerns Catholicism and can harm it. In reality, this is merely a secular matter, not religious, and should be considered politically in light of the commitments of the republic. Remember how you composed your confederations and what acts were promulgated in the process. Can you think that the policy of the Russian empire has changed in three months?"

There was no answer to this speech, only cries: "Free Koszuichowski!" "If you begin to scream," Repnin answered, "I will do nothing. Screams will get nothing from me—ask quietly, politely, in a seemly fashion, and perhaps I will give you satisfaction." Radziwill approached him and began to inquire politely about Koszuichowski. Repnin gave a promise and immediately kept it.

The Diet began and nothing indicated that it might end in a way satisfactory to the Russian envoy. There was no chance of agreement to send negotiators to Repnin for talks on the dissident question. There were cries that such delegates would bring the faith to ruin. "I cannot sufficiently depict the fanatical stubbornness of this nation," Repnin penned. "I have talked with almost everyone, and all answer the same, that they do not have the power to resist. The greater part of them have announced that they are prepared to lose their entire estate and die rather than agree to equality with the dissidents. Others tearfully have said the same to me. No matter how much I work, no matter how many blandishments and threats I employ, no matter how much the king, the cardinal, Radziwill, Brostowski, and the crown treasurer help, there is no success. I foresee, unfortunately, that I shall have to resort to the most extreme measures."

Seeing that the Diet was not disposed to send plenipotentiaries for talks, Repnin wished to suggest to the Diet that it send delegates to him to inquire what the empress desired for the dissidents. If they did not agree to this, no other means was left but to send a memorial to be read to the Diet and to ask a decisive reply. Repnin wished to act in concert with the foreign ministers of the states supporting the dissidents along with Russia. The chief among them was the Prussian minister, Benoit. But Repnin let it be known that secretly Benoit was stalling success in the dissident question by giving assurances that the Russians would only make threats but would never carry them out and that the king of Prussia would not abandon the Poles. Benoit lobbied especially against acceptance of the Russian guarantee. The Czartoryskis also worked secretly and quietly, but diligently, against the guarantee. They met several times at night with the bishop of Cracow. On the Czartoryski side, Prince Liubomirski, the high crown marshal, acted especially forcefully against Russia, but also in secret. The elder Czartoryskis swore young Adam, under pain of loss of his inheritance, not to be a delegate in talks with Repnin on the dissident question.

The October 1 session of the Diet commenced with a speech by the bishop of Kiev, who went so far in his statements against the dissidents as to call the freedom affirmed by law the work of the devil and slavery for the true believers. Then he began to complain about Koszuichowski's arrest, turned to the king and demanded that the latter demonstrate his devotion to the faith in deed as well as word. The king replied that, in addition to ardent support of Catholicism, he was obliged to assure the welfare of the fatherland. He recalled the obligations which the nation itself had incurred through forming the confederation and sending a delegation to the empress. He pointed out the harm that would be done were these obligations not met, and in conclusion demanded that the resolution of the confederations be read. When this was done, a tremendous noise arose; there were shouts from all sides: "Who signed that document?" The secretary of the confederation stated that the marshals signed on order of the united general confederation. Here Soltik rose: "The entire confederation and the breed who composed it originally have not read its letters of accreditation. Truly, they cannot read or write, if they signed such a document. Besides," Soltik continued, "I am not surprised at this, since the confederation was pushed to this step by the force of an absolute power. But now we can and must annihilate all the harm that it has done to Poland, including this document, which is contrary to religion and liberty. Our freedom has been violated completely by the arrests of Czacki and Kosziuchowski. The Diet must send delegates to the Russian ambassador to demand a written answer as to why he has acted as he has, and whether he had instructions to do so. Before receiving an answer from Repnin and the liberation of Czacki, I will allow nothing to be done or said in the Diet. Are all agreed on this?" The majority shouted, "Agreed!" Again the king began to speak quietly. "You yourselves do not know what you want. Such a delegation will insult the dignity of the empress herself. Instead of all this, you must diligently study the plan submitted by Prince Radziwill at the beginning of the Diet, and reconcile it with the act of confederation and the document sent to the empress. For this I will give you until the sixteenth of this month." The session ended.

Having heard of these events, Repnin deemed it indispensible to finish with Soltik. On Tuesday, October 2, a provincial meeting representing Little Poland[34] gathered at the house of the bishop of Cracow. The host spoke even more strongly than at the Diet against the dissenters and the guarantee. He announced that the Diet could not continue longer than two more days, through the next Friday and Saturday, since the usual two-week session for special Diets would end on those two days. Wenceslaw Rzewuski, the governor of Cracow, spoke out even more forcefully than Soltik. He was followed by the archbishop of Lwow and the bishop of Kiev, Zaluski. The whole gathering agreed with them, except Marquis Wielopolski, a representative from Cracow, who vainly opposed their decisions. No one would listen to him. The Russian governor, Prince Czartoryski, was also there and openly opposed the guarantee, but he spoke equivocally on the dissenters and prolongation of the Diet.

When the meeting ended and all had dispersed, Soltik went to have dinner with Marshal Mniszek. Having learned here that the detachment sent by Repnin awaited him upon his return, he arranged to stay with Mniszek overnight. Then Colonel Igelstrom entered Mniszek's house and arrested Soltik. Then he went to Zaluski and seized him. Meanwhile, Lieutenant-Colonel Shtakelberg took Rzewuski and his son Sewerin, the elder of Dolin. All of the arrested were sent with a sufficient escort to Wilno to General Numers, who had orders to treat them decently and not to offend them. On the third day after the arrests, a delegation of one senator from each province came to Repnin. They asked that the arrested be freed and the remaining deputies receive a guarantee of their personal safety. "I will not release the prisoners," Repnin answered, "because they deserved their fate. I will not give anyone except my sovereign an account of my actions. If you wish, you can go directly to her with your request. By the most gracious promise of her imperial majesty, the privilege and security of each citizen of the republic will be observed scrupulously if you on your part adhere as scrupulously to your commitments made in the last articles of the confederation and in the rescript sent to her imperial majesty with the embassy of the entire confederated republic, and if the country's representatives act according to the instructions given them by the local sub-Diets."

Fear had its effect. The Poles drew up a plan and named plenipotentiaries for talks with Repnin. The latter proposed to the delegates to prorogue the Diet until February 1, 1768, and stated: "I will treat anyone who opposes the plan for limitation of the Diet as an enemy of the empress. I will subject them to the same fate suffered by Soltik and his comrades, the carts are already prepared!" The Diet was prorogued. "The fear which the arrest of the bishop of Cracow and his comrades produced led to this," Repnin wrote on October 8, 1767. "I was forced to spread that fear to everyone with my words, especially to the Czartoryskis. I told them plainly that I would arrest them if I discovered any more opposition to this plan, for I knew quite well that they were intriguing against it. Such threats aroused such apprehension in all of them that not one voice was raised in the Diet against this plan. The Czartoryskis did not dare refuse anything and ordered Prince Adam to join the delegation sent to me."

The king could see with some satisfaction how his foes had been deceived in their hopes, after having formed a confederation. Thanks to his recent conduct and pliability in the matter of the dissidents, once again he had grown close to Repnin and received hope of achieving his cherished desire, limitation of the *liberum veto*. Repnin agreed to cooperate with him to this end, but this question was extremely delicate. The ambassador decided not to support the wish of the king directly with Panin. Instead, he presented the matter adroitly in the form of a question, plucking at Panin's most sensitive string—the system of the northern alliance.

Repnin wrote: "The king wishes to determine which questions should be decided unanimously and which by majority vote. If your radiance intends in the future to fashion of Poland something to augment the northern alliance, it seems that the following interpretation might be used with some care: support and preservation forever of the *liberum veto* in important matters which concern the form of government here. For example: in regular Diets unanimity shall be required to increase taxes, enlarge the armed forces, approve any treaty, declare war or sign peace treaties, determine the powers of civil and all state officials, the circulation and value of the currency, and other such important matters. Others which pertain to domestic order, it seems, can be left to majority vote without any danger for, lacking this there will be no order, and without order Poland is useless in the event you have any intentions for it."

Panin did not comment on these words in Repnin's letter; instead there was a note in Catherine's own hand, addressed to Panin: "Remember how dangerous this is. One cannot always say why Diets are dissolved. Furthermore, this totally contradicts your last letter to Prince Repnin."

Repnin's letter continued: "If you do not intend to make anything of Poland, to leave it in disarray and interfere constantly, you need not agree to this stature and merely respond to his Polish majesty that this is not acceptable and that we intend to preserve and not violate the laws. The king also has told me that in his letter to your radiance he attributes his deficiencies to me. I must say to this in all fairness that it is pitiful to view his poverty. It has gone so far that they borrow in bills of 500 or a thousand because sometimes they almost don't have enough to eat, and unfortunately he has no personal credit." Repnin's irritation with Stanislaw Augustus's subjects was expressed in his comments on the emissaries from the confederation to the Russian court. He wrote to Panin: "If in your customary courtesy and kindness you yield even the least bit they will pester you to death with their brainless and endless projects which have neither beginning nor end. Poles are such creatures that they will forget all limits completely the moment you remove fear from them."

Panin demanded that Repnin achieve full equality for the dissidents with the Catholics, with no quotas. Repnin answered that he hoped to do so without danger. "Our partisans," he wrote, "have assured everyone that they favor the dissidents in order to have our protection, but that subsequently they will give them no government posts nor any significant rewards. They deal only with necessary business through the confederation, whereas the dissident question presents so many obstacles that we will be forced to retreat from it. And this in fact is how they have acted in secret. But I knew about this before and now can almost assure you that they are completely mistaken and that the dissidents will achieve equality with the Catholics. I repeat that I am dealing with the latter quietly, with merely a stern demeanor, but I request that the communications of the delegates sent to you be shown to be false. Without this, they will embolden their correspondents and send such rubbish back here that there will be serious disorders. The Czartoryskis already have distanced themselves entirely from the king and of course will have no influence on events. I consider their total absence contrary to our interests. We need not give them preeminence in our party, but we must put them out as scarecrows, which we can use to keep those on our side firmly in hand. If our followers have nothing to fear within the country then, just like the Czartoryskis, they will wish to be independent of us."

Repnin kept his promises in the dissident question. The commission named to make a final resolution ordered that all dissidents of noble background receive equality with the Catholic nobility in political rights, that the king had to be Catholic, and that the Catholic faith remain dominant. Marriage between Catholics and dissidents was permitted. Of the children from mixed marriages, the sons would retain the religion of the father, the daughters of the mother, if there were no special conditions on this matter in the marriage contract. All religious disputes between Catholics and dissidents would be resolved by a mixed court consisting equally of Catholics and dissidents. The dissidents might build new churches, establish schools, maintain consistories and convene synods for ecclesiastical matters. All non-Catholics might acquire Polish citizenship.

Another question remained—the abolition of the achievements during the reign of Stanislaw Augustus concerning constitutional reforms. We have seen already that Repnin did not wish to aggrieve the king by complete annihilation of all these efforts. The ambassador continued to point to the services rendered lately by the king to Russia, and attempted to show that there was no need to make Stanislaw Augustus a sacrifice to his enemies, who were not at all strong. The confederation did not hold the importance which its emissaries in Moscow attributed to it. It was necessary merely to satisfy three or four leaders and everything would quiet down. Repnin maintained that the interests of the empress demanded that they *respect* the king—to prove to him that his own good fortune was connected closely with her friendship. One should acquire his full trust and direct allegiance. A king inclined to Russia would not refuse the empress' ambassador in questions of rewards for people loyal to Russia. Thus, it would be easy to establish a strong pro-Russian party. But how could the king be won over and a party of the best, most worthy people be formed? The king and the better people wished to limit the *liberum veto*.

Repnin wrote to Panin: "If you intend to give Poland even the smallest measure of strength for eventual use against the Turks, domestic order is necessary, for without it we will not obtain the smallest service or use from the Poles. The turmoil and disorder in the citizenry and all other sectors here is of such a degree that no more can be withstood. If you wish that as before all questions without exception be resolved in the Diet unanimously and that as before the Diets be dissolved by the *liberum veto*, I will see that this happens. Our power permits everything at present. But I dare to remonstrate that thereby not only will we not confirm the nation's trust in us and our influence here, but on the contrary we will destroy this and have a wound in the hearts of all rational and worthy men who wish a distinction in the laws (national questions confirmed unanimously, domestic affairs by majority vote). It is on these people alone that we can rely. They alone, in their reason, can stand at the head of the people. Consequently, we will degrade a great part of the nation if we subject it to the previous disorder through complete disruption of the Diets. In doing so, we will prove to the entire nation that we wish one thing—to see it in turmoil, enslaved.

"This will produce distrust of us and consequently will prevent the assembly of a party, independent of everyone but us, of reliable and worthy people, upon whose character and influence among the people we can rely. If we build a party of people who do not enjoy the esteem of the people, they will be only a burden to us, and useless. We will be compelled to do everything solely by use of force, and this will allow no possibility of having our own independent party. What glory there is to create happiness for an entire people and to allow them to emerge from disorder and anarchy! I believe in the possibility of combining politics with love for one's fellow man. I am flattered to be the agent of her majesty's intentions and to cooperate in making happy a people to whom I have the honor of representing her."

Reading this report, Catherine wrote to Panin: "Nikita Ivanovich, you can order answers prepared as to what we have agreed to, for there is hardly any event left where the *liberum votum* [sic] is of use to us. Why not allow our neighbors to make use of some order, to which we are indifferent, which might still be of some use to us sometimes?" As a result, it was decreed in regard to procedures of the Diet that during the first three weeks only economic questions would be considered. These would be decided by majority vote. All questions of state would be resolved in the last three weeks by unanimous vote.

FOREIGN REACTIONS TO EVENTS IN POLAND

We have seen that its ally, the king of Prussia, very much disliked Russia's insistence on resolution of the dissident question. But no matter how irritated he was, or how much he said that the empress of Russia had no right to mix in Poland's domestic affairs and that Poland's neighbors should watch that no changes occurred there, Russia's interference in the dissident question in and of itself was producing a great change and the Russian alliance was still a necessity for him. Without this alliance, Prussia was isolated and weak. When the minister Finkenstein suggested to Frederick that Prussia should not follow Russia's lead any further in Polish affairs, Frederick replied: "But if they were allied with Austria we would have to bear patiently everything they dreamed of doing in Poland."

Frederick himself did not wish to go far together with Russia in the matter of dissidents, and circumstances helped him to sign a new treaty with Russia in which he consigned to Russia the chores and responsibility for further activity in the dissident question by military means. The news of Austria's arming caused the Russian court in April 1767 to sign the following treaty with Prussia: Russia obliged itself to defend by force of arms the rights of the dissidents, while the Prussian king obliged himself to support these rights only by strong but friendly persuasion; if the Austrians invaded Poland and attacked Russian troops, the Prussian king was obligated to create a diversion by attacking Austrian possessions. In return, the empress promised him a suitable reward. The latter obligation was easy for Frederick to assume, for he considered that news of the conclusion of such an alliance between Russia and Prussia would restrain Austria from interferences in Polish affairs, and there would be no war.

Frederick wrote to Solms: "I am sending spies and emissaries into practically all of Austria's provinces to discover the intentions of the Austrian court. Besides this, I am awaiting two epochal events which should indicate what will come of the military preparations there. The first will be when a new confederation is formed and Russian forces invade Poland. The second will be when a new Diet convenes in Poland. What if it appeals to Austria for protection?" But the matter resolved itself simply; Austria feared that the dissidents within its own borders would rise.

Prince Dmitry Golitsyn informed the empress from Vienna of Austria's military preparations. He explained that they were caused by the fact that the Viennese court had learned of the movement into Poland of a significant number of Russian troops and feared disturbances among their own non-Catholic subjects, who might follow the example of the Polish dissidents in demanding return of the rights taken from them. Golitsyn reported further about the fears of the Viennese court that some other intent was hidden under cover of the dissident question. Russia and Prussia might have agreed upon seizure of some Polish territory. In such case, Austria definitely would take military action to thwart such a plan. As for the matter of the dissidents, even though its resolution was unpleasant for Vienna, the Austrians would not take military action in Poland over this alone.

There was greater danger in Turkey. In January Obrezkov reported that enemies of the Russian court were using their entire wits and forces to urge the Porte to intervene in support of the Poles. They told the Porte everything that might justify the Poles' conduct, even the *vituperative* speech of the papal nuncio at the last Diet. They proved to the Porte the baselessness of Russia's pretensions to the right of intervention in Polish domestic affairs. In this, the most passionate partisan was the Crimean khan. At first the Porte tended to look with equanimity upon Polish affairs and forbade the khan to intervene. But the khan again sent a dispatch saying that in view of the hardships forced upon them by the Russian empress for their refusal to satisfy her demands in matters of belief, the most eminent Poles intended to ask the Porte for defense and protection. The khan related that they had announced to their king that if he agreed to the demands of the Russian empress they would deprive him of his throne without fail. The French and Austrian ambassadors then appeared with their previous presentations that Poland was an independent state and the pretensions of Russia and Prussia regarding questions of faith in Poland were contrary to Polish freedom. These pretensions were dividing Poland in two and creating disorder among her neighbors. The Papal internuncio added that his court would not view this calmly. The Porte resolved to await direct representations from the Poles themselves. Informing Panin of this, Obrezkov requested that when Russian forces entered Poland the commander be given strict orders not to approach the Turkish border with even the smallest detachment.

On April 2, 1767 Obrezkov told Panin that the Austrian and French ambassadors had presented the Porte a note which claimed that the Russian court was attempting to annihilate Polish freedom and the old laws of the republic, and was doing this with the same despotism as if it were acting within its own borders. No one had expected such conduct from Russia. This was all the more true since the Ottoman empire had announced in its manifestos to the courts of Austria, France, and other states that it would never suffer harm to be done to the freedom and ancient laws of Poland. In light of such announcements, the Porte, to support its own dignity, should unite with their courts and take measures to defend Poland's liberty and the security of its own borders. The Russian court was acting so boldly in Poland because it relied on its alliance with the king of Prussia. Despite this, Austria and France could not view with equanimity what was happening in Poland.

To counteract this note, Obrezkov presented the sultan a note of his own, in which he advanced proofs of the rights of the dissidents and the right of the empress to defend them. He also transmitted Catherine's declaration to the Polish government, in which she affirmed that in this defense she had no ulterior motives. The Porte answered Obrezkov that it did not understand how Russia could take so great an interest in the dissident question as to deploy troops in Poland. If this matter had any connection with the articles of the treaty it could be settled through a plenipotentiary, without introducing troops on the territory of another power. Perhaps there were other reasons known by the resident for sending troops? Although the empress' declaration explained that her majesty found it unenviable and undesirable to seize Polish lands, nevertheless several of her opponents continued to insist that the dispatch of troops under the pretext of defending the dissidents actually aimed at acquisition of Polish territory. It was evident that the Russian court would not resort to such deception. But since the affair did not merit the sending of armed forces doubts arose involuntarily, and if the real cause of such conduct by the Russian court was unknown to the resident, it was desirable that he request a clarification from his court.

"The dissident question is very important, for its basis is an article of the solemn treaty," answered Obrezkov. "For fifty years Russian ministers in Warsaw constantly have sought to end the persecution of the dissidents, but all in vain. All peaceful means have been exhausted, and therefore troops have been sent. This was not done to restrict anything, but solely to preserve the republic from an inevitable civil war."

Summer passed peacefully. But in October the hospodar of Moldavia told the Porte that in Podolia, close to the Turkish border, a large Russian force had deployed with siege artillery and bombs. Three letters then had been received from Poland, from the governor of Kiev, Potocki, from Soltik, and from the bishop of Kamenets, Krasinski. All three letters said the same thing: that the Porte already knew how long the Polish kingdom had suffered the incursions of Russian forces and how these troops prevented the natural activity of freedom and the operation of the ancient laws of the kingdom. Aside from the Lord, Poland had no other hope of receiving aid except from the Porte. True sons of the fatherland were placing all their hopes on Turkey and hoped to find a safe refuge in the proximity of the Turkish border. They most humbly implored the sultan to order the Crimean khan and other frontier commanders to extend a helping hand to the oppressed.

These letters caused the Porte great anxiety and led to the formation of two parties. The ministry continued to maintain that it was necessary to maintain equanimity in the face of the Russian actions in Poland. But other influential persons, especially the clergy, began to say that it was not in the Porte's interests to endure such lengthy Russian hegemony in Poland. Obrezkov used his funds to spur into action several hidden sources of support and contrived that he be questioned as to the reports of the Moldavian hospodar, reports which, of course, he could refute easily. His reply once again pacified the Turks, who did not answer Potocki, Soltik, and Krasinski, and ordered the khan not to take any part in the troubles in Poland and merely to let the Poles know that the Porte would not suffer the approach of Russian troops to its borders, but that the Poles also should take care not to create disorders along their mutual border.

However, at the end of October the Porte again began to be uneasy as a result of news about the progress of the Diet, the arrest of Soltik and his confederates, and grumbling of many at the lack of initiative of the government, which had allowed Poland to be taken by Russian forces. As a result of this unease, the Khotin garrison was ordered reinforced. The French ambassador presented a note which stated that Poland and the balance of power in Europe were in danger. Since the era of Peter the Great Russia had attempted to destroy the *liberum veto* in Poland. Peter did not succeed in this intent and bequeathed the idea to his heirs. Upon the death of King Augustus III the Russian court raised its own creature to the Polish throne by means well known to all and sparked civil strife among the Poles for their own advantage, after filling the country with their troops. The Porte could not remain indifferent to its own interests and the sole means for it to eradicate the evil was the conclusion of an alliance with France.

The khan sent a Tatar who had just returned from Warsaw with the news that Russia had forced Poland into complete subservience, so much so that that kingdom should be regarded as already having fallen if the Porte did not rush to save it. Russia had arranged the present state of affairs according to its wishes and was moving to force the Poles to cede the provinces lying next to Turkey. For this, a force of 40,000 Russian troops was remaining in Poland indefinitely. Prince Repnin was alleged to have forced the republic to levy a new tax on the Poles to maintain the Russian armies and deployed this force around Warsaw so that foodstuffs were not allowed into the city without a pass. The Poles desired the Porte to dispatch an emissary of some kind to Warsaw on the pretext of greeting the king. This official should prevent the success in the Diet of the harmful Russian enterprises.

In Constantinople, such news was not viewed critically. It was not asked whether the Crimean Tatar was a competent observer of the events in Warsaw and offered only true information. As soon as the Tatar concluded his tales, the grand vizier cried: "Who expected this? How can we report to the sultan now? We absolutely must block these Russian schemes!" Councils were convoked and deliberated for a long time. Finally, it was determined that before a decision was reached an explanation would be demanded of Obrezkov. Were this explanation unsatisfactory, the Porte would proclaim itself the protector of Poland's rights and freedom and send an emissary there.

On December 3 Obrezkov met in secret conference with the reis-effendi.[35] The conversation lasted four hours. Obrezkov, in his words, "put every point in its place and offered such explanation that the reis-effendi seemed to be convinced and satisfied as to its veracity." The reis-effendi stated: "If you assure me that Russia does not intend to expand its holdings at Poland's expense, in return I offer you the hope that the Porte will not pay any attention to any of the aggression, intrigues, or slanders which it receives pending the final resolution of affairs in Poland. The Porte will take no action which might make Polish affairs still more difficult or put off their final resolution. But the Porte promises this upon one condition, that Russian forces should leave Poland within fifteen or at most twenty days after the conclusion of all matters. Besides this, all those arrested should be freed." In his own words, Obrezkov did not see anything unjust or unreasonable in the proposals of the Turkish minister and agreed to these two conditions.

The same kind of struggle was going on in the North between the French and Russian ambassadors in Sweden, which accepted Russia's proposal to speak out in favor of the Polish Protestants, despite the opposition of the French party. The latter stated that the confederation of dissidents was a simple rebellion which should not be supported. To support the Russian party, which insisted upon rejection of the French subsidies, it was necessary to procure for Sweden English subsidies, but England would not agree to pay. On this account, the empress wrote for Panin on Ostermann's dispatch: "They (the English) are dumping everything upon us, and I really am angry that they are so weak and act so blindly. Let Mr. Macartney know this: such actions will win him little esteem." Meanwhile, Ostermann reported that the French ambassador, Breteuil, had frequent secret meetings with the queen in the room of one Fräulein Gorn. Breteuil called upon the lady as if just for a visit, but met the queen there, who came from her private chambers via a secret passage. The king held a private meeting with the French ambassador and the Spanish emissary on the estate of the gentleman of the chamber, Count Delagardie. The king invited them to hunt reindeer there. The retinue was fairly small—only the friends of France. Not long before this the French ambassador was closeted with the king in the arsenal as a result of a supposedly inadvertent encounter.

Ostermann concluded his correspondence of that year with Panin with news of the means which the Swedish court was employing to prevent Stockholm's society, especially young people, from gathering at the house of the Russian ambassador. As soon as the court learned that Ostermann had announced a dinner, invitations were sent quickly to eminent persons, men and women, and then to the king and crown prince. Over the Christmas holidays, Ostermann gave a ball. At court, on the same evening, a lottery was scheduled. The guests whom Ostermann had invited told him that they would come to his dinner after the lottery. But when the court learned of this, it substituted for the lottery a ball which would continue after dinner. "I could have avoided these unpleasant situations by ending my entertaining," Ostermann wrote, "but knowing that the king and queen acted this way purposely to strengthen their party and to deprive me of means of attracting young people to our views, and that they state openly that they are not accustomed to depend upon the Russian yoke for their amusements, I intend to continue my dinners and balls until Lent. Although I do not have the choice of having a select group, I will entertain in my home at least those who have declared for us." Panin noted on the letter: "The friends of France always had such a policy, and it was always successful."

General Filosofov reported in March from Copenhagen that Baron Bernstorff had informed him secretly of the transfer of 500,000 livres from France to Breteuil in Sweden to strengthen the French party. Upon receipt of these funds, Breteuil had two meetings with the queen in the rooms of her chambermaid, but the queen and the ambassador had frequent disagreements over the use of the money. Speaking of this, Bernstorff noted that these weak efforts in no way would resurrect the dead French party and that no intrigues could lead to the convocation of a special Diet. Filosofov made known the necessity for Russia and Denmark, especially the latter, to act in an unbreakable alliance in Sweden and that Denmark need seek there no other friends save adherents of Russia.

Bernstorff answered that although their minister in Stockholm, Shalk, already had received special orders on that account, these orders had not yet been confirmed. He even asked Filosofov to designate a time limit for fulfillment of these instructions (in the original ". . . and he freely allows me to order a time limit for choice."). Filosofov reported: "I left this reasonable minister, so completely devoted to your majesty, free rein with a new royal edict of confirmation to direct Shalk to cooperate with Count Ostermann in all matters."

But a great danger, which Filosofov, along with Saldern, had to avert, threatened this common-sense minister, so completely loyal to Russia. In January Saldern wrote to Panin about his conversation with the British and Prussian ministers, who had begun openly to invite him to cooperate in undercutting Bernstorff. Saldern laughed in reply: "Are you really here, my dear sirs, to overthrow the Danish ministry? I at least am not here for that." The others were silent, and the Prussian minister did not renew the conversation. But the Englishman began again, and Saldern let him know in a friendly manner the whole amusing nature of this proposition. In Saldern's account, the Prussian minister, Borken, was a notorious intriguer, a malicious man, and a liar. Bernstorff told Saldern that Borken often filled the king's head with ruinous thoughts and that he, Bernstorff, considered him a dangerous man. Saldern began to observe and gather intelligence. In consequence of these investigations he informed Panin what Frederick II said to Mitchell, the British minister in Berlin. The king stated that he was dissatisfied with Saldern's embassy and wanted to complain to Panin about Saldern. He looked upon Saldern as a man possessed by his northern system but that he, the king, considered this system harmful to Great Britain and Prussia. Saldern stated further that Mitchell, who was devoted without limit to the Prussian king and obsessed with the necessity of the closest possible alliance between England and Prussia, was telling the cabinet in London that too close an alliance between Russia and Denmark, for which Saldern was working, would shift the balance of power to Russia. England had to unite with Prussia to prevent Russia from becoming the central, chief power in the North. The Russian ministers in Copenhagen must oppose the actions of Prussia and England. To do this, one must support Bernstorff and influence the Danish king. The latter, according to the remarks of Saldern and Filosofov, was very poorly educated. He was not stupid and possessed some learning, but he was too lighthearted and lively and therefore inconsistent in his actions. Indeed, it is natural for a man who has been freed from slavery to lose control of himself in freedom, which is so close to license. The king considers himself higher than the laws. He does not know their nature or power. He does not trust the ministers of his father and distances himself from them. He scorns the court youths, who are all less talented than he. Saldern told the king that he was convinced that the king would trust Bernstorff, without having to like him. "The king," Saldern wrote, "loves to talk and often converses with me. I do not conceal the truth from him when I find a favorable chance to be forthright. The French ambassador is enraged and the Prussian bites his lips because he formerly enjoyed this privilege."

On February 22, 1767 Bernstorff visited Saldern and Filosofov and told them secretly in horror that the king proposed to make great changes in the army. He was taking the direction of the War Department from his son-in-law, the duke of Hesse, and transferring command to Field Marshal Saint Germaine. Almost all of the previous staff of the department would be replaced, and the colonel, Count Herz, would receive command of the Cavalry Department. But Herz's arbitrary and dishonorable character frightened Bernstorff. He could win the heart of the king through intrigue and lead the sovereign to cruel actions. This same Herz was trying to persuade the king to exile the prince of Hesse completely from the kingdom. He had not succeeded, but all the same the prince had been posted away as *Staatsalter* in Schleswig.

The Russian ministers noted to Bernstorff that Herz was not alone in undermining the prince of Hesse. The Prussian envoy, Borken, was in it with him. But of course this did not lessen Bernstorff's apprehensions. The latter voiced his despair that internal measures could not forestall this horrible storm. Then the Russian ministers offered themselves to him as tools to avoid such unpleasant circumstances. They were prepared to intercede in the name of the empress with the king for the prince of Hesse. If the king did not satisfy their requests, they would threaten him with rupture with Russia. Bernstorff answered that the Russian ministers were the only people who could influence the king. Not waiting a moment, Saldern sent to request an audience on the pretext that having regained his health he wished to thank the king for his majesty's frequent inquiries about his illness. The king set a time and Saldern, "in view of his well-known gift for persuasion" (in Filosofov's words), succeeded in demonstrating to the king the entire harm which might come from exile of the prince of Hesse, and the king changed his mind about sending the prince to Schleswig. The entralled Bernstorff called Saldern and Filosofov angels and saviors of Denmark. It was possible, however, only to request that the prince of Hesse remain in Copenhagen, and Saint Germaine became war minister. Saldern and Filosofov had to struggle with the latter to protect the people loyal to them.

At the very end of August Bernstorff let Filosofov know secretly through a third party that at the urging of Saint Germaine the king had agreed to take the Prussian minister, Borken, into his service. If the Russian minister did not force the king in the name of the empress to change that decision, the fall of the ministry was inevitable. Filosofov swiftly demanded an audience and stated bluntly that Borken was opposed to the empress' court—if he was taken into Danish service the alliance between Denmark and Russia would never be signed. The audience lasted three hours. The king remonstrated and assured Filosofov that it had never entered his head to do anything against the empress. Field Marshal Saint Germaine had not mixed into any political affairs and had not tendered him any advice. Then Filosofov demanded a solemn promise that the king would never take Borken into his service nor allow Herz close to his person.

The king replied that he had never even wished to do so. But Filosofov insisted that he promise not to do so in the future. Finally the king gave his word as follows: "I swear to her majesty most solemnly upon my royal word never to take Borken into my service or to allow Herz to become a confidante. I also beseech the empress to lend strong cooperation in having the king of Prussia recall Borken from the Danish court." Departing from his audience, Filosofov said to the king: "I leave your majesty in the assurance that the promise which your majesty has given always will remain sacred and inviolate."

"I call Heaven as my witness," replied the king, "that I consider this promise as binding as a written treaty."

"And despite all this," Filosofov wrote to Panin, "the frivolity of the king and the increase in pressure from the opposing party arouse in me the fear that everything may change, the present ministry will fall, and our conversations will be broken off. The present ministry is extremely timid. Not only does it not dare make strong representations to the king, it fears to give even the smallest appearance of agreement with me. Except for a conference one day each week, at Bernstorf's request I am forced to avoid meeting with him and I receive all my information and other opinions from him through State Councillor Schumacher. As opposed to this, Saint Germaine openly offers his advice to the king and thus gains ascendence over the other envoys."

Bernstorff told Filosofov that a separate article needed to be added to the treaty between Russia and Denmark. This article would obligate the king never to receive Borken in his service nor to allow Herz to become close to him personally. The empress wrote Panin on this account: "It is necessary to act so that the king of Prussia will recall Borken. It is true that the secret article will be strange and will do no honor to the Danish king."

Filosofov informed the empress of Bernstorff's expressions of the deepest thanks for obtaining the solemn royal promise. He accused the minister of timidity and the king of frivolity. But in his letter to Panin at the end of the year Saldern attempted to exonerate the king and indict the ministers for ingratitude, although Filosofov had satisfactorily explained their conduct as timidity. "We have done the impossible," Saldern wrote, "not only in avoiding the threatened danger but in searching out the way to the king's heart, in order to render constant and firm all that which he did out of conviction, voluntarily, and not as a result of fear and force. The king is a young man, extraordinarily vibrant and passionate. He is inclined to self-indulgence not by temperament, but from some frivolity and a desire to know everything by his own experience. He should be pitied. He wishes well, if only he is allowed his little buffooneries. He wishes well and not just in words. It is apparent that he does good also. The misfortune lies in the fact that not one of his ministers enjoys his confidence. It is even more unfortunate that not one of them works to deserve his esteem and trust, to gain entry to his heart, which would unfailingly be receptive were the ministers to incline a bit more to the sovereign's dreams and had more skill in winning his trust. Such is my opinion. It is based upon my own experience. I know that if one plays up a little to his vanity, one may gain influence over him. It must appear that he is acting out of his own desire and according to his own reasoning. But I cannot remain silent about the fact that the ministers here whom we support are ungrateful. Not one of them thanked us properly for our ardor in their cause, while we were the first to congratulate them on their triumph. Not one of them paid us a visit after that. Count Bernstorff with his customary duplicity barely gave us in the third place a hand signal that he knew how much he was indebted to us. Count Reventlow, a coarse and vain man, showed us not the slightest gratitude."

The Danish envoy to the Russian court was Asseburg, who was a friend of Panin and a friend of Prussia. Henry Shirley, in charge of the British embassy after Macartney's departure, said of Asseburg that he should sooner be considered a minister of the Prussian than of the Danish court. This was a bad recommendation to the British ministry, which attributed all the talk in Russia unfavorable to England to Frederick II. This was just, as we know. Shirley wrote to his court entirely correctly about the relationship of the king of Prussia to Russia: "I am convinced that he does not sincerely share the views of this court. He is not entirely a devotee of the northern system. Necessity alone (the alliance of Austria, his natural enemy, with the House of Bourbon) can force him to seek refuge in Russia's protection. If he could act openly without any danger to himself, he would rapidly mount opposition to the intentions of the empress. He views the rapidity with which she increases her power and significance with great discontent. One need only watch his conduct attentively in Constantinople, Poland, Denmark, and Russia to see how he fears Russia and is not at all devoted to its interests. Although he does not declare himself openly and acts only underhandedly, nevertheless he does all he can to impede the success of Panin's system. There is no doubt that he would view an alliance between our king and the empress with great irritation."

This was justified, but it would be strange to suppose, as the British did, that solely upon the urging of Frederick II Russia would refuse to conclude an alliance with Britain, excluding Turkey from the terms of the alliance. Above all, Catherine wanted peace; she was deeply disturbed by the troubles in Poland and Sweden, and thus even less desired war with Turkey. Being assured that Austria and especially France would not bypass any opportunity to feed the Porte hostile representations against Russia, Catherine desired, on the contrary, that England use all its influence to restrain the Turks from war. England intended to do this and would do so out of its own interest, if the alliance obligated it to aid Russia in the event of a Turkish attack upon the latter. This is why Shirley heard from Panin the previous view that, without mention of Turkey, there could be no alliance.

Shirley also attentively followed Panin's fortunes. A curious note of May 9, 1767 from Betsky[36] to Catherine has survived. It expresses a strong animosity against Panin and great discontent with his importance. "I see that to your majesty Nikita [Panin] is a great man. I am going to visit him today, and I advise others to do the same." At the end of the month Shirley wrote to his ministry that the Orlovs' envy of Panin had burst out with new force. They sought his downfall, and used all means to blacken him in the empress' eyes. They alleged that one person should not hold both the function of supervision over the education of the grand prince and the conduct of foreign relations. It was necessary to name Panin chancellor and assign the education of the heir to someone else. They suggested Ivan Ivanovich Shuvalov.[37] But removal of Panin from the palace would be a sign of his fall. Catherine opposed this and tried to reconcile Panin and the Orlovs. To Panin's good fortune, Count Alexis Orlov has fallen dangerously ill. If he lived, he would have to go abroad for a cure, and without him Grigory Orlov will do nothing.

NEW RESISTANCE IN POLAND

At the beginning of 1768 one might think in Petersburg that the burdensome Polish affair was over. "Now we have entered a time of peace and quiet," Panin told Solms. And in Warsaw the king began to ponder various reforms again. At the end of February (March 5 N.S.), Stanislaw Augustus wrote to the empress: "Since everything has been done in Poland according to your wishes, all of the new regulations beneficial to Poland and all of the personal advantages which I have received constitute a new basis for my gratitude to your imperial majesty. I acknowledge these debts and will always do so as openly as I will cooperate in the fulfillment of your wishes. The unswerving directness of my character at the same time prompts me to renew constantly to your majesty the substantive requests regarding subjects which, in my convictions, are vital to Poland's happiness. Leave me the hope that gradually you will agree to my requests and that I will receive from you sooner or later these priceless boons." Catherine answered: "I am happy that I helped the republic gain a permanent, unchangeable constitution which is advantageous for all classes."

The happiness of the empress that a "permanent, unchangeable" constitution had been instituted demonstrated to the king that it was difficult for him to hope for Russian cooperation in altering this constitution, at least in its essential parts. Petersburg wished above all to have done with the matter and to demonstrate that one could not go unpunished for being a false friend of Russia. The Russians saw clearly that the Czartoryskis, and the king under their influence, wished to use Russia as an instrument to change the constitution. When the Russian court, relying on the loyalty of a *Russian* party, tried to use the Czartoryskis as a means of achieving its goals, the Czartoryskis refused to help. This was considered treachery. Russian relations with this family thus were defined, and in the future it was deemed necessary to free the king and country completely from the influence of the Czartoryskis. Arriving from Moscow at the very end of 1767 Colonel Igelstrom transmitted to Repnin Panin's desire that Michael, the elder Czartoryski, grand chancellor of Lithuania, be *driven* from his post. Repnin eagerly set about the task. Through various channels, among them the daughter of the elderly governor of Wilno, Repnin let him know that in his old age he might not survive the misfortunes which might come his way. He should retire voluntarily at his present rank; otherwise, he would lose that rank as a result of indictment by a court of the confederation for inciting a rebellion in his fatherland with his intrigues.

The entire family, including the king, was greatly agitated by Repnin's threats, for conviction by a court of the confederation was considered extremely shameful. The king stated to Repnin that he requested the empress not to allow such a trial and strain his nearest relative. Repnin answered with severity that he would report this to the empress but meanwhile he could not halt fulfillment of the instructions which he had received to strengthen the confederation in all its actions. The whole Czartoryski family then tried to persuade their elder to avoid deprivation of his rank, but the old man answered that he would sooner suffer trial and conviction than display fear. "Thus I do not know," Repnin wrote, "whether I will succeed in frightening him and thereby turn him out of his post. If not, I will pretend that I have felt sorry for them and that her imperial majesty, solely out of compassion, has forbidden such a reprisal." Then Repnin reported that Czartoryski was willing to suffer all possible misfortunes rather than give up his rank, for the latter action might seem to be an acknowledgement that he deserved some sort of punishment. But the old man also did not wish to suffer any woes, and he therefore let Repnin know that not only he, but also his brother August, the Russian governor, would leave Warsaw right after the Diet, go to their estates, and not meddle further in any affairs. They wished to spend the time remaining to them in complete peace and quiet. To this, Repnin expressed the opinion that the old men had been degraded enough, and it was better to leave them in peace. Otherwise, their complete demise might raise their opponents too high and free them of dependence upon Russia. The same had happened with the Czartoryskis, who had been pushed too high by the late Count Keyserling,[38] who had relied too much on their loyalty. The empress agreed to leave the Czartoryskis alone.

But at the same time Repnin received an unpleasant letter from Obrezkov in Constantinople. The letter informed him of the promise he had given to the Porte that Russian forces would leave Poland quickly upon resolution of the dissident question and all those arrested would be freed. Repnin wrote to Panin: "I must say that the immoderation of the Porte in their demands surprised me less than the timid concessions of Obrezkov, who is content with them, as if they were a success. It is not a minister now, but a soldier who speaks to your radiance. It seems to me that to accept such conditions and give such promises can be done only after losing several battles. As far as liberating those who were arrested, there is no way we can release the bishop of Cracow, for the entire public would view him as a god. He would stir up hatred for all his enemies and raise his own repute upon the ruins of their reputations. One must not arouse the confederation or the Diet, where there is a majority of irrational fanatics, to the point where they adjudge Soltik a criminal and deprive him of his standing. The people will view such judges as apostates, and I include three-quarters of the gentry in the people. I see no other means of satisfying the demands of the Porte than to announce that the bishop of Cracow has died and send him for all time to a place whence there will be no news that he is alive. If this seems unmerciful to your excellency, I dare suggest that it would be even less merciful, in freeing him, to deprive those serving us of their status, arouse hatred against them, and plunge the whole land into confusion. Finally, if our attention is diverted, the entire dissident matter will be endangered. I must say exactly the same thing about the lord hetman, Count Rzewuski, who is infected with immoderate conceit and passion for intrigue. Because of his rank, he will be dangerous. He will be worshipped and our adherents will be subjected to scorn, hatred, and *discreditation*. The two others may be released when the Diet ends. The bishop of Kiev is a liar and enjoys no respect, while the young Count Rzewuski, the elder of the Dolina, has no significance himself and was trained to be so audacious by his father." As for withdrawal of the troops, Repnin considered a winter march exhausting. He also thought it not propitious to remove all the troops. In the fall the regular Diet would meet, preceded by the local diets. Vigilance was necessary lest the Catholics catch their breath and undertake something against the dissidents.

In his answer, Panin agreed that "Obrezkov acted with excessive, uncalled for submissiveness," but he explained this by Obrezkov's ill health. "But now," Panin continued, "the deed is done and he cannot be reinstructed without more trouble. We must untie this poorly bound knot by at least offering outward proof of fulfilling our promise. If we grease the palms of the Turkish ministry we can gain some time, which is the best healer in the world." In Panin's opinion, it was necessary to withdraw the forces in May and to send off some units in the winter—at least to give marching orders for the forces nearest the Turkish border by the close of the Diet. It was impossible to hold the troops until fall, given relations with Turkey and the other powers, for there was no justification for such a delay. Panin wrote that, "In light of my unlimited confidence in your radiance, I must reveal to you that the time is not ripe for us to break relations with the Porte."

Repnin had to recognize the justice of these instructions when the papal nuncio presented a protest in the sharpest terms against all that had happened since the convening of the present Diet. "I know this nation," Repnin wrote, "and I do not doubt that as soon as the protest spreads through the public most Poles will become timid, distraught, and perhaps despair completely. A small number of thinking people who regard the protest from the present point of view will not dare utter a single word against it. Finally, I fear that just before the Diet confirms the decrees it has issued, the nuncio will announce that all who vote for approval will be excommunicated. Everyone then will distance themselves from the dissidents' cause and I will not know how to act in such circumstances." Panin counselled the envoy to tell the Poles how degrading the protest of the nuncio was for the republic, since it debased, blackened, and defamed its solemn legislation, for which the republic need answer to no one. Panin wrote: "Pull all strings to convince the king, the ministry, and the confederation to give the Pope a broad, firm reply to the effect that in the future he should not make similar attempts at intervention. Thus you can freely wind up all our affairs. Do not spare any promises or bribes, for both these means cannot be used at a better time. Assure the king and everyone else that if they fulfill this wish of ours, they can count absolutely on the patronage of her imperial majesty. But since it easily may be that arguments and proofs will be of no help, you can arrest those who will most oppose at the Diet ratification of the agreements reached by the delegation or vainly seek time to burden us with new appeals. As for the thunder from the Vatican, which might attack and undermine the entire edifice we have built to aid the dissidents, I recommend that you use money, flattery, threats, and in general all possible measures to bring the king and the magnates to a unanimous view of the danger identical to yours. If it should truly come to pass, then label the nuncio a subverter of the peace, a slanderer, and violator of the peoples' rights, for he denounces the fact that the republic exercises its sovereign right to pass laws and make agreements with a friendly neighboring power. You can even confine him to his own residence, so that he cannot see anyone or pronounce an edict of excommunication. Or, even quicker and more seemly, try to expel him from the country under reliable surveillance and continue his journey while the Diet approves all matters before it. If you succeed in settling all matters in the Diet before the excommunication, it seems that you need worry no more about averting the anathema. You will be able to leave to the Poles' judgment whether this curse will send them to hell. It is very necessary that you embolden the king and cardinal and lead them to tell the Pope that the time has passed when popes managed affairs according to their whims. Instead of good, his unseemly ardor may bring the Catholic faith only harm, and remove Poland from its present submission to the Roman See. Having sufficient means and force to govern in Poland, the king and cardinal, in light of the Pope's unseemly actions, might decide to abolish papal authority there and establish an independent church hierarchy. You may tell the king and cardinal that their honor and the reputation of the republic demand firmness from them. Otherwise, having acceded to this first attempt by the Pope, they will plunge themselves into extreme slavery and the darkness of ignorance at the moment when all other Catholics are ridding themselves of this infection."

Repnin did not consider it possible to take the measures proposed by Panin regarding the nuncio. "The nuncio has quieted down," he wrote. "I am content that the public has forgotten his protest. It is as unthinkable to act against this protest through the Diet or confederation as to use artillery fire—everyone would just be chased off, but the goals would not be attained. Still less can one hope that the government here will confine the nuncio to his house or deport him. They would rather die than do that."

THE SETTLEMENT WITH POLAND

On February 23, 1768 Repnin informed Panin that the Diet had adjourned. It had approved the treaty with Russia, two separate documents, and all points agreed upon by the delegation and Repnin. Consequently, he ordered all Russian forces to remove to the Russian border. The treaty, signed on 13/24 February, read: "Whereas the most illustrious Kingdom of Poland and Lithuania, for eternal steadfastness of all that which it now has enacted for its own benefit, most solemnly has beseeched and now beseeches a guarantee from her all-Russian imperial majesty of the constitution, form of government, freedom, and laws, her imperial majesty, in satisfaction of the wishes and friendly confidence of the most illustrious Kingdom of Poland and Lithuania, solemnly guarantees with this treaty for all time the constitution, form of government, freedom, and laws, and gives a sacred promise and obliges herself and her heirs to protect, preserve, and defend the most illustrious Kingdom of Poland and Lithuania in its inviolable entirety."

A separate document contained the freedoms and privileges of the oriental Greeks, non-Uniates, and dissidents. The Catholic faith received the designation *dominant*. The king and queen were required to be Roman Catholics. Renunciation of Roman Catholicism for another faith was to be a criminal offense. All enactments discriminating against Greeks, non-Uniates, and dissidents in the confederations and constitution were annulled. The Greek non-Uniate churches and dissident parishes, cemeteries, schools, hospitals, and other structures belonging to the churches and clergy might be repaired freely and rebuilt without obtaining permission in case of fire or decay. Services with public processions might be held in these churches provided, however, that no obstacles were posed thereby to Catholic services and processions. The bishops of Mstislav, Orsha, and Mogilev, in the name of the bishop of Belorussia, would govern their dioceses without interference, just as the Roman bishops did. Non-Uniates and dissidents enjoyed the right to establish printing presses and print books for church services, as long as they did not publish heretical works and avoided a polemical style on disputed, inflammatory points pregnant with possibilities for dispute. Marriage between persons of different faiths was permitted. The sons of such marriages would be raised in the faith of the father, daughters in that of the mother. Nobles were allowed to make a contract on this point before the marriage. Non-Uniate Greeks and dissidents did not have to celebrate Catholic holidays and participate in Catholic processions. All churches and monasteries which had been confiscated improperly from the non-Uniate Greeks were to be returned. A joint court of seventeen persons was established for religious offenses. The court was to be composed of eight lay Roman Catholics and eight non-Uniate Greeks or dissidents—the seventeenth member to be the bishop of Belorussia.

Since the equality of the nobility was the basis of Polish freedom and the most reliable bulwark of the rights of the fatherland, all their ancient rights were returned to the non-Uniate Greeks and dissidents. They were declared eligible for all ranks, senatorial and ministerial posts, royal and civil service positions, court and commissioned offices, foreign embassies and missions of the Diet, and receipt of rewards from the king. In sum, the non-Uniate Greeks and dissidents were returned to complete participation in the civil and military services. Also, religion could not bar persons of non-Uniate or dissenting faiths from acquiring full citizenship and noble status.

However, in a postscript to this letter in which he gave news of adjournment of the Diet and ratification of the treaty, Repnin also relayed rumors of a dissident movement in the Bar district, although he expressed doubts of the veracity of these rumors. On March 4 Repnin even took a reassuring tone in informing Panin of the state of affairs in Poland. There was no more foreign influence in Poland, Repnin asserted. The French and Austrians had no party. Finally, the king of Prussia had no friends, since he had insulted the entire country with the Marienwerder tariff[39] and offended the Polish border provinces by the various claims and crude arrogance of his military commanders in dealing with Prussian runaways and conducting impressment campaigns. Consequently, only fanaticism could provoke rebellion in the short run, until the population had become accustomed to seeing dissidents as equal to Catholics. No harm would arise from freedom for the dissidents.

Panin wrote: "I have tried to manage things so as to reward our followers as much as possible while insulting our opponents as little as possible and not leave in their hearts any hatred or thirst for revenge. I have defended our opponents when they were attacked unjustly. I wished to demonstrate clearly that the empress defends justice and all the nation, not just one party. This effort was manifested in the calmness with which I restrained the confederation."

CONFRONTATION: THE CONFEDERATION OF BAR

But Repnin soon sent the true story about the confederation formed by malcontents at Bar. In Repnin's opinion, Russia needed to pay attention to this event. "Shall we abandon the treaty just concluded and her imperial majesty's guarantee, obtained through such labor of the Russian empire? Would it not be an affront to Russia's honor, dignity, and glory if at the very moment of conclusion of this treaty we looked peacefully upon obstacles standing in the way of our proposals? Having been involved in these new rebellions, there is no way that we can withdraw our troops from here. On the contrary, we should use them in a real display, which might tether the Porte, which was promised their return to Russia. The Turks will have even more pretexts if we chase these rebels to the Turkish borders and the rebels learn of our caution about the Turks and stay near the border. Consequently, we must be prepared not to flee in shame from the Turks or Tatars should they think to give us orders forbidding approach to their borders. I know that it is not convenient for us to engage vainly in disputes with the Turks. But if they have no private hostile intentions toward us, they will not seek pretexts for breaking relations. They will be calmed by assurances which our court can give them. If they are not satisfied by this and seek reasons for a rupture, it is better to warn them than to make them even more haughty by extraordinary solicitude for their whims."

It was necessary above all to try to pacify the Turks by peaceful assurances. Panin drafted a letter to the vizier and the empress wrote on this occasion: "With God's help, the thunderclouds will pass this time if you send your letter to the vizier as soon as possible. Please do not dally; if you still find it necessary to take some measures or other in the Ukraine which will give a good countenance, talk to me about it at our next meeting. But it seems to me that Count Rumiantsev's two corps are sufficient for that."

Panin completely agreed with Repnin on the necessity of action against the Bar confederation. He wrote: "It is necessary to disperse the clouds gathering in Bar before they cover the earth or lead one or another power, especially the Porte, into the temptation of undermining the structure we erected at the Diet." In consequence of the unknown circumstances in which the Bar confederation had formed, Panin refused to give Repnin an order how to act against it. He gave the ambassador plenipotentiary powers to employ on the spot those measures which he found best, without further consultations.

The situation soon became clear. The property magistrate[40] of Rozansk, Krasinski, the brother of the bishop of Kamenets, along with Ioasif Pulawski, a well-known lawyer, seized the city of Bar, belonging to Prince Liubomirski, and raised the banner of rebellion in the name of faith and freedom. Mark, a monk from the Berdichev monastery, went around to the various villages with cross in hand and proclaimed the necessity of joining the rebel confederation. In Galicia, another confederation was formed under the leadership of Joachim Potocki, the under cupbearer of Lithuania. Rozewski announced the formation of another confederation in Lublin. But the uprising was unable to become popular in character; the loud cries of *faith* and *freedom* made no impression even upon the majority of the Polish Catholic population. It was difficult to rise for the faith when one relied solely on the word of one Father Mark and did not see who oppressed the faith or how this was done. It was difficult to fight for a freedom which only the nobility enjoyed and used solely to form confederations first against one thing and then against another, while inviting the aid of foreign troops. Now they wished to raise a confederation to restrict these troops, whom they proclaimed the enemies of freedom. It was very hard, moreover, to understand what this enmity consisted of. The conduct of the members of the confederation made it quite incapable of arousing popular sympathy. Their bands spread through the countryside, seized government funds, and robbed friend and foe alike, Catholics and dissidents, clergy and laymen. Having grabbed the money, these bands fled to Hungary or Silesia. Terrible confusion and dissension began to reign everywhere. Brother distrusted brother; everyone had his own interests and intrigues. No one gave a care for the fatherland. One man composed thunderous manifestos against the Russians and joined the confederation, while his brother contracted with the Russians to supply their stores with foodstuffs.

Among the members of the confederation Cavalry Captain Klebowski was distinguished by boldness of a special kind. When he met a pauper, a Jew, or any other sort of pedestrian on the highway, he had him hanged at once on the nearest tree so that, according to his Polish contemporaries, the Russians would need no guides—they could find the confederation members by following the trail of corpses. The gangs did not diminish after being defeated by the Russians because the pay was good, the food sufficient, and free at that. Depravity, absolute power over the inhabitants of the country, and humiliation of the most eminent nobles before the confederation's members, who not long before had been their servants—all this drew to the confederation's banner all sorts of rabble, servants, city dwellers, and peasants who did not wish to work. At the price of several hours of fear when encountering and fleeing from the Russians, lavish parading about the country in the guise of a defender of faith and freedom was sufficient reward.

On April 2 Repnin wrote that in Bar the Poles continued their same waywardness and held close to the Turkish borders. "There is similar ferment everywhere. I note this in various bits of news from all sides. I see that only the fear of our troops located there keeps them quiet against their own will and they await only movements from us to spread the flames of the fanaticism which already burns within them."

Even earlier, on March 27, the Senate decided to request the empress of all the Russias, as the defender of freedom, legality, and the rights of the republic, to use her troops stationed in Poland to suppress the rebels. The troops moved. Lieutenant Colonel Lieven, with one battalion, marched to Lublin and set fire to it. The clergy came out of the city and asked Lieven for mercy, but while they were conducting negotiations the members of the confederation fled through the other gates. Lieven finally gave the clergy twenty-four hours to convince the townspeople and confederation members to surrender, but he did not guess that the latter already had fled the city. Angered by such negligence on Lieven's part, Repnin sent Colonel Kar to replace him. In Gniezno Colonel Burman immediately put down the uprising. The commander-in-chief of the forces acting against the confederation of Bar was Major General Krechetnikov. Major General Podgorichani marched on old Konstantinow, hurried his cavalry detachment, and ordered it to attack. But he had to retire when he saw the impossibility of fighting cannons with only carbines. He implored Krechetnikov to send him infantry and artillery. "Nothing can be done with my small cavalry detachment," he wrote, "but one can lose men, horses, and honor and glory as well. The enemy is about and danger is everywhere. The nobles and the common people are in complete agreement with the rebels and friendly to their spies. Your excellency does not consider them any menace at all. I am sparing no labor; I had nothing like this when I was in the Prussian war.[41] There isn't a moment's peace and the horses are saddled day and night." Repnin assured Panin that the individual commanders were exaggerating the danger. They believed what the Poles were saying, and the Poles magnified everything ten times. "I cannot imagine," wrote Repnin, "that even 10,000 Poles ever could stand against one thousand of our troops as long as they are commanded properly. However, it is perfectly true that all lesser and middle nobles, all except the great lords, are being pushed to fanatical extremes by the priests and monks. Consequently, deep down everyone agrees with the rebels, from which it follows naturally that they help them secretly and supply them privately with whatever each has to offer."

Catherine read the reports of Repnin and the military commanders and wrote to Panin: "Communicate with Count Chernyshev. I have spent the whole day, morn till this hour with him, reading these reports. I think that Major General Podgarichaninov [sic] soon will deliver us from these entreaties, for there is glory, bravery, and skill in him. Pity, what a pity that he did not succeed in taking Konstantinow with the hussars alone, for a laurel wreath would have decorated his old grey head."

Krechetnikov wrote Repnin that only one thing disturbed him—the small number of troops assigned to him. In May Repnin wrote that the matter was becoming more serious by the hour. He proposed that it might be useful for him to go to the scene with some troops because he was better acquainted with the Poles than the other generals. Catherine commented: "I do not wish to risk his person, and I think that Podgorichani will deal with the insurgents, especially when we can be confident that neither the Turks nor the Tatars will aid them." In reality, the news soon arrived that Podgorichani had routed a sizeable detachment of confederation forces near Kmelnik, in the province of Podolia. But Repnin added: "I do not think that this will end the troubles." Indeed, they were not finished even when Colonel Veisman successfully brought to bay the confederation forces under the command of Potocki, the under cupbearer of Lithuania, beyond the Dniester.

It was understood in Warsaw that Russia's troubles had not ended but were merely beginning, and the Poles began to accede only unwillingly to Repnin's demands. Thus, when he stated that the Polish government could not remain a disinterested observer of the struggle of Russian forces against the confederation members, especially since the latter were seizing fortresses and imprisoning royal troops, the military commission resolved, not without dispute, to send royal troops and the regiment general against the confederates. The castellan of the Lublin fortress, Moszinski, protested this decision and resigned as military commissioner. In Panin's name Repnin asked the king to give the Order of the White Eagle[42] to two individuals whom Stanislaw considered his enemies. The king refused, whereupon Repnin wrote Panin a curious letter. "We need not let it go at this, so that he not become used to having his way. If I might dare say to your excellency, you have damaged me somewhat with respect to him. He has concluded from your letters and flattering dealings with Psarski (the Polish resident in St. Petersburg) that you are gracious. He thinks that you will spare him and that I alone am the devil who treats him by my own habit rather than by instruction. On purpose I have avoided this matter in order to correct this impression and to give you an opportunity to admonish him through Psarski. You could have said to him that you notice that the king always finds obstacles when a matter involving our satisfaction comes up. As a consequence he will encounter similar obstacles from us when he wishes something, and we will try to prove to him that he needs more from us than we from him. Thereupon, I can answer that here, after having received such instruction, everyone will act as I wish and our king will straighten out."

Stanislaw Augustus disliked the confederation very much, but he still had not lost his spirit. He wrote to Geoffrin: "Without doubt you thought that all squabbles in Poland ended along with the Diet. But here a new confederation has sprung up in Podolia, next to the Turks and Tatars, whom the confederation wishes to arm to defend Catholicism and annihilate everything done at the Diet for the dissidents. But Muslim blood does not flow willingly for the cross and Christian sovereigns hold no wish to fight with Russia over this confederation. I sent your friend Makranowski to tell the leaders of the confederation that they will bring misfortune upon themselves and perhaps the entire country if they succeed in prodding the restless malcontents into action. Few are rising in defense of religion, while most are trying to fish in muddy waters. As concerns the entire country, this spark will not produce a fire. However, it is very tedious to live constantly with a firehose in your hands and always walk around warm coals. Oh, Mama! What a hard and sad job to be king of Poland! But patience! Good times will come." "Mama" answered that Makranowski would do everything positive he could, but that everything depended on strong measures by "the compass" (Catherine).

Strong measures were indeed necessary, for the confederation took form on the frontier with Turkey. Obrezkov wrote Repnin from Constantinople that to preserve good relations with the Porte it was necessary to end the confrontation with the confederation very quickly. On this subject, Repnin wrote Panin in early June: "Obrezkov's observation is correct. I recommended this happily to Major General Krechetnikov, but I have not had any news from him in quite a long time. The last dispatches to me were on May 12. Thus it has been three weeks now, and he is only four days away by courier. In his last letters he wrote that within three days he would mount an attack against the rebels with his entire force. He wished to start with Priluki and then move to Vinnitsa and beyond. I cannot say anything about why he has done nothing or why I have no news from him. I know only that this is causing unspeakable harm to affairs here." Repnin was especially disturbed that the fight with the confederates might drag out until the meetings of future Diets, for at these Diets "the entire land will be inflamed by the fires of Bar and to quench the flame it will be necessary to deploy twice as many troops." Repnin was disquieted further by the news that Krechetnikov was bypassing him and dealing directly with Petersburg. This might produce "unspeakable dissension."

Finally a courier arrived after twelve days on the road. He brought news that Krechetnikov was besieging Berdichev monastery and had expended so much munitions that he had been forced to send to Kiev for more. Repnin was angered. He characterized these actions as unthinking and wrote Panin: "You can see well enough from Krechetnikov's letter that he has become confused and timid. He does not know how to finish this matter and even fears a desperate attack by the rebels. Judge yourself how much hope I have for such a man, whose head is on backwards. If I have any hope of salvation, it will be when Kar, Igelstrom, and Prozorovsky join him. But I do not know whether he will heed their advice, for sometimes timid and irrational men are also stubborn. The harm caused by his slowness is growing. New revolts emerge hourly. They cannot be averted, for one cannot have troops all over Poland. The Great Polish Confederation led by Ridzinski has been dispersed by Colonel Burman along the Silesian border. But during the night of June 13/14 I received news from Cracow that a confederation has been formed there. Our forces did not succeed in preventing this, arriving a day too late. Thus, a detachment of forces has been assigned to Cracow, which leaves the center of Poland, the province of Sandomir, a part of Russian Poland (Galicia), and the surrounding lands unwatched. We do not have enough troops here, for I do not dare expose the environs of Warsaw, so that similar outrages might occur right under my nose. There is general ferment everywhere." Repnin demanded that the Russian troops in Lithuania march into Poland and that new regiments be sent to Lithuania. He also requested the dispatch of skillful, firm generals without avarice and devoted to the order and glory of the service.

Krechetnikov took Berdichev and Podgorichani defeated a strong confederation force coming to the relief of Berdichev. Major General Count Apraksin took Bar by storm, while Prince Prozorovsky surprised the confederates at Brody. But Repnin took no comfort and continued to accuse Krechetnikov of incompetence and self-seeking. By June the Bar confederates had been scattered completely. The Carmelite Mark was taken prisoner and sent to Kiev. But then a confederation was formed in Sanok. Repnin continued to insist that Krechetnikov be relieved of his command. He sent Colonel Kar to Petersburg to tell Panin about the state of affairs and Krechetnikov's "loathsome conduct."

Repnin wrote: "There is no definite evidence that I can use to remove him from command. But the doubts are so great and so widespread that he must be removed for the honor of the service and Russia's good name. His venality and profiteering are so obvious that they say he has sent several strings of wagons with his booty to Russia and has more ready to send. All Poles and even the Russians in his own quarters openly call him a thief. No one in his command wishes to serve under him. Everyone asks me to be transferred away from him. They say that they fear they will be arrested for his crimes, the likes of which none have seen. On his marches he drags along like a crayfish, about a mile or half a mile per day, God knows whether from insincerity or timidity and laziness. Whoever robs naturally also takes bribes and acts accordingly. Many people are sure that he took a sizeable sum from the governor of Kiev. You are already quite well aware that this governor is a swindler and disloyal. Finally, they say that Krechetnikov is giving out that everything accomplished at the last Diet was done by me alone and that the sovereign knew nothing about it. I have heard this from many Poles. Colonels Kar and Igelstrom, returning from Krechetnikov, also affirmed that he is spreading this rumor to his own advantage around the countryside. For the honor of our fatherland and service, I ask you to recall this man, even if you send no one to replace him. Besides, we have enough worthy generals in the field: Brigadier Generals Saltykov and Bibikov, Major Generals Michael Lvovich Izmailov and Prince Yury Vladimirovich Dolgoruky."

On the occasion of Kar's dispatch to Petersburg, Stanislaw Augustus wrote to his resident there, Psarski (July 7/18): "The first aim of Kar's mission is to report all malfeasances of General Krechetnikov; the second is to portray the poverty and position of need in which I find myself as a result of the fact that I cooperated sincerely with Russia. I have reason to think that in line with Igelstrom's example, Kar will demand your testimony against Krechetnikov. You should not refuse. Let me know who are Krechetnikov's chief protectors in Russia and try to find out what is said in Kar's talks not only about my affairs and Poland in general but, in part, about Prince Repnin himself, since I have strong reason to believe that Prince Repnin is mistaken in considering Kar's comments about Repnin were merely strategems to force those who have spoken ill of him to expose themselves. All the same, it is true that Kar is feared here as a dangerous, two-faced man, whereas Igelstrom is considered a forthright man. Recently Kar asked me insistently several times to forget the caustic remarks he made about me a year ago. I replied that he should demonstrate in deed his loyalty to me and thereby earn my favor. At the same time, I said to him that if the complaints raised against Krechetnikov by all Poland are deserved, it is no less true that his example has harmed the majority of Russian officers and men whose bad conduct leads just as much to bitterness from the Poles as to fanaticism and patriotism. On the other hand, I must tell you that the dissidents themselves strongly desire that the empress agree to diminution of their rights. They see how enmity toward them increases daily."

On July 20 Repnin wrote that in the province of Seradsk bandits or confederates (in his view they were all the same) had been roaming about. "Major Drevits chased them, but he cannot spread himself everywhere. There has been a new revolt in Gostinitsa, only twelve miles from Warsaw. There were only about fifty confederates and not one with a sliver of land. Their leader was Derszanowski, famed to the four corners of the earth for his swindling, for which he would get the noose anywhere. The news from the governor of Lithuania makes one think that there is ferment there, but I know of no medicine for this except cannon and muskets. I will prescribe this to General Numers. Truly it seems that the Devil himself has been everywhere here, for the ferment is genuinely universal in all provinces. Thanks be to God that everything did not catch fire at once. We would not have known then where to turn."

And in August the news was the same. "The ferment continues everywhere." Cracow, where the confederation was headquartered, fell to the assault of generals Count Apraksin and Prince Prozorovsky. Despite the fact that the city was taken by storm, the soldiers looted not a single house or citizen, and behaved themselves as if they were at school. Upon Repnin's insistence, Krechetnikov was replaced by Prince Prozorovsky. On July 19 Catherine wrote to Rumiantsev: "The general howling, from good and bad in all of Poland, against the unauthorized conduct of our Major General Krechetnikov, who has perverted all the glory of our military service and damaged our interests, forces from us such measures that in any other case would be completely contrary to our inclinations and rules of state. This general evidently has overstepped completely the bounds of his post and respect for the honor of our forces. He has been blinded by crass, scornful self-interest and, they say, conducts such self-serving plundering in the country there that already he has sent off many trains with his booty. We have found it necessary to revoke his command."

But even after this, Repnin wrote: "Of course, I will attempt in every way to restore order, but unfortunately everything is not going as might be desired." The *ferment* spread throughout Belorussia. The Czartoryskis began to suggest to Repnin that it was necessary to abolish the edicts concerning the dissidents' rights and the imperial guarantee. The king spoke in the same vein. "I know myself," Repnin wrote, "that the disturbances will end if we accede on these two points. But such quiet would be purchased more dearly than it is worth." Therefore he gave the king the briefest and clearest refusal possible.

The ferment meanwhile was manifested in Lithuania by confederations in Brest and Kowno. The former was completely dispersed at the end of September by Colonel Grotenhelm and Captain Anrep. The Kowno confederates trickled out into Zhmud and announced that they were dispersing to their homes but that their chiefs—Medeksha, Kosakowski, and Scweikowski—had gone to Tilsit. Major General Izmailov had need while pursuing the confederates to go to Nesvizh where Prince Radziwill was located. Izmailov told Radziwill of his mission and received a reply that he should not attack the confederates while near Nesvizh because Radziwill could not be a passive witness to the shedding of his fellow citizens' blood. If a battle took place near his castle, he would bring out his troops. Radziwill also gave shelter to some rebels from the Oshmiansk region pursued by Russian soldiers. In a letter justifying himself to Repnin, he announced that in this he had no intention of fighting with the Russians. On the contrary, he did them a service by convincing the confederates to fulfill Izmailov's demand to quit the confederation, in return for which Izmailov had promised full security of their estates. He had received the confederates at his home in Nesvizh because he was obliged to do so. He could not overlook the spilling of his brothers' blood as long as he belonged to a people among whom freedom and equality reigned. The confederates had revolted because of their religious fervor; such ardor should be in everyone's blood.

At the end of October Repnin described the state of affairs in Poland as follows: "The audacity and impudence of the rebels is increasing in all districts. In Great Poland robberies are committed daily and new bands of such robbers appear hourly. They do not let a single gold piece of state revenues reach here. They seize the mails and plunder those living peacefully in the countryside. No matter how much our troops chase after this whirlwind they cannot catch them and only torture themselves in vain. There was no possibility of holding a Diet, since only thirty deputies came here. Spirits are not merely desperate but, one might say, just about dead. Also, by law it is impossible to hold a Diet inasmuch as not a single deputy has arrived from Lithuania. Within two months the king again will have nothing to eat, for his revenues have been stolen everywhere and nothing is coming in." The word *again* signifies that Repnin already had given Poniatowski a considerable sum for his maintenance.

General Izmailov reported that the Mstislav rebels had announced a desire to leave the confederation and were prepared to give *recesses*, that is, written proof of this. The empress wrote on Izmailov's report: "On the day after giving these promises they will be the same rebels; but if a few were seized and sent to Siberia for settlement their numbers would decrease."

On December 1 news arrived that in Great Poland Major Drevits had defeated the chief rebel there, Malczewski. There were 600 men in his band; some 200 were killed and nine cannon were taken. But Repnin added his customary stanza to this news: "All these repeated lessons remain without effect, however, especially in Great Poland, where there are a multitude of small insurrectionary bands, who rob and commit every crime of violence wherever our forces are absent." The instructions from Petersburg about military operations also greatly irritated Repnin. On December 9 he wrote to Panin: "They are sending military orders here that are completely impossible to carry out, for they are contradictory. From them I see that they seek not only to ruin affairs here and subvert the king, despite the inglorious and harmful consequences which would accrue to us from this, but also try to confuse everything here, blaming it all on me and Saltykov,[43] so that afterwards we can be blamed as guilty of failure. Judge for yourself whether this can be accomplished: they demand that Prozorovsky be held back in Polonnyi, that is, under the nose of the enemy, who hangs over the border. We expect enemy attacks every day, yet they demand that supply depots be set up not only in Polonnyi and on the roads from Kiev and Chernigov, but also at the front, in Podolia itself. Along with this they order in reply to Saltykov that he find a completely secure and peaceful base for his soldiers, when they alone can protect the supplies and reinforce Prozorovsky, who cannot remain in his present position without fear of annihilation of his entire corps without this protection. Still less can the depots be prepared if our forces are not there for their security. If the Turks move in, how can Saltykov and I vouch for the safety of those forces, especially when they are so weak in numbers?

"Having presented our opinion on this matter, we both demanded decisive orders with precise instructions on where to stand firm. But this decision was not made and it was left to us to consider how to achieve conditions of security, tranquility, and correction of all that I have described above. In a word, I would rather be among the first to meet the whole Turkish army with a company of hussars than here in my place with all these whispers. Saltykov, sensing all this, already has written me to yield. He fears that he will perish from all these restrictions. One cannot blame him for his despair in view of all this deceit. I pray to God that an end be put to all this and that decisive orders be given, whatever they might be, just so they do not contradict themselves. I beg you to see what a mess is being made here because of our disarray. I just beseech you, as a benefactor—get me out of this galley. Likewise, I ask that I not be commissioned to decide on the locations of supply depots."

THE TURKISH REACTION

We have seen how Repnin was annoyed by the news of the promise given by Obrezkov in Constantinople that immediately upon adjournment of the Diet Russian troops would be withdrawn from Poland and those arrested would be returned from exile. While using gentle phrasing, Panin still let Obrezkov know what great difficulties this promise could entail. By his own admission, Obrezkov was in "a state of trepidation" that Repnin would write the empress of the impossibility of keeping the promise given to the Porte. He implored Panin to put himself in his, Obrezkov's, position between the hammer and the anvil and to order Repnin at least to give the appearance of fulfilling the promise, for example, by removing at least some units from Warsaw. Meanwhile, every three days Moldavian couriers brought the Porte news from Poland that the Diet had been postponed because of new difficulties caused by Prince Repnin, who imposed new conditions unfavorable to Poland. Many Poles reportedly preferred to quit their native land than to agree to these conditions and suffer the arrogant and imperious actions of the Russian ambassador, and had already gone. Upon this information, the Porte decided to strengthen its forces on the border. To Obrezkov's remarks that he should not believe this news, the reis-effendi replied with irritation that Turkey's honor and interests did not allow it any longer to observe such protracted rule of the Russian court in Poland. Besides, because of the nature of the Turkish people, the sultan and his ministers sometimes were forced to do things they did not want to.

It is easy to understand the degree of Obrezkov's "trepidation" when he received word from Repnin of the Confederation of Bar. The reis-effendi announced to him that although the confederates had turned to the Porte with a request for aid, the Porte did not intend to help such "rogues" who scattered when deprived of outside assistance. Therefore, there was no need to keep Russian forces in Poland, for the negotiations between Russia and Poland were completely finished. This band of vagrants could not prevent implementation of the treaty. Besides, such disruptions often occurred in Poland. One could not keep Russian troops there constantly! Finally, the Porte could never allow Russian forces to attack confederation forces near its borders, not because it wished to defend or embolden them, but because news of such a battle would produce serious unrest in the Turkish people. The last order of the Porte on stationing military personnel in Khotin, Bender, and Ochakov had been issued only to give the common people something to chew upon and thus to shut those mouths and to keep them from accusing the sultan and the ministry of carelessness and timidity.

Obrezkov replied that it was a mistake for the Porte to consider the Confederation of Bar so insignificant. In its manifesto the confederation revolted directly against the treaty concluded between Russia and Poland. Consequently, were the confederation successful, Russian troops would have to return, if they had left, according to the terms of the guarantee in order to restore the violated guarantees. Neither the Porte nor any other power had the right to prevent Russia from doing this. If the Porte truly desired restoration of tranquility in Poland and withdrawal of Russian troops, the best means of attaining this would be to allow Russian forces to seek out the rebels, even close to the Turkish border.

But the reis-effendi steadfastly refused to agree to this. He repeated that the confederation would vanish the moment the insurgents were deprived of hope of aid from the Porte. He demanded that Obrezkov renew his promise regarding withdrawl of Russian forces from Poland. But Obrezkov this time firmly refused to give any promise. After a two-hour argument the reis-effendi stated that the Russians should pacify the confederates, but that they should not approach the Turkish border and pacification should occur as smoothly as possible, without sound and fury. Obrezkov knew that the *ulemas*[44] insisted that Turkey interfere in Polish affairs on the basis of the religious principle not to turn away from the oppressed asking assistance. Therefore, he thought it necessary to give the reis-effendi three thousand gold pieces, in consequence of which a decree was sent to the Crimean khan to instruct the French consul not to interfere in political matters and to let the leaders of the Bar confederation know that they should not hope for help from Turkey or the Crimea and should hurry to end their uprising. Another decree to the khan was prepared, for the expulsion from the Crimea of the French consul, Tott.

Spring and early summer passed quietly. But on July 7 Obrezkov transmitted a communique from the Porte that a sizeable detachment of cossacks in pursuit of Polish rebels had entered Balta, a village belonging to the Crimean khan lying right on the Polish border. While

destroying the confederation forces, they killed several Tatars, Moldavians, and Turks. Then the cossacks proceeded to another estate of the
khan, Dubossarai; there they demanded that the steward surrender the
confederates. Not receiving satisfaction, they burned Dubossarai where
some 1,800 Tatars, Moldavians, and Turks died. How did this happen?
Who were these cossacks?

RELIGIOUS AND NATIONAL FERMENT IN THE UKRAINE

On February 29, 1768 Georgy Konissky wrote to Catherine: "The
people here of the Polish state who profess the Greek-Russian faith
have not received real, complete protection from the all-wise providence,
devoted care, and unmeasurable generosity of your imperial majesty.
Through me, your subject, they offer their most heart-felt and loyal
thanks. In the present change of their circumstances, which they have
desired for a century and a half but of which they have never despaired,
they consider themselves like the ancient Israelites, freed from the
Egyptian bondage, like the early Christians, resting after persecution of
the pagans, and like old Russia, beginning to serve God unhindered, as
it received enlightenment. They pray to God with tears, not of sadness
but from an excess of joy. Your imperial majesty has done the deeds of
Moses, Constantine and Helen, Vladimir and Olga,[45] all in the flower of
her health. They pray for the long life and preservation of your majesty's
intentions, so pleasing to God and useful to Christianity, so that your
majesty may confirm that which has been done and offer salvation to
those who still have not received the strength, here and in other places,
which has been sent to your majesty by God, so that they may be delivered from their suffering. Thus, I beseech your highest majesty most
humbly to issue an edict to whom it need be, that, borrowing the ardor
and zeal of your majesty, for the holy faith they should apply the
proper effort to fulfill every thing specified in the treaty benefitting
those whom you have defended, and especially that those should not be
defended weakly who before the signing of the treaty by the Diet committed themselves to return or convert from the Uniate or Roman faith
to our belief."

From the last few lines, one can see that in early 1768 there were
still people suffering from persecution of the Orthodox faith. One also
can discern that there were people who recently had returned from the
Uniate or even the Catholic church to Orthodoxy; that is, they had
abandoned Orthodoxy involuntarily and now reconverted. Konissky
asked that primarily they be defended, for according to the last treaty
abandonment of the dominant faith was considered a criminal matter.
Events in the so-called "Ukraine"[46] explain Konissky's words.

In this Ukraine, on the banks of the rivers Rosi and Tiasmina, ancient Rus had struggled interminally with the Polovetsians and other barbarians of various names, half-nomad and half-settled. In the seventeenth century, Russia, Poland, and Turkey had struggled there, and the cossacks had shifted now to one side, now to the other, then to the third. In the Ukraine (which had been declared a no-man's land in the Treaty of the Pruth[47] in order to avoid conflicts) in the period under discussion, as is the nature of all such borderlands, disparate elements came into conflict. It was settled by runaways from the closest countries—Russian peasants, Uniates, and Orthodox Christians. The Uniate clergy attempted to subordinate the Orthodox and eliminate their clergy, but encountered resistance. In the dense forests on the right bank of the Dnieper Orthodox monasteries were tucked away in various places, and the monks were always more capable of battle than the scattered and therefore weak white clergy.[48] Zaporozhe was not far off, and the Ukraine was well-known as the favorite country of the haidamaksi,[49] knights of the steppe and terrible bandits, but men whom the Russian Orthodox believer always regarded above all as the indefatigable enemies of Poles, Jews, and Uniates.

A strong religious movement had been evident in the Ukraine since the famous dissident question was raised. At this time in the other Russian districts belonging to the Kingdom of Poland and Lithuania the degraded Orthodox nobility, deprived of all means of representation, tilled the soil themselves. The townsmen and peasants, chased here and there and accustomed to every burden, were awaiting salvation from the strong hand of the Russian monarchy, which was active through its prince-ambassador in Warsaw. However, in the Ukraine, because of the very character of the country and the population, Orthodoxy could not tolerate such suffering, especially when a man appeared who drew others to him. Such a man was the monk Melkhizedek, abbot of the Motreninsk monastery. To bring order and the influence of Orthodoxy to the Ukraine, he fashioned an ecclesiastical union between the population there and the nearest bishopric, that of Pereiaslavl. He became the active mediator between the bishop of Pereiaslavl, Gervasius, and his flock on the other, west bank of the Dnieper, in Poland (or Egypt, as Konissky put it). Finding support in the Russian church hierarchy, Melkhizedek did not wish his people to remain in suffering. He began an open struggle against the Uniates. He began to lure the Ukrainian population away, to strengthen Orthodoxy at the expense of the Uniate faith, and to entrench Orthodoxy's position by building churches and establishing greater clerical discipline. Melkhizedek also spent some time in Petersburg and in Warsaw with the usual complaints about persecution and the usual requests for intercession. Panin told him: "Be reassured that it will be done in the common good through the most holy Belorussian, Georgy [Konissky]."

But the Ukrainian Uniates did not wish Melkhizedek and the Orthodox to be reassured. Melkhizedek's activity, the open struggle which he had begun, the loss of parishioners—all this aroused terrible fury in the Uniate clergy, a fury shared by Polish officialdom, for the same fanaticism of which Repnin complained in Warsaw reigned also in the Ukraine, only with more unruliness, given the local conditions. The Uniates began openly to attack, rob, and torment the Orthodox population. Since the Motreninsk monastery was the center of the movement, the peasants brought their Uniate priests there to swear an oath "to piety," which was revolt in the eyes of Uniates and Catholics. Since the Motreninsk abbot was the chief culprit in this, the fury was directed mainly at him. He was accused of fomenting rebellion and converting Uniate priests to Orthodoxy. They seized Melkhizedek and held him in fetters in the closest confinement, from which he somehow managed to escape in some secret manner to Pereiaslavl.

At the beginning of 1768 when the equality of Greeks and non-Uniates with Catholics was proclaimed, Gervasius wrote to Konissky that in the Ukraine the Uniates continued their outrages, beating and tormenting the Orthodox population and clergy, for they had nothing to fear from any quarter. In the most recent estimates, some eighty-six assaults were reported. The news from Warsaw of the restoration of the dissidents' rights roused a terrible bitterness among the Uniates, to whom it seemed that revenge from the Orthodox population soon would be forthcoming. Abusing an Orthodox priest and tearing off his hair and beard, one official stated: "I am tonsuring you now, but you might peel off my skin." The Uniates foresaw vengeance upon themselves, and this vengeance came.

Two Liubomirski princes, the lord high marshal and his brother, the governor of Liubel, forced a third Liubomirski, a feeble-minded drunkard, a Lithuanian courtier and the holder of enormous estates, to bind over these estates to his children, he and his wife receiving a sizeable yearly sum from the revenue. Since the Liubomirski children were minors, guardians for them were appointed. This agile maneuvering did not please Sosnowski, a secretary of the grand duchy of Lithuania, and Princess Liubomirska's lover, for it balked his hopes to better his own situation. He persuaded the princess to kidnap her husband from Warsaw in order that he reassert control of his estates. Then she would control her feeble-minded husband and his estates rather than the Liubomirski family or some guardians. The princess aroused her husband, stole him away from Warsaw, and prevailed upon him to sign contracts in Lwow in 1768. Upstanding people there would have nothing to do with him. But some cardsharps came in from Warsaw, won in a game with Liubomirski, and forced him to pay his debt with his estates, under guise of a sale. The buyers knew quite well that this matter would not proceed easily and that the guardians of the Liubomirski children would not let them set foot on a single estate. It was necessary to find someone to obtain power of attorney from Liubomirski, assume the struggle with the guardinas, and gain the buyers entry to the estates. Such men were found—two petty nobles, Bobrowski and Wolinetski.

Bobrowski was dispatched as a commissioner to Liubomirskii's estate "Poberezhe" [By the Shore]. No one paid any attention to him, and hardly anyone came out to greet him because one of the guardians, Scweikowski, learned of the doings in Lwow and sent orders to the estates that none of the managers should dare listen to Bobrowski and Wolinetski, no matter what papers from Prince Liubomirski they might show. Bobrowski, tossed out of "Poberezhe," conferred with Wolinetski and both decided to go to another Liubomirski estate, Smilianscszizn, and rouse the peasants there by promising to do away with the Uniates. To get other help they went to Bar to Pulawski, the marshal of the confederation, and asked that he recognize them as councillors of the confederation and give them forms to make out various orders in his name. In return for this they promised to bring the confederation one thousand armed cossacks. Pulawski easily assented to their wishes.

Having received their papers, Bobrowski and Wolinetski triumphantly proceeded to Smila, a fortified castle belonging to Liubomirski. But the gates were locked and there were no orders to let them in. The steward, Wondz, was not at home but his wife did an excellent job of handling everything. In the castle there was a garrison of fifty cossacks, gunpowder, and many other supplies. "My husband does not know any commissioners of Prince Liubomirski except the guardians of the young princes," the wife answered to Bobrowski and Wolinetski and their threats and demands to open the castle. Then the commissioners turned to the cossacks living on the estate lands and persuaded them to attack the castle. But the cossacks in the garrison repulsed the attack. Bobrowski and Wolinetski then thought up a strategem—seize the wives and children of the cossacks in the castle garrison and put them in the front line of the cossacks storming the castle. But this did not help; the garrison cossacks fired despite the fact that their wives and children fell as a result. Seeing such a terrible sin, the cossacks halted the attack and refused to obey the commissioners. Bobrowski and Wolinetski, who had promised them several days earlier to fight for Orthodoxy, now began to threaten them that the Confederation of Bar would come, massacre them to the last man, and let dogs drink their blood for their disobedience. This threat had no effect; the cossacks did not storm the castle. Then Bobowski and Wolinetski decided to go to Bar. In order to keep the promise made to Pulawski, they ordered the leader of the cossacks, Timberski, to follow them to Bar with all his cossacks. Timberski did not dare disobey an order written in the name of the marshal of the confederation (on Pulawski's blank form) and ordered the cossacks to follow the commissioners.

Timberski was a man of enormous height and girth. It was difficult for him to ride horseback, and hard for a horse to carry him. He asked Bobrowski and Wolinetski to allow him to leave the horses and ride in a wagon. They permitted this. But as soon as Timberski settled into the wagon, the cossack elders, captains, hetmen, and lieutenants stopped the vehicle and asked him "Where are you leading us, lord colonel?" "I have an order from the marshal of the Confederation of Bar to appear with you at Bar," he replied. "If you wish, lord colonel," the elder said, "go to Bar by yourself" and, turning to the cossacks, he cried: "Fellows, let's head back home to Smilianscszizn." And that was that. Bobowski, Wolinetski, and Timberski galloped into Bar alone, fearing pursuit from the cossacks.

It should be remembered that Wolinetski threatened the peasants and cossacks with attack by the forces of the confederation, which would wipe them all out. As luck would have it, within several days a rumor arrived that a column following two Polish royal standard bearers was going by, taking with it some haidamaks caught plundering in order to impale them at the scene of their crime, Smilianscszizn. The cossacks feared that these troops had been sent to punish them for turning out Bobrowski and Wolinetski and began to flee to the Russian border, across the Dnieper near Pereiaslavl, where the Russians let them through with their horses, keeping their arms at the barriers.

One of the haidamaks impaled was the cousin of the abbot, and himself the steward of the bishop of Pereiaslavl. The abbot, incensed by the shameful death of his relative, convinced the Zaporozhe Cossacks then in Pereiaslavl on a pilgrimage and their chief, Zhelezniak, that they should go to war with the Poles for the faith, for the Poles had formed the Confederation of Bar against Orthodoxy. To strengthen their conviction, the abbot showed Zhelezniak a parchment edict of the empress to rise against the Poles for the faith. The heading was written in gold letters and the signature and seal were counterfeit. Zhelezniak told the abbot that he could not begin such a project with only several hundred cossacks. The abbot said: "But not far from here, at the barriers, are many runaway cossacks who fled the confederation's troops because the Poles wished to slaughter them all. Join these cossacks and invade Poland. Slaughter the Poles and Jews. All the peasants and cossacks will be with you."

Zhelezniak went to the cossacks and showed them the counterfeit imperial edict. All together they pushed across the Dnieper, aroused the local cossacks and peasants, and killed Poles and Jews. On the trees they hung Poles, Jews, and dogs together with the sign "Pole, Jew, dog— their faith is the same."

This is the story of the haidamak revolt as told by a contemporary Pole who heard the details from people closest to the events. At the beginning of his story, he states: "This affair appeared to occur at the instigation of the Russian government, but in reality the causes were different."

The haidamak incident greatly irritated Repnin. He singled out the bishop of Pereiaslavl, Gervasius, and the abbot of Motreninsk, Melkhizedek, as "a partial cause" of the uprising. He was especially up in arms against Melkhizedek. We know how Repnin looked upon the spread of Orthodoxy at the expense of the Uniate and Catholic faiths and how he had defended a draft project in the Senate for the introduction of Uniate bishops. Therefore, he could not look favorably upon the activity of Gervasius and Melkhizedek against the Uniates. Repnin demanded that all Orthodox Polish provinces be put under the jurisdiction of the bishop of Belorussia, who might thereby be lifted from his poverty, so harmful to the dignity of Orthodoxy.

But the king, Stanislaw Augustus, took a surprisingly impartial and even-handed approach to the matter in a letter to Geoffrin. "Several fanatics threatened the peasants of our part of the Ukraine with every misfortune if they did not switch from non-Uniate to Uniates, that is, stop explaining the Trinity as they do in Petersburg and use the Roman explanation instead. Consider, could the unfortunate peasants there understand anything? But this was enough to outrage them, and the uprising of these people is not a joke! There are many of them, and they are armed and fierce when outraged. They are now killing their lords, along with the wives and children of the latter, as well as Catholic priests and Jews. Thousands of people already have been killed. The revolt is spreading rapidly because religious fanaticism is combined with thirst for freedom. Greek and slave fanaticism is fighting with fire and sword against Catholic and noble fanaticism. One thing is sure—without the Confederation of Bar this new misfortune would not have been."

The revolt spread, seized Smilianscszizn, and threatened Uman, belonging to the governor of Kiev, Potocki. One Mladanowicz was Potocki's chief steward, and his treasurer was Rogascewski. The steward and treasurer secretly sent some Jews to the governor to talk things over. To determine who was right and who wrong, Potocki sent to Uman the nobleman Tseselski, who told Mladanowicz and Rogascewski the kind of denunciations made against them to the governor. The two, instead of suspecting each other, suspected Captain Gonta, whom Potocki liked and had assigned to settle his villages. Gonta therefore often went to visit the governor. The steward and treasurer took their revenge on Gonta by demanding one hundred gold pieces for keeping his captain's office—this at a time when a cossack revolt was boiling in the neighborhood.

The Confederation of Bar sent a demand that the governor of Kiev send his entire militia and all his cossacks to Bar. But the governor ordered otherwise; he directed Tseselski to collect the cossacks and post them in the steppe on the river Siniukha, the border with Russia. He wrote to Pulawski that instead of cossacks, who would not willingly fight the Russians, he had ordered a cavalry and infantry militia to be formed from the nobility. He would send this militia with three months' pay and provisions to Bar. Tseselski, Mladanowicz, and Rogascewski imposed a special levy for this purpose on the cossacks so that the governor's treasury would not be exhausted by formation of the militia. All of this was done while the cossack revolt boiled in the neighborhood and the Uman Cossacks were out in the steppe along the Siniukha under the command of Captains Duska, Gonta, and Yarema, ready allies for Zhelezniak.

Some Jews sensed disaster and came to Tseselski protesting that it was necessary to beware of Gonta, all the more now that he was chief, Duska having died on the steppe. The Jews stated that in all probability Gonta would deal with Zhelezniak. There was a rumor to the effect that Gonta already had proposed an alliance with Zhelezniak to Duska, but the latter had supposedly answered: "We will lord it over them for seven weeks, but for seven years they will hang and quarter us."

Frightened by the Jews, Tseselski sent an order to Gonta to appear immediately in Uman. He hurried there and at once was thrown into irons and brought out to the gallows the next day. But the women saved everything from the lucky hand of Khmelnitsky's cossack knights.[50] The wife of Colonel Obukh begged mercy for Gonta: "Leave him alive, I vouch for him." Tseselski was touched by the requests of the noblewoman Obukha and released Gonta and sent him once again to command the cossacks at the encampment on the Siniukha! The Jews saw that their fate was in the hands of a man whom they had been about to lead to the gallows. They collected bolts of cloth, other materials, and money, and went to Gonta with hat in hand: "Little father, protect us." Gonta told the Jews: "Get Lord Tseselski to give me an order to proceed against Zhelezniak." The Jews obtained the order, but Tseselski ordered three colonels to take command of the cossacks. This did not help. On the road, Gonta told the colonels: "You may, your lordships, now get out of here. We don't need you any more." The colonels hastily left for Uman, and Gonta joined with Zhelezniak. Soon the entire mob appeared before Uman. In a nearby wood they spread a carpet on which Zhelezniak sat with Gonta. The cossacks formed a circle and a scribe read the false manifesto of the Russian empress. Then the carousing began and lasted all night.

Tseselski remained no longer in the Uman fortress, and disappeared. The command fell upon Mladanowicz. The commander, Lenart, called on him and said that the drunken cossacks were sleeping on the estate grounds and that it would be nothing to make a sortie out of the fortress and disperse them. But Mladanowicz could not make up his mind. He called the Jews and ordered them to load carts with precious materials and take them as gifts to Gonta and Zhelezniak, along with a request for capitulation. The latter, both drunk, received the gifts with satisfaction, but postponed negotiations until morning.

On the morning of the next day both leaders with their entire entourage rode up to the town gates, in front of which there was a bridge thrown across a deep ditch. Commandant Lenart ordered four cannons loaded with grapeshot, but Mladanowicz and Rogascewski, seeing this, cried out: "What are you doing? You will kill us all!" The noblemen fell upon the guns and chased off the cannoneers while Mladanowicz hurried to conclude negotiations with Zhelezniak. They decided: (1) The cossacks would not kill Catholics, nobles, and Poles in general, nor harm their estates; (2) the cossacks were at liberty as far as the Jews and their estates were concerned. Upon conclusion of the agreement, the Poles retired to the Catholic church and the cossacks plundered the town and began to attack the Jews. Then, when all the Jews had been killed, they set upon the militia which the authorities at Bar had ordered to be organized. Finishing with the latter, the cossacks proceeded to the Catholic church, dragged out men, women, and children, and beat them. They married several of the women who pleased them and adopted their children. Mladanowicz and Rogascewski perished at Gonta's hands, the entire town was strewn with corpses, and the well in the market was filled with murdered children. Meanwhile, the peasants in the outlying villages attacked the Jews, bound the monastery elders and the nobles, and dragged them into Uman where drunken cossacks killed them.

After these exploits, Gonta proclaimed himself governor of Bratslaw and Zhelezniak governor of Kiev. He sent detachments off in various directions to kill nobles and Jews. But Zhelezniak and Gonta did not rule long. They were arrested upon the orders of General Krechetnikov.

The revolt of the haidamaks fizzled out but its consequences were demonstrated in an unexpected manner. One of the haidamak detachments sent out by Gonta and Zhelezniak, under the command of Captain Shila, went to Balta, a little place along the border which the river Kodyma separated from the Tatar settlement of Galta. Balta was famed for its fairs, to which people brought horses, cattle, and sheep. Remount officers from Prussia and Saxony came there to buy horses. The little town grew rich from these fairs. Many Jews lived there, along with Greeks, Armenians, Turks, and Tatars. There were plenty of people for the haidamaks to kill and much to plunder. Shila and his detachment appeared in Balta and began by beating up the Jews. Then, after spending four peaceful days, he gathered his force and left Balta. Having seen that with this the affair was over, the Turks raised an outcry and together with the Jews moved from the Tatar to the Polish side of the town. Some went up the hill in pursuit of the haidamaks, while others set about beating the Orthodox population, Serbs and Russians, stealing their goods, and burning the outskirts of the town.

Having heard that Turks and Jews had attacked the Orthodox inhabitants, Shila returned, drove the foe over to the Tatar side, followed right after them into Galta, and pillaged and destroyed everything there. The next day the battle was renewed with an attack by the Turks, who again were driven back into Galta. After this the haidamaks made peace with the Turks and returned much of the plunder to them. But as soon as Shila left Balta a second time, the Turks and Jews appeared in town again, began to abuse the Christians, shot and stabbed many of them, and plundered the churches. On the heels of the infidels confederation forces appeared and things got no easier for the Orthodox population. Every day the Poles "inspected the Christians," and beat and killed them. The Orthodox population turned to the Russian colonel, Gurev, with a plea for defense and explained the situation in their request. The entreaty ended as follows: "The confederates want very much to catch and kill us now. We ask therefore that you not leave us but show us mercy. We ask you to give us poor folks an escort so that we can collect our possessions. To this report the entire brotherhood of our Greek merchantry have affixed their signatures."

WAR WITH TURKEY

The Porte was so agitated by the news of the events in Balta that Obrezkov was barely successful in keeping the Turks from declaring war immediately, assuring them that this event had occurred contrary to the intentions of the empress, who would grant the Porte full satisfaction. Even so, the Porte ordered an army corps of 20,000 men to the border. Obrezkov wrote that although the Porte did not even now intend to break the peace, one could not guarantee that it would not be forced to start a war "pursuant to irrational and precipitate popular inclinations." On July 11 the reis-effendi demanded of Obrezkov that all Russian forces be withdrawn from Turkish borders and that Russian troops completely evacuate Podolia. Meanwhile, rumors about the happenings in Balta and Dubossarai proved false. Obrezkov presented the Porte with the true story, that rebellious Ukrainian peasants along with haidamaks had attacked Galta, a village belonging to the khan, which lay along the river Bug opposite the Orel district Russian frontier post. In addition, he argued that Russia was not obliged to answer for all bandits in the area. But the machine, as Obrezkov put it, already had been set in motion and the Porte did not have the power to stop it quickly. The Porte continued to demand evacuation of Podolia and promised in that case to expel all confederates hiding in its districts and force them to settle down. Obrezkov repeated that war was possible and pointed out that the Turkish government resembled a republic more than an autocracy. The ministry had been assured that Russia was not demanding from Poland anything contrary to the interests of the Porte, but the public, along with several heads with long gray beards, thought otherwise.

On August 25 the grand vizier, "a well-intentioned and peace-loving man," was removed. Obrezkov feared that a change in the post of reis-effendi soon would follow. He wrote: "This will deprive me completely of my best instruments. If Russia withstands one or two campaigns in a defensive war on its borders and forces the Turks to suffer all the difficulty of campaigning, this undoubtedly soon will leave the Porte in despair, especially if the Russian commanders adhere to the principle of Prince Eugene,[51] who usually attempted to avoid general battles in the beginning of a campaign and gave battle only at the end. The Turks are always passionate and bold at first, but work soon makes them apathetic and timid; they often even revolt."

In his difficult position, Obrezkov requested some sage advice from Panin. The latter relied upon Obrezkov's skill and enthusiasm, and to help him he sent a letter to the vizier filled with expressions of Russia's desire for peace. He also sent a purloined dispatch of Tott to Duke Choiseul[52] which revealed that Tott had bribed the Balta commander Yakub to send false reports to the Porte. "Her imperial majesty intends," Panin wrote, "to combine flattery and firmness in our explanations to the Turks. On one hand, she will show them all possible consideration of their wishes, but on the other hand will not accede to their whims when our interests and advantages or the dignity of the crown are involved. Should it be necessary to lend your words to the Turkish ministry more force through the flattering glint of gold, her imperial majesty has deigned to order 70,000 rubles sent to you."

At the beginning of September Obrezkov wrote that the vizier had been replaced because of his age and weakness. In his place had been appointed the pasha of Kutais who, according to rumor, was an arrogant and crude man. Only the sultan and the common people desired war, while the ministers and clergy were against it. They were convinced in Constantinople that Russia was dragging out matters in Poland in order to have a pretext to keep its forces in Poland permanently. Russia therefore was not trying to crush the confederation, and was using a small number of troops without one well-known general in command. There was also no small amount of grumbling among the Turks over the fact that the Polish king and republic were completely voiceless, and that all orders emanated solely from the Russian ambassador. This made it clear that Russia was ruling despotically in Poland, and this annoyed the sultan more than anything.

The results of this irritation soon became apparent. On September 14 the reis-effendi was removed and on the 25th Obrezkov was summoned to an audience with the new vizier. At his entrance he found the chamber filled with a multitude of people of different ranks. When he sat on his stool and began his greetings the vizier cut him off with the words: "This is what you have brought things to!" Trembling with malice, he began to read a paper which stated: "Poland should be a free power, but it is oppressed by military forces. Its people are being ravaged terribly and killed inhumanely. Barges belonging to subjects of the Porte have been sunk on the Dniester. Balta and Dubossarai have been plundered and many Turks killed there. Instead of offering satisfaction, the governor of Kiev haughtily answered the khan that this all was done by the haidamaks when it is well known that everything actually was done by Russian subjects. You have assured us that your troops would be withdrawn from Poland, but they are still there now. You claimed that there were no more than seven thousand men without artillery, but there are more than 20,000 there now, with cannon. Therefore you, you traitor, answer yes or no: will you pledge that all troops will be withdrawn from Poland, or do you want war?"

Obrezkov replied that upon completion of its business Russia would remove all its troops from Poland. He swore to this and the Prussian envoy vouched for him. The vizier ordered him into another room. After a two-hour wait the Porte's translator came to him and announced:

"You must also pledge that the Russian court will repudiate the guarantee of everything enacted at the last Diet and protection of the dissidents. You must leave Poland in complete freedom." Obrezkov answered that there had been no talk of this and, therefore, he could not know the opinion of his court. If it pleased the Porte, let these demands be put in writing; he would forward them to his court and immediately inform the Porte of the reply. The translator went to the vizier and returned with the demand that Obrezkov give the required pledge right away— otherwise there would be war. Obrezkov stated that it was not in his power to undertake such an obligation.

After a little while, the master of the ceremonies entered and announced the arrest of Obrezkov and the eleven other members of his embassy. They placed Obrezkov on a horse, led him through the entire city past great mobs of people, and incarcerated him in the cellar of a tower, with light coming through just one tiny window. The prisoners spent one full day there, and when the commandant reported that they could not withstand even three days of such confinement because of the dampness and oppressiveness, they were moved to two little huts, into which light came through the doors and some small windows in the ceiling. The demands of the English ambassador and Prussian envoy that Obrezkov be freed had no effect. Despite his imprisonment, with the aid of the British ambassador Obrezkov found it possible to send news to Panin of the state of affairs in Constantinople and advice as to how to conduct the war. Thus he counselled that despite the prejudice of the new commanders, the chevaux de frise and pike should not be abandoned in fighting the Turks. In December Obrezkov grew desperately ill and bribed the doctors and commandant to move him to better quarters.

EUROPEAN REACTION TO TURKEY'S DECLARATION OF WAR

The Prussian envoy, Segelin, who had tried in vain to avert war, informed his court of the events in Constantinople in almost the same words used by Obrezkov. Frederick did not want war because, according to the terms of the alliance, he was obligated to help Russia with money, but not troops, in the event of a Turkish attack. He grew angry and said that Russia itself was responsible for the troubles in Poland—why had it pushed the dissident question so far? In September he wrote Catherine that if Russian troops did not approach the Turkish border the Porte would look calmly on the defeat of the confederation. But to inflict that defeat more troops were needed in Poland. Panin inquired whether Frederick could not send his troops into Poland, but the king refused, citing the treaty. If Russia could not deal with the confederation by itself, it should come to terms with it. Speaking with Count

Finckelstein about Obrezkov's arrest, Prince Dolgoruky singled out the court of Versailles as the chief instigator of the affair. But Finckelstein answered that in his sovereign's opinion the Viennese court also had participated. The basis for this was that when the news of the fall of the old vizier was received in Vienna, the Austrian minister in Constantinople received a raise in salary.

Prince Dmitry Mikhailovich Golitsyn wrote from Vienna about the *modest* conduct of the court there regarding the Polish disturbances. In August, on the occasion of the Russian seizure of Cracow, Kaunitz[53] had a conversation with Prince Golitsyn. He said beforehand that he was speaking to him not as a minister but as a private citizen. "In my opinion," Kaunitz stated, "it is not necessary now to deal harshly with the instigators of the confederation. One should not increase the number of aggrieved people in Poland. Far away an unpleasant thundercloud now is gathering, and it would not at all be bad if you tried to avert the storm by settling all the affairs in Poland in a manner satisfactory to the Poles who disagree with you." These suggestions showed clearly how contented Vienna was with Russia's difficult position.

The French showed no modesty. Duke Choiseul acted openly against Russia everywhere. The Confederation of Bar aroused in him the hope of once again beginning a successful struggle with Russia in Poland. He succeeded in inciting Turkey, which declared war on Russia. He prepared the last stroke in Sweden. He attempted to break up the alliance of Russia with Prussia and turn the latter closer to Austria. In all this Choiseul spared not even the smallest means of expressing his hatred for the young power which dared to compete with the elder, France, in the breadth of its political role and to create its own northern system in opposition to the southern system set up by France. In documents sent from the French to the Russian government suddenly the adjective *imperial* disappeared in front of the noun *majesty*. To the inquiry of the Russian minister as to the meaning of this, the answer was received that the expression *majesté impériale* was not consonant with the spirit of the language. The French kings, taking the title *majesty* and adding no other epithets to it, could not grant such an epithet to any other crowned head. Catherine wrote on the report about this from the Russian minister in France, Prince Golitsyn: "It is against the rules of the Russian language to receive documents without the proper use of titles." The Russians stopped accepting French documents, and a chargé d'affaires, Khotinsky, replaced Prince Golitsyn. Duke Choiseul told Khotinsky bluntly: "We will not give in." "And neither will we," retorted Khotinsky. From Choiseul's words, Khotinsky could not miss the enmity to the former minister, Prince Golitsyn. Choiseul said to him of

Golitsyn: "He wrote many falsehoods to his court about affairs here. We know accurately what is said in Petersburg, just as if it were said in Paris."

The success of French diplomacy in Turkey forced the Russian court to redouble its attention to Sweden. Ostermann began the year with a request that 26,000 rubles be sent to embolden and strengthen the "well-intentioned" party. "After the blow suffered by the French party at the last Diet," Ostermann wrote, "one might expect more quiet and less dissemination of French thoughts. And, in reality, the French party apparently has become quieter, but has not stopped secretly instilling perverted ideas in people. Perceiving, then, that the peace-loving party, relying on its superiority in the Senate and the justice of its cause, is somewhat inactive, the French party, united with the court, has grown bolder than before and openly expresses the hope of attaining its goals. The following circumstances support it: (1) the court has turned all its influence to the advantage of French views; (2) members of all higher and provincial institutions buttress the views of the court and the "hats;"[54] (3) French money for the necessary expenditures; (4) the court shows favor to the members of the French party, raises them in rank, awards them posts and orders, and in contrast attempts at every favorable opportunity to degrade the dignity of the Senate, construe the distribution of state ranks in a bad light, and strengthen general discontent.

"Spies are everywhere. Emissaries to all localities spread malicious news, arouse discontent, blame the party of the "caps" for the heavy taxes levied as a result of not receiving twelve million livres which France had set aside for Sweden. They hold out the hope of lower taxes if the legislature convenes. They say that Sweden is under a Russian yoke. They frighten people of little spirit with the displeasure of the court. They buy up privileges of the nobility and prevent the collection of state revenues. They advise the people not to pay taxes and raise hopes that the Diet will free the people from their obligation to pay. The goal of all this is to call a special session of the Diet and change the form of government and established system of foreign relations. Such a situation in Sweden requires the most rapid assistance."

The king decided on an unparalleled step. In the Senate he announced the necessity of convoking an extraordinary diet, for he found no measures in the Senate to avert the ruin of the country. The Senate did not agree and the king proclaimed that in consequence of this refusal he placed all responsibility on the Senate. Ostermann wrote that the chief, although secret, mover of the royal proposal was the crown prince. Thereupon the party of the "hats" announced publicly in the market

places that the whole kingdom was entirely ruined. Reporting this, Ostermann wrote that now was the time for the Russian side also to begin its
operations, namely, to publish works of members of the "caps" party
to refute the opposing party's brochures, distributed daily to the public.

In this state of affairs it was easy to understand the kind of impression produced in Sweden by the news of the Confederation of Bar and
Russia's conflict with Turkey. The "hats" rejoiced, while the "caps"
despaired. In October people at court were talking of the inevitable war
of Russia with the Porte, a change in the Prussian king's system, and of
the rapprochement of the Danish king with the views of the French,
who pointed out to him the possibility of taking Holstein while Russia
was busy with the Turkish war. The crown prince spread these rumors
assiduously. In November the College of Foreign Affairs offered the
Senate the opinion that to preserve Swedish credibility in Constantinople
it was necessary to instruct the Swedish emissary there, Zelsing, not to
interfere in the smallest way in the disagreement between Russia and
the Porte. But the Senate did not accept this opinion and contended
that by such detachment Sweden merely would arouse groundless suspicion from one side or the other. The Senate resolved to instruct Zelsing
to take measures to pacify the Porte and to coordinate his actions with
those of the ministers of the powers allied with Sweden. But the king
offered the written objection that in the present case Sweden should
act so as not to lose the friendship of either Russia or Turkey.

Meanwhile there arrived in Stockholm a new French ambassador,
Count de Modein, replacing Breteuil. Ostermann learned that his letters
of accreditation were composed differently from those of previous envoys. There was no mention in them of preservation of friendship with
the state or nation of Sweden, only with the king. In compliance with
this, Modein only once visited Baron Frizendorf, the senator charged
with supervising foreign affairs. Instead, he carried on constant, protracted conversations with the king in public gatherings at court. The
content of these conversations was revealed when the king once again
raised the question in the Senate of the necessity of calling an extraordinary diet. He added that if the senators did not agree this time, he
would refuse to govern the country, for he could not bear the cries of
the suffering. The frightened senators capitulated. Ostermann wrote:
"The 'well-intentioned' party has asked me to place them under her
imperial majesty's most merciful protection and to ask her not to abandon them in their present dire situation, but to preserve their freedom."
He promised to use his entire influence to oppose the force being inflicted upon them. The leaders of the opposing party refrained from
discussing changes in the constitution, but their agents everywhere cried

out that it was better to live under the king and the guidance of a wise Senate than the Russian yoke. The king announced that he was not especially inclined to any party and would solicit only the general welfare. But the crown prince stated that he belonged to the royalist party.

In Denmark the French party was weak. But the king determined to travel and to visit France where he might fall prey to local counsel. In February Filosofov informed Panin that the king suddenly had announced his intention to make a protracted journey through Europe. Filosofov wrote: "Time will tell whether this young and unimaginably frivolous sovereign will gain anything from his trip. One must fear that, being so prone to willful actions, he will be subject to just criticism, prejudicial to his honor and glory." The king set out on his journey and Filosofov went to Aachen for a cure. But in June he broke off his stay and went to Neuss to see the king, or more accurately Bernstorff, who was travelling through that city. He found Bernstorff in great despair. "It is true," said Bernstorff, "that until now the king has done nothing willful, but then he has gained nothing useful from his travels. He is bored everywhere. He does not want to see any of the sights. If protocol demanded that he go look at something, he did so without any enthusiasm and paid no attention to the explanations or descriptions offered him. His sole pleasure was being alone with his favorite, Count Holk. The latter tried to harm me. The king and his favorite have agreed to shorten the journey and after visiting Paris to return home in the fall or beginning of winter. Hourly I must fear still more irrational undertakings from two such frivolous young people. I must allow that in all the seventeen years of my ministerial service I have never been in such a difficult position. I do not know how to preserve my own esteem and the honor of my sovereign."

Filosofov received instructions to accompany the Danish king on his trip. He was with him in England and then in France, whence he wrote Panin in October: "I paid a visit to Duke Choiseul, but I was not received by him and I did not hear a word from a single Frenchman. The French court hates everything Russian and seeks to spread its poison by every means, various slanders and outbursts against all our actions and enterprises, and the sacred person of our sovereign."

If the French did not speak a word to the Russians, they talked a great deal with the Danes. Choiseul tried to convince Bernstorff to break the alliance with Russia and ally with France, which would pay Denmark a subsidy twice as large as the Russian. Bernstorff replied that alliance with Russia was necessary because of Denmark's position, and to end the troubles with the House of Holstein. After this conversation they turned their attacks upon the king personally. Choiseul was alone with him twice and aroused him on the issue of Russia's power-hungry schemes. He offered as an example affairs in Poland. But the king constantly interrupted his addresses with talk about the weather and other such subjects, so that Choiseul parted from him very discontented. The French then turned to the favorite [Holk] and found success. The favorite convinced the king, without saying a word to anyone, to grant permanent access to his chambers to Duke Durras, sent to him from the French court. Not even Count Bernstorff enjoyed this privilege. Since there was no way to deal with the matter directly, it fell to Filosofov to convince the king that he should grant the same right to Bernstorff and Baron Schimmelmann, a man loyal to Russia.

When the Turks declared war on Russia, the French ceased all restraint of their slanders. The bishop of Kamenets, Krasinsky, came to Versailles, as he said, "to hurl Poland into France's embrace." He then went to Saxony after receiving 200,000 livres and the promise of the French court that in the winter this sum would be increased to three million. Without entering Poland, Krasinsky was to aid in the subversion of King Stanislaw through agents by forming a general confederation and choosing Prince Condé or the Saxon Prince Albert as king. Then the newly-chosen king was to marry the Austrian archduchess. In France officers were chosen to be sent to various Polish confederations to train the rebels in the military arts.

France's enmity lent great significance to Russian relations with England, France's constant rival. Having learned that Britain had elevated its representative to Russia from minister of the second rank, as before, to ambassador, Petersburg issued a similar instruction. Brigadier General Count Ivan Chernyshev was named ambassador, replacing the plenipotentiary minister, State Councillor Musin-Pushkin. The instructions to the new ambassador stated: "The rules we have adopted to maintain our own interests independently place us in such a position that those courts which have grown accustomed to influencing other regions are filled with envy of us. For natural reasons, other courts can rely more firmly on our friendship and alliance, all the more since our empire possesses no such scattered and varied interests in Germany or in all of Christian Europe as the other chief powers. Therefore one may conclude that courts having neither the interest nor the inclination to involve themselves in distant troubles, but whose circumstances demand somewhat closer unity with powers holding the balance in their hands, according to circumstances preferably can lean toward the political system of our empire."

But St. Petersburg was happy also with this change in the rank of the English representative because they could recall Musin-Pushkin, whom they considered incompetent. One of Musin-Pushkin's reports began thus: "By almost ceaseless solicitations I finally acquired a note on the motivating causes of the additional duty on several of the linens imported here from the blessed empire of your imperial majesty." To this report, Panin wrote: "The ministry and relations of this minister are comprised solely of grandiose words, such as 'blessed empire,' 'wealthy treasury,' and suchlike, but are not founded on action. For some thirty years, whenever the British parliament tried and many times came close to levying these tariffs on Russian linens and sailcloth, so harmful for the factories here, the efforts of the various Russian ministers at the London court prevented enactment of this measure. Now, when this matter was brought up once again in the latest parliament, timely representations to avert the measure were not made. To the question of why precautions were not taken in good time, the reply was that no special instructions had come from here. But it was impossible to expect such instructions in time, nor was it necessary to demand them. It goes without saying that every minister is obligated to protect the interest of his court without instructions. If he had read the ministerial archive of his predecessors, he would have found sufficient guidance there for his conduct in this case."

Chernyshev set out for his post through Prussia. In Potsdam he was presented to Frederick II, who spoke with him about Polish, Turkish, and British affairs. In regard to Poland, the king asked whether Russia was well informed about everything that was going on there. It seemed to Chernyshev that Frederick had doubts about this. "I think," said Frederick, "that all of Poland soon will be divided up in its parts in confederations. All this is the work of the great lords, who fear to join a confederation openly and have their creatures join instead. It is unpleasant that this is dragging on a long time, although I am sure that sometime it will end according to your wishes. Of course, there is reason to doubt that the Turks will interfere in this affair, but one cannot count much upon them, all the more since other powers are influencing them greatly. Therefore, it is my opinion that the Polish affair should be finished as quickly as possible. This cannot be done other than by sending more troops there, up to 15,000, and by sending them to Lithuania, so as not to arouse Turkish jealousy. I do not doubt that the Russian forces in their present numbers could terminate the matter successfully, if they could do so in one place. But the opponents are scattered and one should not chase them all over. Because of my nearness, I know all their discontents. The chief complaint stems from some trifling tax imposed for the king's benefit at the past Diet, amounting to six or seven hundred thousand, and from the removal of power from the high officials."

The king repeated three times that it was necessary to send more troops into Poland. When Chernyshev noted that the forces already had been augmented, Frederick answered, "Too little!" Count Finckelstein conversed with Chernyshev about England and said: "The British are now strictly following the Bute system[55] of not undertaking any obligations on the continent. I do not understand what need we all have to enter into obligations with them and mix in their quarrels with France. Let the two weaken each other. We should only take care that a balance is maintained."

But when Chernyshev arrived in England, Lord Rocheford, the director of the northern department, assured Chernyshev of his sincere and heartfelt desire to bring to conclusion the matter of the alliance between Russia and England. He considered this alliance of general usefulness, and especially useful in that it would curb that proud intriguer, France. But such a statement also had a personal basis—Rocheford was terribly irritated with France. Previously, he had been ambassador in Paris. When the French took Corsica, the British government ordered him to protest (to the French) the irregularity of this action, which might have bad consequences which Britain could not witness peacefully. Rocheford made his presentation in such form that Choiseul said to him: "When one declares war, one does it with greater civility." Choiseul sent a complaint about Rocheford to the British ministry, which replied that it had not instructed him to make such a statement.

No matter how much Rocheford assured him of his hatred for France and devotion to Russia, no matter how much he said that in the king's council he performed more the function of Russian ambassador than British minister, Chernyshev could not convince him of the necessity of giving a subsidy to Sweden and thus shaking French influence there. All agreed that it was necessary to give a subsidy. "The sum was not great," said Rocheford, "but what could be done, when we have decided not to give subsidies in peacetime and when the members of the present ministry were in opposition, insisting on respect for this decision."

After the Turks declared war, England offered its services as mediator to restore peace. Chernyshev stated that this was not the time to speak of mediation. The empress expected from the British the sole service of insuring and protecting Russia from another enemy. The surest way to do this was to conclude a subsidy treaty with Sweden. To think of mediation would not be consonant with the dignity of the empress, who had been insulted so terribly by the treatment of her minister, Obrezkov.

Rocheford transmitted to Chernyshev the reports of the British ambassador to Vienna, Lord Stormont, who among other things described his conversation with Maria Theresa. She spoke directly about the

Russo-Turkish war and said that this flame personally was more disturbing and dangerous because it had burst forth so close to her. "I will not conceal the fact," said the empress, "that for many reasons I cannot wish the Turks success or expect that they will be successful. I greatly regret that the Turks have been drawn out of their inactivity. I think that if the Russian empress wished, there would still be time to avoid war by condescending to make several concessions about what was done in Poland at the last Diet. But who will begin? You cannot because of your close friendship with Russia. I cannot because of my close friendship with France. Who? I would willingly undertake to do all that was demanded of me. I was against the choice of Poniatowski as king. But once I have recognized him, I do not wish to replace him." Kaunitz swore to Stormont on his word of honor that the Austrians had not participated and would not participate in raising the Turks against Russia. This would be opposed completely to his and Maria Theresa's system. The Prussian envoy had spread the rumor about Austrian intrigues in Constantinople.

The French moved the Porte to declare war. These same French would force Sweden also to war with Russia were they to gain decisive advantage in Stockholm. What could be more dangerous than a war with Sweden, along with one against Poland and Turkey? Therefore it is not surprising that Petersburg decided to employ all means to prevent the French party from triumph in Sweden, which would have the consequence of subverting the existing constitution. In conversations about the British alliance the Russians decided to abandon their chief demand, which had served as a constant bar to conclusion of the alliance. They decided to abandon the demand that Turkey be mentioned in any alliance and instead to insist that England conclude a subsidy treaty with Sweden.

Macartney's successor, Lord Cathcart, did not arrive in Petersburg until August 1768. Panin produced a very pleasant impression upon him. "I have rarely seen a man," he wrote, "with whom I could do business more pleasantly, securely, and advantageously." Catherine made a strong impression on him. He was able to refer to her only by citing Virgil's lines about Dido (Talis erat Dido, etc.). He wrote that the empress need fear nothing and no one because of the superiority of her mind, and that all was going excellently. In England they suspected that the lord was somewhat carried away and they pointed out to him the dangers for Dido. They demonstrated that she was distracted from important domestic matters by foreign affairs. There was the unsatisfactory situation in Poland. France was striving openly to arouse the discontent of the Porte and to change the constitution in Sweden.

The Russians soon got down to business. Saldern, who recently had returned to Petersburg, let Cathcart know that the article about alliance against Turkey would be deleted from the treaty and replaced by an article about subsidies for Sweden. "Does this mean that we must purchase an alliance with Russia?" asked Cathcart. "No," Saldern answered. "The empress is buying your alliance, and giving you free a system acquired at some cost. She demands only that you help support it. Besides the funds spent by the empress in Sweden and Poland at the time of the choice of the king and in support of the dissidents, she will continue to spend much more money than you." Cathcart understood and wrote his ministry that in his opinion the article was acceptable. But they answered him that he should repeat the same things in Petersburg that were said to Chernyshev in London: England found it extraordinarily difficult to change its practice of not paying subsidies during peacetime.

The break with Turkey pushed all other matters into the background for the moment.

NOTES

Additional information on personalities and topics found in the text and notes is available in Joseph L. Wieczynski, ed., *The Modern Encyclopedia of Russian and Soviet History* (MERSH); Harry B. Weber, ed., *The Modern Encyclopedia of Russian and Soviet Literatures (Including Non-Russian and Emigre Literatures)* (MERSL); and David R. Jones, ed., *The Military-Naval Encyclopedia of Russia and the Soviet Union* (MERSU), all published by Academic International Press.

CHAPTER I

1. Soloviev refers here to Catherine's *Nakaz,* or *Instruction to the Legislative Commission*, a document composed by Catherine at least a year before convocation of the assembly, and presented to the delegates for their guidance in considering revision, reform, or emendation of existing Russian law. Catherine drew heavily upon modern political theory, especially the thought of Montesquieu and Beccaria, in composing this programmatic and quite liberal statement of her political, social, and legal principles.

2. Pomestie and votchina were historically the two major kinds of landholding in Russia. Pomestie refers to estates granted by the ruler in return for service, generally in the military, but later also in the civil service. Votchina describes an estate held and inherited free and clear of any obligations to the ruler or state. The distinction between the two was effectively eradicated during the reign of Peter the Great, but was revived in debates among the nobility as the nobles were emancipated from their earlier service burdens.

3. This is a free translation of the title *syn boiarskii*, literally "boyars' sons," who constituted the lesser gentry in the pre-Petrine Muscovite state.

4. In ancient and medieval Russia the bulk of the population, including most of the peasantry, had been free. The term used here for slave is *kholop*, one of several types of non-free residents of ancient Russia before the development of serfdom.

5. *Dvorianstvo* is the Russian term commonly translated as "nobility," "gentry," or "landed gentry." Russia in 1767 had not developed as homogeneous a nobility as many western European states, and therefore the term dvorianstvo once had a far more specific meaning than the translations above indicate. The dvorianstvo was the military service class which arose upon the consolidation and extension of Muscovite power in Russia and eastern Europe. The dvorianstvo received estates from the grand prince or tsar in return for service, and therefore their claim to nobility was based solely upon their position in the service of the ruler, not upon older familial ties. By the mid-eighteenth century the dvorianstvo constituted the bulk of the Russian nobility, thanks especially to the levelling

effects of the reforms of Peter the Great, who eliminated many of the old titles and positions, such as boyar. The Russian nobility was still not a homogeneous class or estate in the French or British sense, and many titled nobles of older or more prominent families felt no class identification with the common service nobility.

6. The system of ranks referred to here is *mestnichestvo* (right of place), established during the reign of Ivan III and abolished only near the end of the seventeenth century during the reign of Fedor II. Mestnichestvo provided that no noble in the service of the tsar could be appointed to a post in which he would be required to take orders from a man from a family, any member of which had served under any ancestor of the noble. This was a means of maintaining family precedence in the tsar's court, but often led to irreconcilable conflicts in making appointments according to both family precedence and ability. Under Peter the Great a new, formal system of ranks was established by the Table of Ranks, which instituted fourteen ranks in the military and civil services. Any man attaining the eighth rank on the table (the lowest level of commissioned officer or the equivalent) was automatically to receive hereditary nobility.

7. *Raznochinets* refers to a non-noble, free resident of Russia, usually a crown servant or his descendents on a level below rank eight in the Table of Ranks. Literally a person of various ranks, raznochinets soon came to mean one without rank, a pejorative for the lower classes of state bureaucrats.

8. Shcherbatov's instruction refers here to one of the most touchy questions of the day, the right of non-nobles to own serfs. There were two main legal groups of peasants in Russia, those who lived on crown lands (state peasants) and those living on lands of the service nobility (private peasants, estate peasants, or serfs). Peter the Great had attempted to spur the development of a heavy manufacturing industry by allowing factory owners chartered by the government, even if not nobles, to own and use serfs in their factories. This created a third, fairly small, but troublesome category, known as possessional peasants.

9. Landrat is a reference back to the system of local administration which Peter the Great had attempted to introduce into Russia in the 1720s, modelled on the example of Sweden and its Baltic possessions. The terms from the Swedish or German were appropriated directly into Russian, which hitherto had had no or few words for organs of local self-government or administration (neither was ever really well-developed in Russia).

10. The College of Church Landed Property was one of the administrative colleges established by Peter the Great to replace the old government departments (prikazy) as the highest central executive administrative offices of the state. The College of Church Landed Property was founded in 1726 from one of the departments of the Holy Synod (see note 26, below). Its mission was to oversee the estates and possessions of the clergy and to collect taxes from them.

11. When Peter the Great issued a formal legal decree obligating all nobles to state service for life, he also established schools and required that all nobles obtain an education. However, many nobles objected to going to the same schools as commoners. In 1731 in St. Petersburg the Corps of Cadets was established as a school for nobles; it admitted only nobles and guaranteed placement as a commissioned officer upon graduation.

12. The Treasury College was established in 1718 to supervise the collection of state revenues.

13. Soul (dusha) is the term customarily used to refer to an adult male, usually a peasant. Hence the "soul tax"—a head tax imposed upon all adult males

not exempt from state taxation (that is, nobles and a few other exceptions). Wealth generally was measured by the number of "souls" that one owned, so the term often was used interchangeably with serf.

14. The Russian term is *Obrok*, the obligation of the peasant to his master when paid in money or goods. The closest English equivalent is either rent or quit-rent. Some serfs fulfilled their obligations to their lords in labor, a practice called *barshchina*, roughly equivalent to the French *corvée*.

15. The merchant class was divided into three guilds and registered by the government according to property holdings and occupation in legislation issued by Peter the Great in 1699 and 1720. Catherine eventually reorganized the legal structure and divisions within the merchant class in her Charter to the Cities in 1785.

16. The village elder, or starosta, generally was chosen by the peasants in an informal election or (more commonly) by consensus. His duties involved mainly dealing with representatives of the lord or the crown and in assuring that all the peasants in his village contributed their fair share to the obligations which the village as a whole owed the master or the crown. Sometimes the starosta was appointed by the owner of a village and acted in greater part as his agent.

17. The Votiaks or Udmurt were a tribe of Finno-Ugric derivation, located mainly in the wilds east of Viatka and north of Kazan.

18. The College of Audits was one of the original colleges founded by Peter and was in charge of financial inspection and auditing of other government agencies.

19. *Meshchanstvo* is a catch-all term referring to all legally free city dwellers who were not registered as nobles, merchants, clerics, or peasants. The meshchanstvo generally included the lower urban classes, such as artisans, small traders, day laborers, and so forth.

20. The head tax (or "soul tax"—see note 13, above) imposed by the government on all adult males subject to taxation (generally all but members of the nobility), was introduced by Peter the Great in 1724.

21. *The Russian Justice* (Russkaia pravda), the first code of laws in Russia, was issued during the reign of Iaroslav the Wise in the mid-eleventh century. The reference here, "keeper of the keys," is to the old Russian office of *kliuchnik*, the senior servant in a noble's house, and responsible for managing the property and meting out punishments and rewards to other servants.

22. Catherine has left us various notes expressing her discontent with the views of the members of the Commission about the serfs: "If the serf cannot be recognized as a human, then he is not a man. But to allow him to be viewed as cattle will have the entire world attribute little glory or love of our fellow man to us. All that follows about a slave is a consequence of this paternalistic position and is done to cattle by cattle." (Soloviev)

23. The Free Economic Society was the first learned society in Russia (besides the Academy of Sciences, a state institution). It was founded by Catherine in 1765. Its members generally were drawn from the nobility close to the court. Its mission was the study and dissemination of Western agricultural and economic knowledge in the hope of strengthening Russia's rural economy.

24. Alexander Petrovich Sumarokov (1718-1777) was one of the first great poets, dramatists, and men of letters in Russia. He was from a noble family, well educated in the eighteenth-century French manner, and dedicated to the neoclassicism which dominated eighteenth-century European literature. He was a staunch disciple of Voltaire and probably the most prominent literary authority of his time in Russia.

25. Beardé de l'Abaye, also spelled Beardé de Labbay, from Aix-la-Chapelle, and holder of the degree of doctor of laws, was a French political and economic thinker of the mid-eighteenth century.

26. The Holy Synod was the supreme governing body of the Russian Orthodox church. When the office of patriarch became vacant in 1700, Peter the Great declined to make a permanent appointment. In 1721 Peter abolished the Patriarchate and substituted the Synod, a collegial body headed by a chief procurator, as the supreme ecclesiastical authority in Russia.

27. The third estate (tiers état) was composed of bourgeois notables, deputies from towns to represent the people in assemblies. The third estate is composed of municipal magistrates and noted bourgeois citizens, people who were at one time almost all serfs. The sovereigns will raise it up and by degrees admit their charges. The third estate was composed of bourgeois representatives for the deputies of the towns. Some people a bit acquainted with the principles of this matter believe that the entire clergy, as an indistinct mass, should comprise the third estate. This is an error that is easy to refute. It is true that those of the clergy who are not nobles by birth or otherwise cannot be placed elsewhere but in the third estate. But those who would enjoy the title and prerogatives of nobility either by their extraction or by virtue of some office to which nobility is attached or by virtue of certain ennobling learning ought not at all to be mixed up with the third estate. One cannot contest their right to be included in the order or estate of the nobility the same as other nobles whose profession they know and which gives the latter their nobility. (Soloviev, quoting Catherine)

28. A verst was the common Russian measure of distance, some 3,500 feet, or roughly one kilometer. See the table of weights and measures at the beginning of this volume.

29. Before full conquest and assimilation of the Ukraine by Russia, the cossacks had organized themselves into an independent local unit called the *sech*. The closest western equivalent might be the old town meeting, but this does not fully convey the disorganized, rambunctious, but often quite authoritarian nature of cossack self-government. The sech would choose an *hetman* (the term *ataman* also is used), generally by consensus and not through formal electoral procedures. The hetman was the military as well as political leader of the cossack band, but usually was not separated socially from the rest of the cossacks. After Mazeppa's treachery in 1708 the Russian government attempted steadily to erode the institution and authority of independent, elected hetmen. Catherine in effect ruled the Ukraine through her plenipotentiary representative, military governor Prince Rumiantsev.

30. Grigory Nikolaevich Teplov (1720-1770) was a member of the Academy of Sciences and tutor and companion to the appointed hetman of the Ukraine in the 1750s, Kirill Grigorevich Razumovsky. Soloviev has treated Teplov's writings on the Ukraine in some detail in an earlier volume.

31. Zaporozhe, the location of a set of rapids south of Kiev, became the site of one of the largest Cossack settlements in the Ukraine. The Zaporozhe *sech* along the Dnieper was the most famous of all the old cossack communities.

32. This is a reference to the capitulation of 1449, an agreement between the Livonian knights and the papacy. This agreement established the privileges and landholding rights of the Baltic nobility. The laws based upon this charter were preserved in the Treaty of Nystadt, signed after Russia's victory over Sweden in the Great Northern War in 1721.

33. *Speculum*, a literary work of a moral and educational nature.

34. For some reason Soloviev chose here, in a footnote, to list the major requests of the various groups of deputies to the Commission. The list is as follows: " . . . from government deputies: (1) to let laymen of any rank enter the clergy and allow clergy to enter lay service of any rank and free the clergy from unseemly labors; (2) to teach children the catechism, to found schools for youths in the cities, and not to take as private tutors men and women without references; (3) on the purchase of serfs by clergy and other church workers; (4) reduction of the number of holidays; (5) pass a law on how to act in cases when death results from beatings administered by a landlord; (6) do away with women leading a dissolute life; (7) forbid fist fights; (8) do not shoot with muskets and other weapons inside houses and do not allow base people to carry any weapon with them; (9) give monastic immovable property to the crown and establish funds to feed the monks and support the church; (10) institute a law requiring that various kinds of people live in harmony; (11) suppress excessive luxuries; (12) pass a law on runaway people and peasants and punishment for keeping or owning them, with or without land; (13) do not allow anyone else to become a cossack and supervise all who are registered as such; (14) give debtors to designated people to work off the debt in the event they are not fit for exile at hard labor; (15) identify and distinguish virtuous citizens; (16) have the police publish news about all new events; (17) rule on paper money; (18) do not allow paupers through city gates; (19) do not allow people to ride fast or unbroken horses inside the cities; (20) on post boys and riders not having knouts and whips; (21) establish public places in the cities for the enjoyment of the permanent residents.

"The nobility presented these requests: (1) to have educated priests on salary, sell the church lands, and have clerics teach peasant children to read and write; (2) make Little Russian ranks equivalent to Great Russian ranks; (3) make a law about renting out villages; (4) sell ecclesiastical lands to the nobility; (5) on the gift or sale to nobles of cleared lands, virgin fields, and lands and various services of service people; (6) on the introduction of special liberties for regiments in the cities and for removing them from districts [in the countryside]; (7) establish special schools in the cities for nobles' children; (8) establish banks in the cities; (9) for state bread stores; (10) for pharmacies and doctors; (11) shops and factories should be in the cities; (12) to forbid the sowing of grain on advantageous city plots; (13) on allowing peasants in the cities to engage in retail trade of their products; (14) on allowing peasants to enter into contracts; (15) on the presence of peasants as agents of merchants in their stores or roadhouses only in the winter, so that they return to cultivate their fields in the summer; (16) not to take supplies from the peasantry but instead establish post stations; (17) not to assign peasants to guard duty and similar work; (18) on the increase of peasant dishonors (that is, fees for dishonor) and on the increase in their sums (that is, the sums of the payments) for those who wish to be called merchants, and not to allow them to be registered in the cities by their wives' families; (19) to take money instead of fodder in some places, and in others, where it is necessary, to take fodder and provisions instead of the soul tax; (20) to levy the soul tax on some free cultivators; (21) to settle foreign colonists in various districts and cities so that the peasants might receive an instructive example of better home management from them; (22) not to allow the Cherkassy to move from place to place; (23) to make the wives of those conscripted into the army obedient to their lords; (24) on the destruction of iron, glass, powder, and other factories to preserve the forests; (25) on the choice of governors and their aides by ballot among the nobility of their district; (26) to forbid those who are not allowed the rights of the nobility to have farms or mills; (27) to issue a strict law to prevent the flight of peasant women and girls; (28) to inflict, as before, capital punishment in the cities on felons, bandits, and murderers.

"The city dwellers petitioned that: (1) they be confirmed in the honor of the Christian faith; a law be issued on how to protect the Lord's treasures when a church unexpectedly caught fire during a service; disturbances not be raised in church during a service; (2) free exercise of religious observance to be extended to people of other faiths; (3) those desiring should be tonsured in the appropriate monastic ranks; (4) on fines from those not going to confession; (5) on the construction of churches and the writing of contracts on all church matters without any taxes; (6) on the allocation of money for the construction of churches, iconostasis, and decoration of the churches; (7) on the maintenance of parish clergy on a fitting basis and allocation of a salary to them; (8) on not making any demands from the clergy except those indicated for church needs; (9) on the founding once again of appropriate offices in the cities; on the establishment once more of city courts, as has been done in other states; (10) on the subordination of the police in the cities to the magistrates and *ratusha* [city councils]; (11) on confirmation of the Magdeburg Law; on affirmation of nobles' rights for the cossacks and retention of these rights gained by cossacks in previous posts; (12) on the choice for all time in all things of leaders for all citizens; (13) on the choice of special deputies from the merchantry and allowing them to enter all [government] offices on merchant business; (14) on the rights and preeminence of the Russian merchantry, not calling them unseemly names, and allowing the leading merchants to wear swords; (15) on the founding of a state bank in the cities to aid the merchants' commerce and increase trade; (16) on the suppression of luxury and the banning of all foreign things coming into Russia; (17) on the elimination of the present census by soul and the use of the previous method, by household; (18) on exemption from the soul tax of nobles, *deti boiarskie* [lesser gentry], merchants, and people of other callings and also exemption of them from the draft; (19) on removal of the money tax from horsemen (in Little Russia) and redistribution of the tax on landowners and people subject to tax *(tiaglie liudi)*; (20) on the establishment of cooperatives; (21) on the abolition in Little Russia of tariffs; (22) on not giving any industries or goods out as monopolies; (23) on not allowing soldiers to insult or beat merchants and making them pay money for goods taken from merchants; (24) on not allowing the peasants in the districts to insult the merchants or to rob to pay others' debts; (25) on the establishment of quick, hearings courts, even courts of three, instead of formal courts for all disputes between merchants and people of various ranks *(raznochintsy)*; (26) on justice and rapid resolution of business in government offices upon requests submitted by merchants; (27) on forbidding civil servants to hear or work on affairs at home; (28) on lessening the number of courts and on fines for judges; (29) not to bring city dwellers to court in civil offices by force without a summons having been delivered; (30) to impose a prohibition so that no one will dare abuse another faith; (31) on the purchase of peasants and house serfs by clergymen, merchants, and people of various callings; (32) to forbid churchmen to purchase land; (33) to make the bishops and monasteries renounce the lands taken from them; (34) on the establishment in cities of academies, universities, and schools and on instruction in them of the children of merchants, people of various ranks and orphans in various languages; (35) on the establishment of hospitals and orphanages maintained by the state; (36) on the election by the Little Russian people of a hetman and elders by free vote and on subjecting the cossacks to the justice dispensed by the elders;

(37) not to force merchants to shave their beards and wear German clothes; (38) take the Old Believers living among the Orthodox in the cities, judge the amount of deceit spread by them in society and their avoidance of civic services, and resettle them in special places; (39) to allow Old Beliver priests, monks, and nuns returning from Poland and Turkey [to Russian jurisdiction] to conduct services in vestries and churches according to the old books; (40) not to have a special police force in the cities and to give such duties to the magistrate.

"The poor nobles and free farmers asked: (1) to designate clerical teachers for the sciences and exhortation to deeds worthy of God, and secular teachers for the establishment of well-being, knowledge of the law, and good conduct; (2) to construct state barracks and stables for quartering troops in the cities; (3) for defense from soldiers passing by; (4) not to send service people in the cities into the countryside to make edicts public, but to send for this church servants to the various churches; (5) to have the whole society of the district choose judges and to appoint district residents special members of government office staffs to hasten the conduct of business; (6) defendants' advocates be present in meetings in government offices; (7) to lessen the five year term of governors and to change governors and secretaries upon request of district residents; (8) to remove Russian governors from Little Russian cities; (9) about the oppression of themselves and other people by government offices and by government officers themselves; (10) about the oppression visited upon poor nobles and free farmers by nobles and their peasants; (11) for hearings courts; for the designation for trials among permanent residents of commanders or elders of their choice, and not to have them in any matters under the jurisdiction of government offices, except involving the soul tax."

This long and sometimes curious list is indicative of the wide range of interests which were expressed and debated in the Commission on the Law Code. The requests range from the important to the petty and sublime, and indicate how often the decrees and authority of the autocrat were ineffective or thwarted in local administration. Soloviev illustrates and discusses most of the important requests in the text proper.

35. *Zertsalo* was the emblem of legality in tsarist Russia, placed on desks in courts and other government institutions. Introduced by Peter I, it was a three-cornered prism, with a two-headed eagle and on each corner a copy of the three basic decrees of Peter on legality in Russia.

36. Nikita Panin (1718-1783) was one of Catherine's chief advisors during the first half of her reign, and tutor to Paul, heir to the throne. Panin was especially influential in the formulation of Russian foreign policy and is mentioned much in Chapter II of this volume. He was also the main figure in the party which opposed the influence of the Orlov brothers over Catherine.

37. The *pud* (or *pood*) was a unit of weight in Russia, roughly equal to 16.38 kilograms or 36.13 pounds (US). See the table of weights and measures at the beginning of this volume.

38. Schlüsselburg (later Shlisselburg) is a fortress built by Peter the Great where the Neva flows out of Lake Ladoga, about forty miles east of St. Petersburg. Like the Peter and Paul fortress in the capital, it rapidly came to be used for the incarceration of political prisoners rather than for military purposes. It was one of the most infamous of such prisons in the imperial era.

CHAPTER II

1. Nikolai Vasielevich Repnin (1734-1801) was sent by Catherine to Poland in 1763 as ambassador plenipotentiary to deal with the dissident question. Son of a noted military commander and from an old noble family, Repnin had served in the military and briefly as director of a military school before this assignment.

2. Waclaw Rzewuski (1706-1779) was the scion of one of Poland's most eminent noble families. He served as high crown marshal (see note 3 below) and military commander of Cracow. He was also a noted literary figure.

3. The high chief hetman and the chief hetman (from the Russian *velikii getman* and *getman pol'nyi*) were respectively the royal commander in chief of the armies of Poland (called up in time of war) and his replacement in case of death or incapacity. The offices were first established during the reign of Sigismund I in the sixteenth century.

4. I have used Diet throughout as a translation of the Polish *Sejm*, the parliamentary assembly in Poland of this time. One should note that the Sejm was composed almost entirely of representatives of the upper nobility and clergy, and that unanimity was required before any measure could be approved by the Sejm.

5. Georgy Konisski (1718-1795) was the archbishop of the Orthodox diocese of Belorussia. He was one of the most ardent defenders of the rights of Poland's Orthodox subjects (numbering some 600,000) and spent much of his life championing his faith in the face of Catholic oppression. He was one of the leaders of the dissident movement of the 1760s.

6. Otto von Saldern was a native of Holstein who had been sent to serve the Russian court in 1762, during the reign of Peter III. He remained in the Russian diplomatic service, performing missions such as the one outlined in this volume, and eventually rose to become Russian ambassador to Poland at the time of the first partition.

7. This is the date of the coup which overthrew Peter III and placed Catherine on the throne.

8. Francois Ravaillac was the assassin of King Henry IV of France, the monarch whose election at least temporarily ended the religious conflict of the late sixteenth century in France. St. Bartholemew's night refers to the slaughter of Huguenots by Catholic forces in Paris on August 24, 1572, an event which generally is agreed to have begun the open religious civil war of the late sixteenth century in France.

9. The coronation Diet refers to the meeting of the Sejm in 1764 at which, with pressure from Russia, Catherine's former lover, Stanislaw Poniatowski, was elected king to succeed Augustus III. The Potocki family had attempted to resist the Russians and place a candidate favorable to France on the throne, but they were outmaneuvered by the Czartoryski family, to whom Poniatowski was related and who favored Polish alignment with Russia. The Czartoryskis later fell out with the Russian court over some reforms proposed by them which would strengthen the monarchy and partially eliminate the paralyzing need for unanimity in the Sejm.

10. In Greek mythology Nessus was a centaur killed by Hercules with a poisoned arrow. A shirt soaked in Nessus's blood by Hercules's wife, as a love charm, subsequently brought death to Hercules.

11. Benoit was the Prussian chargé d'affaires in Warsaw and ambassador to Russia.

12. As mentioned, the Polish Diet required unanimity before it could agree upon any action—election of a king, declaration of war, passing of financial

legislation, and so forth. The *liberum veto* (literally "I reject freely," from the Latin, or "I forbid," from the Polish *nie pozwalat*) was a privilege accorded all members of the Diet by the constitution based upon the assumption of the political equality of all Polish citizens. (In this era the Poles extended such political equality only to the nobility and upper clergy.) Every measure before the Diet had to be adopted unanimously, and any member of the Diet, by exercising his right to a veto, could block the passage of any measure and force dissolution of the Diet. This procedure originated in the sixteenth century and was aimed at avoiding the tyranny of majority rule.

Instead, the *liberum veto* allowed any faction, no matter how small, to immobilize the Polish state and opened up countless opportunities for bribery, intrigue, and foreign intervention. Eventually members of the Diet resorted to the expediency of forming confederations, which would adopt a platform by majority vote and then vote in the platform unanimously at the session of the Diet. Nevertheless, Poland was still trammelled by the *liberum veto*, since it took only the recalcitrance of one member of a confederation to wreck months of preparation and dissolve a Diet before it could accomplish anything.

13.   Adam Casimir Czartoryski (1734-1823), at the time the youngest of the clan, had been educated abroad and returned to Poland to serve as commander of the Polish army in Podolia. He was a candidate for the throne in 1764 but renounced his candidacy in favor of his cousin Poniatowski. He later served the Polish and Russian governments in various capacities. He should not be confused with his son, Adam Yuri (George) Czartoryski (1770-1861), the intimate of Alexander I, member of the unofficial committee, and leader of the uprising against Russia in 1830.

14.   Julius L. Falkenstein (1708-1776), a noble official of the Court of Frederick II.

15.   The Stadhoulder, in the old republic of the Netherlands, was the chief executive officer of the state. The office was made hereditary in the House of Orange in 1672.

16.   Fontenoy is a small town in Belgium where on May 11, 1745 the allied armies of Britain, Hanover, and the Netherlands suffered a crushing defeat at the hands of the French army.

17.   Popillius Laenas, Gaius, was a Roman consul in 172 B.C., when he defended M. Popillius, whose conduct in Liguria had incurred the disapproval of the Senate. He was Roman envoy to Greece in 170 B.C. and in 168 B.C. he led the expedition to Egypt which after Pydna forced Antiochus Epiphanes to withdraw his army immediately from Egypt. Popillius drew a circle around King Antiochus and demanded a decision about his troops before the monarch stepped outside of the circle.

18.   Alexis Mikhailovich Obrezkov was the Russian chargé d'affaires in the Ottoman empire in the late 1760s.

19.   Ivan Andreevich Ostermann (1725-1804), a count, was the son of the famous Andrei Ivanovich (Heinrich-Johann) Ostermann, favorite of the Empress Elizabeth. The younger Ostermann served in the Russian army and guards. He went abroad after an unpleasant incident, and later served as a member of the Russian embassy in Paris before being assigned to Stockholm as head of the Russian mission in the 1760s.

20.   There were two major factions in the Swedish parliament and court at this time, one leaning to Russia and the other to France. Ostermann constantly refers to the pro-Russian faction as the *blagonamerennye*, literally, well-intentioned people. I have tried to preserve this usage as much as possible.

21. Count Frederick Axel Fersen (1719-1794) was descended from a branch of the Scottish MacPherson clan which had migrated to Sweden in the sixteenth century. He served in the French army, and later in the Swedish army during the Seven Years' War. He became a leader of the aristocratic party in the Swedish parliament and after the victory of his opponents in 1765 he became one of the closest political advisors of the monarch.

22. Louis August le Tonneille, Baron de Breteuil (1733-1807) was the French ambassador first to St. Petersburg and then Stockholm in the 1760s. In the 1780s he was appointed a minister of the French court, where he became known for his ultra-absolutist political views.

23. The name "hats" (shliapy) was used to denote the aristocratic party, hostile to Russia, which had the king's ear in Sweden. This party favored the return of more power to the monarch, while the opposing party, the "caps" (shapki), favored retention and expansion of the independent powers of the parliament.

24. George Macartney (1737-1806), later made an earl, began his career in public service in Britain by leading a particularly delicate trade mission to St. Petersburg from 1764 to 1767. Later he was a member of Parliament, chief secretary for Ireland, governor of the Caribbean Islands, Madras, and the Cape of Good Hope.

25. Alexis Petrovich Bestuzhev-Riumin (1693-1766) rose during the reign of Elizabeth to become chancellor of the Russian empire from 1744 until his fall in 1758 for recalling a Russian commander without Elizabeth's authorization, since he believed that Elizabeth would not recover from an illness afflicting her. Later he was pardoned and recalled from exile by Catherine.

26. In an effort to hasten development of his new capital, St. Petersburg, Peter the Great decreed in 1713 that a number of raw materials be exported only through the port of St. Petersburg. In 1715 St. Petersburg's share was reduced to one-half of the total exports of the original commodities, but in 1718 a series of decrees essentially restored the prohibition against extensive export from Russia's White Sea ports. St. Petersburg was to be the point of export for two-thirds of the total volume in most materials, and the export of grains and import of silk and brocade through Archangel was forbidden altogether. These decrees were modelled on the British Navigation Acts, a set of restrictions enacted by Britain in the last half of the seventeenth century to limit the amount of foreign shipping intruding into the trade between Britain and its colonies. Peter was familiar with the laws governing shipping within the British empire as a result of his visit to Britain and study of its shipbuilding and shipping industry.

27. Prince Vasily Vladimirovich Dolgoruky (1667-1746) was a prominent government personage in the first third of the eighteenth century. He served Peter the Great in a number of capacities. He was a member of the Supreme Privy Council under Peter II and as such one of the most powerful men in Russia. He was the only member of the Privy Council to oppose the limitations initially put upon Empress Anna, so he survived in good odor some six months longer into her reign than did his colleagues and relatives who favored limitation of the autocracy. Exiled in December 1730, he was recalled to the court in 1741 by Empress Elizabeth.

28. The Chernyshevs were an old Russian noble family with a pedigree dating from the fifteenth century. Soloviev is referring here to Zakhar Grigorievich Chernyshev (1722-1784), a field marshal and official in the War College, and his brothers, Ivan Grigorievich and Peter Grigorievich.

29. This is the Polish office of referendarz, established by Sigismund I in 1507. There were four such offices, two for Poland and two for Lithuania, with

one for each kingdom being drawn from the clergy and the other two from the laity. The original duties of the *referendarz* were to hear the complaints of subjects and transmit them to the king and his ministers. Later these officers only announced the government's actions on petitions. In 1766 a system of courts (Russ., *referendarskie sady*) was set up better to handle the load of petitions, especially those arising from disputes between peasants on crown lands.

30.   Karl Stanislaw Radziwill (1734-1790) had been the military governor of Wilno. He was a well-known daredevil and humorist and especially popular among the Polish nobility. A member of one of the most illustrious Lithuanian princely families, he owned enormous properties and reportedly supported 10,000 regular troops out of his own pocket.

31.   Maria Theresa Geoffrin (1699-1777) was the hostess of one of the most renowned literary salons in Paris. The wife of a manufacturer of glass and mirrors, she rose from petty bourgeois origins to meet and entertain most of the leading figures of French and European literary society. She opened her own salon in 1748 and her soirées served especially as a place for foreigners to meet and talk with such French figures as D'Alembert, Diderot, Holbach, and others. She aided Poniatowski when he was a young man living in Paris. For her aid he was never to forget her and often referred to her as "mother." She had just visited Poland in early 1766.

32.   Soloviev uses the term mile here without any qualification. The distances could be Polish miles, which would be equal to about five English statute miles (putting the troops between fifteen and twenty-five miles from Warsaw), or they could be old Lithuanian miles, also roughly equal to five statute miles.

33.   Sicilian vespers: a massacre of the French in Sicily which took place during the hour for vespers on Easter Monday in 1282. The term now is used to refer to any bloody and treacherous attack, especially with religious overtones.

34.   Little Poland (*Malopolska*) was the southern area of Poland, united with greater Poland by King Wladyslaw II (1260-1333), and generally includes the areas around Cracow, Sendomir, and Lublin.

35.   The reis-effendi was the master of the court of the Turkish sultan, in other words, the chief minister and advisor of the sultan.

36.   Ivan Ivanovich Betsky (1704-1795) was one of the leading figures in the eighteenth-century Russian enlightenment and one of the first innovators in Russian education. He was born in Stockholm, the illegitimate son of Prince Ivan Yurievich Trubetskoy, then a prisoner of war. After being returned to Russia, Betsky was sent to Copenhagen for an education and then entered the Danish military service. He was injured, had to leave the military, and travelled widely through Europe. He entered the Russian diplomatic service in 1729 and served in various European capitals. He won great rewards for his support of Elizabeth's coup in 1741. He served as official guide for Catherine's mother when she first came to Russia in 1745 and then retired when Catherine's mother departed. He spent the next fifteen years in Paris, became well acquainted with the Encyclopedists, and absorbed a great many of their educational theories, which he later attempted to apply in Russia. He returned to Russia upon the command of Peter III, and after Catherine came to the throne was very close to her, but held no official position. He concerned himself only with education and did not mix much in affairs of state. He became head of the Academy of Arts and the Infantry Cadets' Academy, and toward the end of his career was richly rewarded with estates and orders by Catherine.

37.   Ivan Ivanovich Shuvalov (1727-1797) was one of several of the Shuvalov family who rose to prominence in the reign of Elizabeth. He was more modest

than his kin, refusing the title of count and estates when offered, and is best known for his part in the founding of Moscow University in 1755 and the establishment of other educational and learned institutions in Russia. He went abroad shortly after Catherine took the throne and remained out of Russia for the next fourteen years.

38. First Baron, later Count Hermann Karl Keyserling (1695 or 1696-1764) came from an old German family. He was educated in Königsberg under Bekenstein and Bayer, who later became members of the Russian Academy of Sciences. In 1730 he entered Russian service in the College of Justice. After a brief stint as president of the Academy of Sciences, most of his career was spent in the diplomatic service. One of his posts was that of emissary to Poland, especially concerned with defending Poland's Orthodox subjects from governmental persecution.

39. Marienwerder was located near Dantzig on the Vistula river, and was the capital of the westernmost part of East Prussia. Tariffs levied by the Poles and Prussians on goods moving between the two parts of Prussia and from Poland to the Baltic were a constant source of friction between Poland and Prussia.

40. Property magistrate: Soloviev uses here the term *podkomorii*, denoting an official in the *sad podkomorski*, or property court in old Poland and Lithuania. The property court was generally a court of three with one party representing each of the two litigants and the property magistrate, generally appointed by the crown. The court was not empowered to settle questions of ownership, only disputes over boundaries between parcels.

41. The reference here is to the Seven Years' War.

42. The Order of the White Eagle is an old Polish military decoration, eventually merged with the Order of St. Vladimir after full Russian absorption of Poland in 1831.

43. It is not clear here whether Repnin is referring to the otherwise anonymous Saltykov who served on the Russian command staff in Poland, or to a more prominent military figure, such as Prince Nikolai Ivanovich Saltykov (1736-1816) or Count Ivan Petrovich Saltykov (1730-1805), both of whom were involved in the Seven Years' War, the events in Poland, and the first Turkish war under Catherine.

44. *Ulemas* are scholars or priests trained in traditional Muslim theology and law. In the Ottoman empire these educated churchmen carried considerable weight when they intervened in political affairs.

45. All these are revered for protecting or spreading the faith. Moses should be familiar to all; Constantine was the Roman emperor who first converted to Christianity, and Helen was his mother; Olga was the first Christian ruler of Russia (945-962), and Vladimir, her grandson, converted the Russians to Orthodox Christianity in 988.

46. Ukraine is used here in its original meaning of frontier as much as in reference to a recognized geographical entity organized into some sort of state or province. The terms Ukraine and Ukrainians did not come into common usage to describe the land and its inhabitants until later, and this land and people in South Russia were still called Little Russia (Malorossiia) and Little Russians in the eighteenth century.

47. The Treaty of the Pruth refers to the peace signed between Russia and Turkey in 1711, after Peter the Great and his armies had been surrounded by the forces of the sultan during a campaign aimed at the Danube basin and the Balkans. In this treaty Russia generally renounced its aims to territory along the north coast of the Black Sea and gave up Azov and the other lands gained in Peter's earlier campaign against Turkey at the end of the seventeenth century.

48. The Russian Orthodox clergy were separated into two branches, the black and white. The black clergy was monastic and celibate, and supplied the higher ranks of the administrative hierarchy of the church. The white clergy was the mass of common parish priests and lower clerics. They were allowed to marry, but could not rise above the status of local priest without taking monastic vows and joining the black clergy. White clergy therefore tended to be scattered more evenly among the general population and were not capable of organizing themselves to the extent of the black clergy, based in and around their monastic strongholds.

49. The term haidamaks (gaidamak) is derived from the Arabic *gada*, to disrupt, and the Russian *gnat'*, to chase off, and evidently came into use in the seventeenth century. It referred to people in South Russia who had left their old homes during the Time of Troubles and organized themselves into loose, uncontrolled, roving bands on the steppes. The term first was used officially in 1717 to apply to bands of bandits and raiders in the steppe, but soon acquired the connotation of a group rising in protest against the established social and political order. In Russian legend the haidamaks therefore are often portrayed sympathetically, like Robin Hood's men in British tales—hence Soloviev's reference to the "knights of the Steppe."

50. Bogdan Khmelnitsky was the hetman of the Zaporozhe Cossacks who led his people in revolt against the Poles in 1648, after the Poles had attempted to place a number of restrictions in excess of the existing regulations upon the Dnieper cossacks. After changing aides (sometimes unwillingly) several times, Khmelnitsky eventually reached an agreement with the agents of Tsar Alexis and led the Ukraine into union with Russia in 1654. He is a Ukrainian national hero, but his behavior typified the rather ambiguous feelings of cossacks toward full unification with the Russian empire.

51. Prince Eugene of Savoy (1663-1736) was the son of a prominent noble at the French court. Insulted by the refusal of Louis XIV to give him his own regiment, he entered Austrian service, where he won great honors through his military prowess in various campaigns against the Turks and several European powers.

52. Etienne-Francois Choiseul, Duc d'Ambrois (1719-1785), rose to the rank of major general in the War of the Austrian Succession. He then retired, married the daughter of a wealthy banker, and entered the French diplomatic service. After being posted to Vienna and Rome, he received his title and was made minister of Foreign Affairs in 1758. He dominated French politics and diplomacy through the 1760s, before being exiled to his estate in 1770.

53. Prince Wenzel Anton Dominic Kaunitz (1711-1794) was chancellor of the Austrian empire at this time. As the youngest son in his family he was destined to enter the priesthood, but instead decided upon a diplomatic career. He served in several foreign posts in the 1740s, and became chancellor in 1753. He then was able to work at his cherished goal of an alliance between Austria and France. When this alliance failed to destroy Prussia in the Seven Years' War (because Russia fortuitously changed sides), he remained flexible, amenable to Russian interests, and gained some territory for Austria in the first partition of Poland.

54. The aristocratic party, favorable to France. See note 23, above.

55. The Bute system refers to the international posture adopted by Britain under John Stuart, Count Bute, prime minister from 1762 to 1763. Born in 1713, he rose through connections among the upper gentry and eventually became tutor to the future George III. When the latter took the throne, Stuart attempted to isolate the king and dominate him. As prime minister he concluded peace with France in 1762, raised tariffs, and attempted to maintain a policy of British non-involvement in continental alliances and affairs, while still assuring a balance of power in Europe.

INDEX

Aachen, 190.
Academy of Arts, 206.
Academy of Sciences, 34, 36, 198-199, 207.
Aix-la-Chapelle, 199.
Aksakov, Ufa vice-governor, 40.
Albert, Prince, 191.
Alcohol, proposed tax on, 39.
Alekseev, peasant, 53.
Aleksin, 18.
Alexander I, 204.
Alexis, Tsar, 208.
Alfimov, Kurmysh deputy, 32.
Alois, agent, 119-120.
Amsterdam, 92.
Anna, Empress, 115, 205.
Annisk, 54.
Anrep, General, 171.
Antioch, Syrian ruler, 100.
Antiochus Epiphanes, 204.
Antonov, Yaransk deputy, 24, 26.
Apraksin, Major General Count, 130, 168, 170.
Archangel, city, 205; province, 1, 26.
Arctic Ocean, 24.
Armenians, 183.
Asseburg, envoy, 155.
Assumption, cathedral of the, 1.
Astrakhan, 1, 63, 64.
Attic (Czartoryski), 121.
Augustus III, 149, 203.
Austria, 83, 92, 94-102, 109, 115, 146-148, 156, 187, 208; foreign affairs: Prussia, 95-96, 147; Russia, 100-102; Turkey, 98, 115, 187.
Azanchevsky, Lieutenant, 133.
Azov, city, 207.

Bakhchisarai, 102.
Bakhmut hussar regiment, 36.
Balkans, 207.
Balta, village, 174, 183-185.
Baltic, 41, 47, 48, 59, 207.
Bar, district, 162-165, 168, 178-179, 181-182; Confederation of, 163-173, 174, 179-181, 187.
Bashkirs, 40, 41, 43.
Batiushkov, cornet, 64, 65.

Baturin, Colonel Ioasph Andreevich, 64.
Bavaria, 92, 97.
Bayer, 207.
Bearde de l'Abaye, 33, 199.
Beccaria, 196.
Beer, proposed tax on, 39.
Bekenstein, 207.
Belgium, 204.
Belgorod, 1.
Belorussia, 138, 171, 203; Archbishop of, 127, 162, 180.
Belozersk, 60.
Bender, 174.
Benoit, 83, 91, 100, 133, 140, 203.
Berdichev, 164.
Berlin, 93, 100, 101, 112, 133, 152.
Berlin Congress, 69.
Bernstorff, Baron Count, 111, 151-155, 190-191.
Bestuzhev, 114.
Bestuzhev-Riumin, Alexis Petrovich, 205.
Betsky, Ivan Ivanovich, 156, 206.
Bibikov, Alexander Ilich, Kostroma deputy, 3, 5, 51, 53.
Bibikov, Brigadier General, 169.
Bistritsk, 122.
Black Sea, 207.
Bobrowski, petty noble, 178, 179.
Bohemia, 101.
Bolonkin, Michael Alekseev, peasant, 53.
Borken, envoy, 152, 153, 154, 155.
Borov, district, 15.
Bourbon, House of, 15, 92, 94, 95, 96, 97, 156.
Boyar's son (syn boiarskii), 6.
Boyars, 6.
Branitski, high crown hetman, 130.
Bratslaw, 183.
Braunschweig, 92, 95.
Breslau, 60.
Brest, 171.
Breteuil, Count of (See also: Tonneille, Louis August le), French foreign minister, 106, 189, 205.
Britain, 156, 204-205, 208. See also: England.
Broadcloth, 23.

ACADEMIC INTERNATIONAL PRESS

THE RUSSIAN SERIES

1 S.F. Platonov *History of Russia* Out of Print
2 *The Nicky-Sunny Letters, Correspondence of Nicholas and Alexandra, 1914-1917*
3 Ken Shen Weigh *Russo-Chinese Diplomacy, 1689-1924* Out of Print
4 Gaston Cahen *Relations of Russia with China . . . 1689-1730* Out of Print
5 M.N. Pokrovsky *Brief History of Russia* 2 Volumes Out of Print
6 M.N. Pokrovsky *History of Russia from Earliest Times . . .* Out of Print
7 Robert J. Kerner *Bohemia in the Eighteenth Century*
8 *Memoirs of Prince Adam Czartoryski and His Correspondence with Alexander I* 2 vols.
9 S.F. Platonov *Moscow and the West*
10 S.F. Platonov *Boris Godunov*
11 Boris Nikolajewsky *Aseff the Spy*
12 Francis Dvornik *Les Legendes de Constantin et de Méthode vues de Byzance*
13 Francis Dvornik *Les Slaves, Byzance et Rome au XIe Siecle*
14 A. Leroy-Beaulieu *Un Homme d'Etat Russe (Nicolas Miliutine) . . .*
15 Nicholas Berdyaev *Leontiev* (In English)
16 V.O. Kliuchevskii *Istoriia soslovii v Rossii*
17 *Tehran Yalta Potsdam. The Soviet Protocols*
18 *The Chronicle of Novgorod*
19 Paul N. Miliukov *Outlines of Russian Culture* Vol. III (2 vols.)
20 P.A. Zaionchkovsky *The Abolition of Serfdom in Russia*
21 V.V. Vinogradov *Russkii iazyk. Grammaticheskoe uchenie o slove*
22 P.A. Zaionchkovsky *The Russian Autocracy under Alexander III*
23 A.E. Presniakov *Emperor Nicholas I of Russia. The Apogee of Autocracy*
24 V.I. Semevskii *Krestianskii vopros v Rossii v XVIII i pervoi polovine XIX veka* Out of Print
25 S.S. Oldenburg *Last Tsar! Nicholas II, His Reign and His Russia* 4 volumes
26 Carl von Clausewitz *The Campaign of 1812 in Russia*
27 M.K. Liubavskii *Obrazovanie osnovnoi gosudarstvennoi territorii velikorusskoi narodnosti. Zaselenie i obedinenie tsentra*
28 S.F. Platonov *Ivan the Terrible* Paper
29 Paul N. Miliukov *Iz istorii russkoi intelligentsii. Sbornik Statei i etiudov*
30 A.E. Presniakov *The Tsardom of Muscovy* Paper
31 M. Gorky, J. Stalin et al., *History of the Civil War in Russia* 2 vols. Out of Print
32 R.G. Skrynnikov *Ivan the Terrible*
33 P.A. Zaionchkovsky *The Russian Autocracy in Crisis, 1878-1882*
34 Joseph T. Fuhrmann *Tsar Alexis. His Reign and His Russia*
35 R.G. Skrynnikov *Boris Godunov*
43 Nicholas Zernov *Three Russian Prophets: Khomiakov, Dostoevsky, Soloviev* Out of Print
44 Paul N. Miliukov *The Russian Revolution* 3 vols.
45 Anton I. Denikin *The White Army* Out of Print
55 M.V. Rodzianko *The Reign of Rasputin—An Empire's Collapse. Memoirs* Out of Print
56 *The Memoirs of Alexander Iswolsky*

THE CENTRAL AND EAST EUROPEAN SERIES

1 Louis Eisenmann *Le Compromis Austro-Hongrois de 1867*
3 Francis Dvornik *The Making of Central and Eastern Europe* 2nd edition
4 Feodor F. Zigel *Lectures on Slavonic Law*
10 Doros Alastos *Venizelos—Patriot, Statesman, Revolutionary*
20 Paul Teleki *The Evolution of Hungary and its Place in European History*

FORUM ASIATICA

1 M.I. Sladkovsky *China and Japan—Past and Present*

THE ACADEMIC INTERNATIONAL REFERENCE SERIES

The Modern Encyclopedia of Russian and Soviet History 50 vols. 1976-
The Modern Encyclopedia of Russian and Soviet Literatures 50 vols. 1977-
Soviet Armed Forces Review Annual 1977-
USSR Facts & Figures Annual 1977-
Military-Naval Encyclopedia of Russia and the Soviet Union 50 vols. 1978-
China Facts & Figures Annual 1978-
Encyclopedia USA. The Encyclopedia of the United States of America Past & Present 50 vols. 1983-
The International Military Encyclopedia 50 vols.
Sports Encyclopedia North America 50 vols. 1985-

SPECIAL WORKS

S.M. Soloviev *History of Russia* 50 vols.
SAFRA Papers 1985-